PRAISE FOR
The Sex Lives of African Women

"Touching, joyful, defiant—and honest."

—*The Economist*, a Best Book of the Year

"Nana Darkoa Sekyiamah is changing the way African women talk about sex."

—*Harper's Bazaar*

"The stories, as written by Sekyiamah, are mesmerizing. The women shared with her, and by extension with us, with true generosity."

—*Glamour*

"The honesty and frankness with which these women share their experiences of falling in love, lust, and their traumas, too, is fascinating. . . . It's the kind of book that inspires you to reconsider your own romantic preconceptions and to imagine new, healthier dynamics."

—*BuzzFeed News*

"Sekyiamah's book seeks to provide the roadmap to recovery through a collection of shared experiences. . . . Readers will resonate with the honesty of these stories, and hopefully feel more courageous to live their truth each day."

—*BUST*

"A book like none you will have read before. . . . With sensitivity, this book has facilitated astonishing breaking of silences. . . . Sekyiamah has delivered an extraordinarily dynamic work, true to her own precept that 'Freedom is a constant state of being . . . that we need to nurture and protect. Freedom is a safe home that one can return to over and over again.'"

—Margaret Busby, *The Guardian*

"Groundbreaking volume. . . . The result is a candid, subversive and empowering read."

—*Ms. Magazine*

"Dazzling. . . . The tone is hopeful, resilient, and accepting. Marked by the diversity of experiences shared, the wealth of intimate details, and the total lack of sensationalism, this is an astonishing report on the quest for sexual liberation."

—*Publishers Weekly*, starred review

"An ambitious, moving account of women controlling their bodies and their destinies."

—*Kirkus Reviews*

"These intimate confessions come from pansexual women, polyamorous women, queer women, trans women, and those who identify as heterosexual. Some of their stories are heartbreaking, while others are liberating. Instead of having their stories told for them, they take the reins and find freedom in that, something that every woman deserves."

—Del Sandeen, *Sisters from AARP*

"Its stories are raw, unencumbered, exhilarating and, at times, enraging."

—*The Independent*

"Talking about sex is still taboo in most cultures and communities and these personal stories reveal a mind-blowing variety of sexualities, sex lives, and relationships."

—Bernardine Evaristo, *The Times* (UK)

"Reading these stories is a reminder that the sexuality of African women is far from a monolith. . . . A refreshing and emotional read."

—*The Continent*

"Everyone will come away standing a little taller and breathing a little lighter, buoyed by the affirmation that we are all normal and that the marginal is central. *The Sex Lives of African Women* is a safe space: it is pure, unadulterated freedom."

—Jane Link, *bigblackbooks*

"Overflowing with candor, vulnerability, and juiciness, this collection of raw, tender stories that Nana Darkoa Sekyiamah has so lovingly gathered will upend all of your assumptions and stereotypes. These mothers, activists, writers, sex workers, and others share painful truths, evolving glories, and journeys toward love and freedom, in their own words. They are trans, queer, heterosexual, kinky, and say, 'To hell with labels.' Facing down dangers and double standards, they are healing. *The Sex Lives of African Women* captures the breadth and depth of the Diaspora with the intimacy of looking in a mirror. Marvelous!"

—Deesha Philyaw, author of *The Secret Lives of Church Ladies*

"*The Sex Lives of African Women* is a Pan-African feminist love offering to our ancestors, women living across the Diaspora and future generations to come. Nana Darkoa Sekyiamah delivers this love with honesty, levity, and delicious prose. This book satiates my appetite for stories that take the interior lives of Black, African, and Afro-descendant women seriously. It is simply unparalleled and right on time."

—Charlene A. Carruthers, author of *Unapologetic: A Black, Queer, and Feminist Mandate for Radical Movements*

"I really haven't read anything like it, in its treatment of African women's lives, sex lives, and sexualities. It breaks silences, it challenges stereotypes, it dismisses taboos, it throws social norms out the window, and most importantly, it defends our complexity and it gives us shelter and room for healing."

—NoViolet Bulawayo, author of *Glory*

"In these emotionally charged and refreshingly honest essays, this collection gives literal shape to women's sexuality and desires. Nothing less than stunning. Essential read! I couldn't put it down."

—Nicole Dennis-Benn, bestselling author of *Patsy*

"This collection affirms what we've known all along: African women are reclaiming their bodies and taking ownership of their sexual destinies. Every single story leaves you feeling deliciously empowered."

—Lola Shoneyin, author of *The Secret Lives of Baba Segi's Wives*

THE SEX LIVES OF AFRICAN WOMEN

THE SEX LIVES OF AFRICAN WOMEN

SELF-DISCOVERY, FREEDOM, AND HEALING

NANA DARKOA SEKYIAMAH

ASTRA HOUSE · NEW YORK

For information about permission to reproduce selections from this book, please contact
permissions@astrahouse.com.

Astra House
A Division of Astra Publishing House
astrahouse.com
Printed in the United States of America

Library of Congress Cataloging-in-Publication Data
Names: Sekyiamah, Nana Darkoa, author.
Title: The sex lives of African women : self-discovery, freedom, and healing / Nana Darkoa Sekyiamah.
Description: First edition. | New York : Astra House, [2022] | Summary: "From her blog, "Adventures
from the Bedrooms of African Women," Nana Darkoa Sekyiamah has spent decades talking openly
and intimately to African women around the world about sex. Here, she features the stories that most
affected her, chronicling her own journey toward sexual freedom. We meet Yami, a pansexual
Canadian of Malawian heritage, who describes negotiating the line between family dynamics and
sexuality. There's Esther, a cisgender hetero woman studying in America, by way of Cameroon and
Kenya, who talks of how a childhood rape has made her rebellious and estranged from her missionary
parents. And Tsitsi, an HIV-positive Zimbabwean woman who is raising a healthy, HIV-free baby.
Across a queer community in Egypt, polyamorous life in Senegal, and a reflection on the intersection
of religion and pleasure in Cameroon, Sekyiamah explores the many layers of love and desire, its
expression, and how it forms who we are. In these confessional pages, women control their own bodies
and pleasure, and assert their sexual power. Capturing the rich tapestry of sex positivity, The Sex
Lives of African Women is a singular and subversive book that celebrates the liberation, individuality,
and joy of African women's multifaceted sexuality"—Provided by publisher.
Identifiers: LCCN 2021044278 (print) | LCCN 2021044279 (ebook) |
ISBN 9781662650819 (hardcover) | ISBN 9781662650826 (epub)
Subjects: LCSH: Women—Sexual behavior—Africa. | Women, Black—Sexual behavior—Africa. |
Sex—Africa.
Classification: LCC HQ29 .S455 2021 (print) | LCC HQ29 (ebook) | DDC 306.7082096—dc23
LC record available at https://lccn.loc.gov/2021044278
LC ebook record available at https://lccn.loc.gov/2021044279

ISBN: 9781662601989 (pb)
First paperback edition, 2023
10 9 8 7 6 5 4 3 2 1

Design by Richard Oriolo
The text is set in Bulmer Regular.
The titles are set in Franklin Gothic Demi Condensed.

For my daughter Asantewaa,
and African girls and women
wherever they may be.

CONTENTS

Preface | 1

PART 1: SELF-DISCOVERY | 5

Nura | 11

Nafi | 21

Keisha | 31

Bibi | 40

Ebony | 48

Elizabeth | 55

Naisha | 64

Naike | 73

Philester | 81

Krystal | 90

Estelle | 100

Bingi | 108

PART 2: FREEDOM | 113

Fatou | 118

Helen Banda | 127

Alexis | 140

Miss Deviant | 150

Gabriela | 158

Amina | 164

Laura | 172

Solange | 184

Yami | 194

PART 3: HEALING | 201

Salma | 206

Mariam Gebre | 214

Shanita | 218

Maureen | 227

Esther | 238

Baaba | 246

Vera Cruz | 254

Tafadzwa | 258

Tsitsi | 264

Waris | 270

Nana Darkoa | 278

A FINAL NOTE | 283
LETTER TO THE READER | 285
JOURNALING PROMPTS | 287
GLOSSARY | 297
ACKNOWLEDGMENTS | 299
ABOUT THE AUTHOR | 301

THE SEX LIVES OF AFRICAN WOMEN

PREFACE

·

FOR MORE THAN ten years, I shared my personal experiences of sex on "Adventures from the Bedrooms of African Women," a blog I cofounded with my friend Malaka Grant. I also facilitated conversations about women's experiences of sex and pleasure in a variety of public settings, ranging from intimate living-room conversations in Mombasa, Kenya, to public events in Berlin, Germany. I have often spoken and written about the importance of owning one's body, and my continuing journey in negotiating my own sexuality and desires both within and outside the bedroom. Speaking in public about a subject that is often deemed taboo—especially in the part of the world where I originate, Ghana—is a political act. I think and write about sex in order to learn how to have better sex. I encourage other women to share their experiences of sex in order to build our collective consciousness around the politics of pleasure. This is critical in a world where women too often lack access to a truly comprehensive sex education.

Black, African, and Afro-descendant women are often told that sex should only be within particular constraints—between people of opposite genders, for instance—and within certain parameters. In some countries, these parameters are marriage. In other countries the law prohibits some types of sexual acts, or tries to control the choices girls and women have when they experience an unwanted pregnancy.

In *The Sex Lives of African Women*, individual women from across the African continent and its global Diaspora speak to their experiences of sex, sexualities, and relationships. It was really important to me as a Pan-African feminist that a book about African women's experiences of sex centered continental Africans, and included the experiences of Africans who have been violently displaced by the legacies of slavery and colonization, as well as those who have voluntarily migrated to other parts of the world. For this reason I was especially pleased to interview women of African descent from places like Haiti, Barbados, and Costa Rica.

The stories in this book are based on in-depth interviews I conducted between 2015 and 2020, with women between the ages of twenty-one to seventy-one, from thirty-one countries across the globe. I made conscious efforts to interview women who came from a broad range of backgrounds: across socioeconomic lines, women of faith and women who practice no particular religion, women for whom English was not their first language, and women representative of communities that have been historically marginalized in society. The biggest challenge for me personally was interviewing women who were not native English speakers because in one instance it meant speaking through a translator, and it also meant that I ended up speaking primarily to women who were also fluent in English. I can see how my book would be even more rich in content if I had interviewed women in a variety of African languages, for instance. When I started working on this project, I focused on interviewing people face-to-face, a goal that was made possible by the privilege of my job, which allows me to travel across the globe. That changed with the COVID-19 pandemic, and I started to do more interviews via video. One particular woman and I ended up concluding our conversation via a series of voice notes because she lives in a country with poor internet connectivity that also experiences frequent power outages.

In my introduction to each story I describe each woman as she self-identified. This allows me to show the diversity of ways in which people see themselves, whether they identify as cis women, femmes, trans, heterosexual, or pansexual, for instance. I also share people's ages and their country of origin and residence in order to contextualize their experiences. A significant proportion of the women I interviewed represented more than one nation, and had their sexual encounters shaped by the various countries they had lived in and cultures they had experienced. After speaking to more than thirty women for this book, I started to see several common threads weaving through the stories, threads that I also see reflected in my own life. My conclusion is very much this: we're all on a journey towards sexual freedom and agency. In order to get there we need to heal. Healing looks different for everybody. For some of the women in this book, healing came about through celibacy and spiritual growth. For others, healing came through taking back power as a dominatrix and sex worker. For some others, healing is still part of the journey they need to travel.

Many of the women I spoke to inspired me with the realities of how they live their best sexual lives. This included deeply personal stories: for example, about navigating freedom and polyamory in conservative Senegal, or resisting the erasure of lesbian identity and finding queer community in Egypt in the midst of a revolution. African women grapple with the trauma of sexual abuse, and resist religious and patriarchal edicts in order to assert their sexual power and agency. They do this by questioning and resisting societal norms while creating new norms and narratives that allow them to be who they truly are. The journey towards sexual freedom is not a linear one, or one that is fixed and static. Freedom is a state that we are constantly seeking to reach.

All names used in this book are pseudonyms unless indicated with an asterisk.

PART 1: SELF-DISCOVERY

AT TWENTY-TWO I WAS STILL TECHNICALLY A VIRGIN. THIS WAS IN spite of the fact that Eric had told my boyfriend Jeremy six years ago: "I fucked your girlfriend by a gutter near her house." The day I met Eric, I was walking down from Community 11 along the snaky bend of the road aptly named)w) junction towards Community 10 in the city of Tema, Ghana. I had on my new favorite miniskirt that my aunt in the US had gifted me on one of her infrequent visits to Ghana. My mum was horrified by the skirt, a double strip of faded denim with brass rings punched through the second strip. "It's all the rage in New York," my aunt explained when Mum attempted to object to the gift. I wore it every chance I got, and was wearing it when the red sports car came hurtling around the side of)w) junction and, in what seemed like seconds, overturned into a nearby gutter. I stood there like a mumu, frozen to the spot. What should I do? There's no one else around. Is the driver hurt? As these thoughts tumbled about in my head, I saw a flash of red and blue as a smallish light-skinned man extricated himself from the wreckage only to start kicking the car in anger. I was still frozen to the spot when he saw me and ran over. "Hey, can you watch my car for me? I just need to go and get my brothers to come help me." I nodded, still lost for words, and was still in the same spot minutes later when he came back with a group of boys piled into the back of a pickup. "Thanks for watching my car, can I have your number?" His name was Eric, and I spent the rest of the summer hanging out with him. We would spend all day together and at dusk he would walk me to my house, or I would walk him home. In the quiet spots behind the houses, or on the part of the road where the streetlights failed to come on, we would kiss with open mouths and tongues like I had seen on TV. "Why do you kiss with your eyes open?" he asked one day, and then I knew that one must always kiss with eyes closed.

By the time I met Fiifi I was ready to lose my virginity. At twenty-two, it had started to feel like an unwanted weight that I was carrying between my legs. I no longer worried about being called a mattress, or any of the names that guys gave girls they slept with. I had firsthand knowledge now that most of the guys were lying about the girls they had slept with; besides, I now lived in London, where most girls my age were already sharing flats with their boyfriends. I don't remember much about the first time I had sex with Fiifi, except that he fucked me three times. When I told my friend, she exclaimed, "Weren't you in pain?" I was, but I also believed him each time he told me, "It'll be easier the next time round," and in a sense he was right. I don't remember much about the sex we had over the five years we were together. Our sex was vanilla: missionary mainly, me going down on him a lot, me begging for the first three years of our relationship for him to go down on me. And then he found out I had cheated on him. "Why did you wait for us to get married before you cheated on me?" he asked. I had no words to offer to him. If I had, I might have said:

I spent years avoiding sex with guys because I didn't want anyone to gossip about me. I wish I had realized sooner that no matter what I did guys would claim to have fucked me every which way under the sun.

I spent years scared that sex would result in a pregnancy, and that would mean dropping out of school and having my life ruined forever. I wish I had known about contraceptives, and that sex could be enjoyed for its own sake.

I spent years thinking that once I had sex with a guy I would need to stay with him forever, and then once I was married I realized I should have done what a lot of guys are encouraged to do and sown my wild oats. I too have wild oats to sow.

But I had no words to offer him, and he had gone insane at the thought that this girl, this woman whose body had been wholly his, had been possessed by someone else . . . and in his words, someone had put his dick where he used to put his mouth. Thinking about this over and over again made him hurl words at me in the middle of the night when we were sleeping, or even in the park where we had picnics in a vain attempt to get back to how things used to be.

What did you do with him?
Tell me again.
You enjoyed it, didn't you?
Let's have sex now.
Look, you're wet. Talking about him turns you on. You weren't wet before.
Look at you; you're growing fat while I grow lean.

One night when he had reluctantly gone to work the night shift at his job, I packed a suitcase and left. I knew he would call me on the house phone just before midnight, as had become his new habit. I made sure to leave before that phone rang. I walked out of the relationship three times before I found the strength to leave permanently.

What I have learned over the years is that you don't discover yourself by sticking to well-trodden paths. You discover yourself by embarking on your own personal odyssey, which is experienced differently by everyone. The journey towards self-discovery may be long and winding, but it is also one filled with the infinite possibilities that come with adventure.

It is imperative to break out of the boxes circumscribed by society in order to discover one's self, and the multitudes we hold within us. This requires practicing an audacious form of bravery, and often requires one to go against the grain of everything that has been presented as the norm.

The women whose stories I share in this section speak to the quest that many women need to undertake to discover their true sexual selves. Sometimes, this involves a literal journey, like moving to another country for love, as was the case for Nura, who married a man she had never met before and subsequently moved from Kenya to Senegal. For others, self-discovery requires stepping out of the relative safety of the familiar to explore different relationship models based on consent, openness, and love. Getting to know one's self may even mean a reckoning with the gender that was assigned at birth.

Travel features a lot in the stories shared here. Travel to a city where one can work legally as a sex worker, in the case of Krystal; or in the case of Elizabeth, migrating from Lagos to London just as she was falling in love with her childhood friend. For many Africans in the Diaspora, their very existence has been shaped by travel—the journeys their ancestors may have taken to the countries where they currently live. They are forged not just by where they are immediately from, but also where they originated. This is visible in stories shared by Estelle, for instance, whose ancestors came from Africa, the Middle East, and Europe, an ancestry that is visible in the color of her skin and the texture of her hair.

In many ways, we are all on a journey and are on different parts of the road towards our true selves and sexual freedom. The women in this section model bravery and vulnerability. They challenge us all to continue our own paths towards discovering our true selves, even if that journey remains an ongoing one.

I met Nura on a trip to Senegal in January 2020. It was my last international trip before many countries started closing their borders due to the COVID-19 pandemic. I had decided to take myself on a personal retreat, to write, read, and rejuvenate for the year ahead. My friend the writer Ayesha Harruna Atta opened her home to me, and my days consisted of waking up early to write, conducting virtual interviews, and allowing myself to get lost while exploring the nature reserve and beaches of Popenguine.

In Senegal, like in many other countries where I find myself, I have an almost ready-made African feminist community. One day, a Kenyan friend told me that she was going to visit a compatriot who had moved to Senegal and was now in a polygamous marriage and in need of finding a community of sister friends. I was intrigued, and I, my friend, and two other women made the hour-long trip to the town where Nura now lived.

Over water and pineapples, Nura shared with us snippets about the romance that had led her to get married and move to Senegal at the age of forty-two to start a new life in a country where she had no friends, and did not speak Wolof, the dominant language. She was living in a flat owned by her sister-in-law, and in a few short weeks was going to move to the house where her husband lived with his other wives. She was keen to build a healthy relationship with the other women her husband was married to. I initially interviewed Nura before she moved in with her husband, and reconnected a few months later to find out what life was like in a polygamous household.

I was especially curious to find out what Nura's experience of polygamy was like because my parents were also in a polygamous marriage. Even though polygamy is legal in Ghana, over time it has acquired a tinge of illegitimacy due to the dominance of Christianity, which promotes heterosexual monogamous marriage as the only valid relationship structure. Yet polygamous practices are dominant in the country. My friend Kobina Graham coined a word, "fauxnogamy," to describe a practice where married men in relationships that are meant to be monogamous have multiple relationships without taking on any of the responsibilities that come with being legally married to multiple women.

NURA

.

MY SISTER WIVES and I have nothing in common. Well, that's not exactly
true. We have *His Excellency* in common. We are all married to the same man.

Ishmael and I met in 2018 on Muzmatch, a dating app for Muslims looking to get married. By then I had been a convert for about four years, and I
knew that I needed to expand my circle of potential suitors. I wasn't born into
a Muslim family, and so I couldn't rely on my own networks to meet the kind
of man that I wanted to be with. The Muslim men I met in my own country,
Kenya, were incredibly conservative, and I wanted to meet a man who was
more like me: well traveled and with a global view of the world. When Ishmael
and I started chatting our conversations felt very easy. I found myself laughing
a lot. He was also respectful. He didn't even hit on me. Around the same time
my aunt who lives in Canada had started a relationship with a Congolese man.
She told me how much he adored her, and how loved she felt. I started to wonder if this was just how Francophone men were. Then Ishmael told me he
wanted to travel to Nairobi to see me. I told him that I didn't want to meet him
unless we were meeting as husband and wife, and so an Imam married us
online. When we met, I thought his pictures and even our video chats had not
captured him accurately. He looks like the stereotype of a Senegalese man: six
feet tall and skinny. The phrase "melanin popping" was coined to describe
people like him. He also has this air of a quiet, confident masculinity. He
practices martial arts and is really strong. You wouldn't think he was in his
late forties if you met him. That first time we met, we spent four days together
in a hotel. All we did was fuck and pray. That was really important to me.
Sensuality and spirituality are two sides of the same coin, and I wanted to be
with a partner I could learn the faith with, from a place of curiosity, and not

oppression. I found Islam in my late thirties. I had been searching for a spiritual practice that spoke to who I am as a Black African woman, and in the Islamic faith, I found one that also spoke to the social and environmental justice issues that are important to me.

When Ishmael left Nairobi I was in a daze. I had found this man, married, and had the most incredible bonding experience with him, and now he was gone. Two months later I flew to Senegal and visited him for two months. He arranged for me to stay in an apartment owned by his sister, and the whole experience felt like dating while married. That period taught me that I can actually be committed to someone else. When you're legally bound to a person, you just don't walk out on them. You have to show up not only for yourself, but for the partnership you're in. It's not a simple matter of "Can I deal with this person?" because it's not about the other person changing. It's about how you deal with who they are intrinsically, and how they are evolving. That initial experience taught me that you can love and care for someone even if they are very different from you. Ishmael is a traditional man. He's always done what he's expected to do as a responsible Senegalese man. The most radical thing he's done has been to marry me. A woman who is in her forties, an Anglophone, someone from a foreign country who doesn't speak Wolof or French and doesn't know his culture and traditions. The expectation in Senegal is that if a man is going to stray out of the constraints of who he is expected to marry, then he would be with a white woman.

My biggest struggle is with the gender norms that I am expected to conform to. To look pretty but not too pretty. To sit in a corner quietly and not voice my opinions in public. To agree with my husband when we have an audience. That is not how I grew up. I'm the firstborn of a single mom. My dad died when I was sixteen years old, and so my mom was very clearly the head of the household, while I as the firstborn child had to take on a lot of responsibilities. It pisses me off that I now have to perform this subservient role. Meanwhile you only have to look at Islamic history to understand the active role that women have always played in our communities. Women actually went into battle with the Prophet, peace and blessings be upon him. One of his wives was a scholar who taught women and men. There were women who were trad-ers, and so the idea that a woman's space is in the domestic realm, and her role is to be docile, is one that I struggle with.

Our private life is completely different. We're playful when we spend time together. I feel like I can let my inner child out with him and that's really important to me. We talk a lot about faith and politics. He teases me about being an artist. He likes to say, "I am a simple Senegalese man and you're a philosopher." People who know him in the outside world would be shocked to see what he's like with me in private.

Until a few years ago I had absolutely no desire to get married, and then I converted and with that came this deep desire for heterosexual partnership. That shook me. I was never one of those girls who wanted to get married or who had visualized exactly what their future wedding was going to be like. The desire for marriage came from the healing that my faith brought me, including reckoning with the loss of my father. Prior to converting, I had never fully grappled with that deep hunger I felt for a father, and Islam allowed me to acknowledge that. I began to recognize that I was looking for my father in everything I did. Another part of the deep desire that I had for marriage was a need for companionship and sex. I also knew that marriage could give me a type of leverage, an opportunity that could help me move from one space to another. We live on a continent where our status as women is very precarious. I believe this applies across the board, whether you're a bi, straight, or queer woman, and so heterosexual marriage at least provides a measure of protection to women. I think this is a question that Black and African women need to ask themselves more often. What can I do to preserve myself and my children in a way that allows them to move to the next level?

In December 2019 I packed up my life and moved to Senegal. I spent the first month living in the apartment of my sister-in-law so that my husband could finish building the place he had started constructing for me. In Janu-ary 2020 I moved to my new home. The first-floor flat belonged to the first wife and her children, the second floor to the second wife and her children, and the third floor, the latest addition to the building, was mine. My husband has eight children between the ages of twenty years and six months. I have no children at all.

It's been four months since we've been in this new arrangement and it hasn't been exactly what I expected. In hindsight, yes, I was naive. I assumed I would have some common values with my husband's wives, but apart from our faith, and *His Excellency*, we have nothing in common. My intention had been to cultivate a respectful, sisterly interaction, but instead I am met with a lot of passive aggressiveness. I'm a stranger here. I don't speak Wolof or French, although I am learning. When I ask where I can go to buy a particular item, I am told, "Don't you know?" No, I don't know, otherwise I wouldn't be asking. Initially I tried to befriend the second wife; I would even occasionally go and visit her, until she decided to publicly shame my cooking. One day for our meal I prepared fufu with a side of meat, and then loudly in front of everyone she said, "Where are the vegetables? Why didn't you add any to the meal?" I didn't know I needed to add vegetables to fufu. I'm still learning how things are done here.

Everything centers around the arrival of *His Excellency*. He spends two days in each household, and so the day before his arrival I spend the day preparing. Whichever wife he is staying with is responsible for cooking for the entire household, and so I'll go to the market with my domestic staff and we'll buy enough food to feed the household for two days. The first time it was my turn to cook, I had someone make me tcheb, a popular Senegalese rice dish, and then I made some mashed potatoes and chicken and sautéed a range of vegetables: eggplant, carrots, and French beans. That's the kind of food we eat back home in Nairobi. Then I served everything in one large communal dish because in Senegal everyone except for the man of the house eats out of one bowl. All the wives and children had arrived by then, and so I set an individual plate for my husband and went to inform him that dinner was ready. When I came back half the wives and children had already left. They didn't even touch the food that I had spent hours preparing. This has happened time and time again. It really gets to me because meals are not just about what goes in your stomach. The process of cooking a meal is about creativity, and the act of feeding others is about nourishment. When you spend over three hours cooking a meal and people come to eat, there should be conversation, laughter, and joy. Instead what I experience is very sterile. There is silence, some people leave straight away when they see the food, others stay and pick at their plates. It's gotten to a stage where I'm even beginning to wonder if my husband eats my food out of mere politeness. One time my husband was unwell, he was staying with one of his other wives at the time, and she had made him a meal that was supposedly good for his health. He was due to visit me next and so I asked her if she could tell me the name of the dish she had made. She said no.

In all of this my husband has said nothing. He's either oblivious to what is going on, or has an attitude of, "I'll let you women figure it all out amongst yourselves." I also don't feel like I can raise this directly with him. I've told him in general terms that I find living here challenging, but it's not like I can say, "Your wives are being bitchy towards me." I'm very much aware that I'm the newest member of this household. I know that I am the one who is supposed to figure out a way to fit in, and that I should be grateful that they have allowed me to come into their lives.

I started out expecting there to be kindness between the wives. We're all women from this continent. Yes, we have different levels of privilege, but we all live in this male-dominated society. I feel like we could achieve much more if we worked together rather than against each other. I can imagine that in the case of the first wife, for example, she married Ishmael when they were both young. Chances are she was a virgin. They started a life together, and then twenty years later he married a second wife, and then after another five years later he marries yet another wife. Even if that's part of your culture, that shit must hurt. I have no idea what my husband told his wives when he married me. I doubt that he asked their permission. He is not obliged to do so, and I never asked him what he told them about marrying me because that's about his relationships and it's none of my business.

One of the things that makes me happy is that the children feel comfortable enough to come and hang out in my apartment. They walk in and out as they wish. Sometimes they come to hang out with their dad. Other times they come here even when they know he is not around. It is really important to me that children feel secure, and I want the children to know that they can always reach their dad or come to me if they need anything. I don't know how the other wives feel about the time the children spend here, but it's important to me that they continue to see this space as one that they are also invited to share. Before my dad died, when I was still fairly young, he'd always been around. I grew up in a situation that is very different from this one. My parents were in a monogamous marriage, and my dad and mom were extremely close. Sometimes it felt like they lived in their own bubble, and we, the children, were just an extension of that. It's been a big stretch going from observing the marriage my parents had to this one, and yet there are many things that I like about my own marriage. I like that I don't have to see my husband every day. I don't even have to talk to him every day. This gives me a lot of time for myself. I can read, I can study, and I have time to work on my art. To a certain extent I am also comfortable, my basic needs are taken care of, and I have my own flat and someone at home to help me with the work. Our sex life is also really good. I have no issues there. As a woman I'm insatiable. I love to explore and sometimes I even ask myself if I am too much. One time he said to me, "Oh my goodness, I am so tired. I thought we were only going to have sex like once a month." I told him, "That's not going to happen." Apparently he had assumed that because I am over forty my libido would be much lower than it is. On the contrary, I feel like I am just starting my sexual journey. Sexually speaking, it feels to me like this is the best chapter of my life. I'm the most self-aware that I have ever been. I am flexible. I am juicy. I am up for sex whenever, however, whatever. Before my husband comes over I make sure I'm well rested. I get a good night's sleep, I drink lots of water, and I meditate. I make sure the house is clean, I burn lots of incense, and I use my crystals so I am prepared to deal with whatever energies he may be bringing into the house with him. Sometimes you have to be ready to repel any negative energy that may be coming through the door with him. I work on my face and my body. I make sure I look good. I prepare for sex by performing these rituals that I was taught by Somali women. I burn some oud and then I stand over the incense while wearing a long flowy dress and use that to move the essence all over so my body retains the heat. When he comes home I'm uncovered. I don't wear a head covering like I normally would. He arrives an hour before dinner, and so that is also the time we have to ourselves before everyone else gets there. He already knows that's our window to be intimate.

I have a confession to make. I'm skeptical about marriage. I was never one of those girls who dreamed of wearing a long, flowy white dress and walking down an aisle to meet the man or woman of her dreams. And then I got married at the age of twenty-five. I am sure you can guess what happened next. You don't get a cookie for any correct guesses, but if you can hold on, and if you are one of those folks who reads in order, you will eventually discover my own personal story over the course of this book.

Years ago, I wrote an article titled "Don't Tie the Knot." I've had a marriage counselor tell me that she's shared that article with young people whom she counsels. One of my friends constantly reminds me of how pivotal that piece was. I come from a part of the world where marriage is still seen as a natural destination. People who are married have social recognition and status. People who are not married are looked at suspiciously and considered immature. This has real-life consequences. Some unmarried people get passed over for promotion or are not considered suitable for certain high-profile roles. Older unmarried women, especially those living life on their own terms, are often considered sexually immoral. For all these reasons I consider it an act of bravery when a woman chooses to end a marriage that no longer serves her.

Nafi is a thirty-four-year-old cis heterosexual Fulani woman from Cameroon. In my conversation with her she spoke to me about her ongoing divorce proceedings from her husband and how they went from an illicit long-distance, cybersex-filled relationship to a marriage with two children and no sex. I too know the thrill that comes with the ping indicating a message from a lover or romantic interest. I remember spending hours chatting with a man I had met only virtually, breaking up with my then girlfriend so that I could date him, and when we finally met in person thinking, Uh-oh. Sometimes the burning chemistry one experiences virtually cannot be sustained in our physical realities.

NAFI

·

I FIRST GOT introduced to the man I married in 2007. My cousin had said to me, "Can you believe my mum is trying to marry me off to a man who is just your type?" Her mother was obsessed with getting her children married and had introduced her daughter to Hassan in the hope that there would be a connection. She showed me his picture, I thought he was cute. We kind of look similar. He's light-skinned, skinny, and tall. Later I would find out that he loved music and enjoyed reading. That's totally my type: the silent brooding guy who is also an unofficial DJ or just really loves music. A bit on the introvert side but not really a nerd. Someone who could still go out to a club but for the music.

I had always thought I would never marry another Fulani person because our culture tends to be very conservative. We're socialized from a really early age to think of ourselves as Fula first before anything else. As a woman your identity is first linked to your father, and then your husband. We also have a lot of child marriages because you're not regarded as a woman until you're married and so even children tend to desire marriage for the recognition that it brings them.

Growing up, my aunts would tell me, "Nobody will marry you if you have sex before you get married." I was quite lucky because my parents are educated and never pushed me to get married. When I was about ten years old, my mum used to get my siblings and me to watch this French show called *Le bonheur de la vie*. It featured *une famille recomposée*, a blended family of an old white grandmother who spoke to her Black male grandchild and her white female grandchild about their bodies, sex, masturbation, and homosexuality. In the nineties it was one of the few French shows that featured a Black person. So on one hand I had some sexual education from this show, which would say, "Listen to your body," "This is how you're going to feel," "You need to know your body," against the backdrop of conservative Fula culture. I've always had these kinds of contrasts in my life. I didn't want to be in a relationship with a Fula man because I had this fear of being judged. Then I meet this man who comes from the same place I come from, but is super open-minded, loves to read and listen to music, and has lived in Europe most of his life.

When I was initially shown Hassan's picture I thought he was cute but that was it. At the time I was still dating the same guy I had dated from the age of sixteen. During the summer of 2007, my cousin came to visit me in South Africa, where I lived at the time. When she went back to Cameroon, she met up with Hassan, who was there on holiday with his girlfriend. She showed him pictures of her time in South Africa and pointed me out to him: "This is my cousin Nafi." Two months later I traveled to Brussels for work and messaged my cousin. She told me Hassan was also in Brussels visiting his girlfriend and connected herself, Hassan, and me via a group chat. That night we all started chatting together; eventually my cousin went offline, but Hassan and I continued until late in the night. We didn't meet up physically on that occasion, but stayed in constant touch afterwards.

Soon, our conversations became more and more intimate and we started having phone and video sex although we were both in relationships with other people. He was the first person I ever had cybersex with. This virtual sexual relationship went on for a year. There was even one time when we were both home in Cameroon at the same time but didn't see each other in person. By then we had had lots of conversations about how physically attracted we were to each other, but he was in a long-term relationship, and I had just ended my own long-term relationship and did not want to start a new one, especially one that would be at a distance. Over time, Hassan became my confidant. I even told him when I met someone new, so we would go from him giving me advice about how to talk to the new guy I had just met, to having video sex fifteen minutes later. Then I had another work trip to Brussels and Hassan was there around the same time because he was visiting his girlfriend. We decided to finally meet in person.

I was a bundle of nerves because he had never seen me in person. I thought, Is he expecting to see a skinny girl? At the time I had become obsessed with my body and was convinced that I was overweight and unattractive. When he arrived I found him quite shy. I was a bit surprised that he came on his own. I had half expected him to come with his girlfriend since our own relationship was an illicit one. We sat in the bar and had a couple of drinks. At the end of the night he assumed we would go back to my hotel together, but I said no. He got upset and we had an argument. I think that's typical of men, especially African men. They feel entitled to your body, especially if you're in a relationship with them or have had some sort of intimacy with them before.

I left Brussels and continued on my work trip, which was taking me to various cities in Europe. In Germany, my cousin contacted me. Hassan had reached out to her and begged her to intervene on his behalf. She said to me, "He's having a really hard time in his relationship." My last stop in Europe was in France, where Hassan lived. We met up again and this time we had sex. It was the first time that I had actually enjoyed sex with anyone. Part of the excitement for me was that I wasn't trying to be in a relationship with this guy. I didn't have any emotional baggage attached to him. I didn't think that I had to behave in a particular way. Plus there was all that buildup from months and months of cybersex. We spent the entire weekend in bed. I remember moments of feeling embarrassed because I got quite loud and one of my colleagues had the hotel room next door.

When I got back to South Africa I just got on with my life. I didn't text or call him. He started to send me all these messages and eventually we got chatting again and resumed our cybersex relationship. After a few months he told me his relationship had ended. I was single too but still not keen on a long-distance relationship, so we continued with the weird connection we had going on. I became more and more interested in Hassan and lost interest in dating other men although we had not defined our relationship. On my next trip home to Cameroon, he was also there visiting, and we decided that we would officially start dating. By then we had known each other for three years and so I felt it was well worth pursuing the relationship. Being close to him was one of my motivations for choosing to study in Switzerland—I knew there would only be a three-hour journey between us.

A few days before my journey I got a message from an unknown woman on Facebook. She told me that Hassan was still in a relationship with his old girlfriend and had never left her. I was heartbroken. I didn't understand why he had lied to me. I had never asked him to leave his girlfriend. I stopped picking up his calls. A few days later I got a message from Hassan's girlfriend. The same woman who had messaged me had also messaged her. She said to me, "Can you explain your relationship with Hassan?" I didn't know what to say. I had only agreed to date him because I thought they were no longer together but I had also willingly slept with him when I knew he was in a relationship. I felt stuck. I didn't know how much information to share with her.

When I moved to Switzerland, Hassan came to see me. He told me, "I lied because I wanted to be in a relationship with you. I'm really sorry that this has to end. There is a lot happening that's outside of my control." Later on I found out that his girlfriend had tried to kill herself, and her father had called Hassan's dad, who had held a family meeting and told him to fix it. After that we broke off all contact for a couple of months.

And then my parents got robbed at home. It was a violent robbery and people died as a result. The story spread throughout our community and Hassan reached out to me. He said, "I'm really sorry that you're going through this. I know you don't want me in your life, but maybe we can be friends. I'm here for you." I'm sure you can predict what happened next. We resumed our strange virtual relationship. He was still with his girlfriend while he and I were chatting all this time, developing an even closer bond and friendship. And yes, our cybersex life was also back online.

At some point in time I decided to end things with Hassan once and for all. I had a male best friend, a guy I had known from childhood, and he had confessed to me that he had always been in love with me. He already knew about my complicated relationship with Hassan. I told him I still had feelings for Hassan and he told me not to worry, that we would figure things out. I was determined to have a fresh start. I told Hassan we could no longer be friends. I wanted to give my new relationship a real try.

My new guy was great. He's the kind of person that anyone would be lucky to be partnered with. He has such a kind heart. For the first time I felt like an equal partner in a relationship. Since we had known each other from childhood, I could truly be myself with him. With Hassan I had started to feel like the lesser being. My new man and I had a pact that we would be completely honest with each other, and so eventually when I cheated on him with Hassan, I told him. He told me that he didn't think I could have a complete relationship with anyone else unless I stopped seeing Hassan altogether, but I insisted that we were only friends, and because we didn't live in the same country and rarely saw each other, it wouldn't happen again. It happened again. Although I cared for my new man and we had a decent sex life, I just didn't feel as passionate towards him as I did with Hassan. Sex was technically good, but he didn't set my body alight. He started to feel fearful that eventually I would leave him. I also realized that I had started to try and make him someone he was not. He was a businessman. He had never been interested in higher education and I kept trying to persuade him to go back to university to complete his degree. I could see he wasn't happy and so one day I sat him down and said, "This isn't working." He agreed and went on to say, "This relationship is ending, and our friendship is also ending. I cannot be your friend anymore. I'd like you to respect that."

Shortly after our relationship ended I heard about a tragedy that had befallen Hassan's family. I had moved to Kenya for work at the time and I had heard he was back in Cameroon with his family. I sent him an email that said, "Let me know how I can support you." He replied, "I just need you to come here." I remember looking at my computer thinking, Do I want to get sucked into this dynamic again? I knew he was still with his girlfriend. A few days later I bought a ticket, flew to Cameroon, and spent two weeks there. We spent most of that time talking about his feelings. It was like I was his therapist because he didn't want to burden his family, who were already going through a difficult time, and he didn't feel like he could openly share with his girlfriend. In the meantime their relationship had also progressed. He had now moved back permanently to Cameroon, and she was meant to be moving there too so they could get married and be together. I even helped him house hunt. By then I had said to myself, "You need to forget this relationship. You guys are never going to be together. You need to figure out what you want from life and relationships." Yet we kept sleeping together. All my friends told me that until I ended that relationship, I would never be able to fully move on with my life. Then Hassan suggested that we should date seriously. His girlfriend had broken up with him—she had gotten frustrated because he kept delaying her move to Cameroon. I didn't want to be his rebound relationship, and so initially I said no, which shocked him. I asked him for some time to think about it and then I gave him an ultimatum. I told him, "We can date, but if we're still together in a year's time, then we either get married or we break up for good."

I had never been interested in marriage but I think the years of being in a grey area with him made me want something that I thought would be permanent and secure. Our first year was great. I was totally in love. At the end of the year he said to me, "My family is ready to come and ask for your hand in marriage." I thought it was a joke because he hadn't even proposed to me. And then one day my dad called me and said, "Hassan's family has gotten in touch with me, and they want to come and ask for your hand in marriage. Why didn't you say anything to me directly? Why am I hearing this from strangers?"

We ended up having multiple elaborate wedding ceremonies. There was the traditional wedding, the religious wedding, and the legal wedding. Usually Fulani people spread all these events over several days, but because Hassan and I were not interested in all the pomp and pageantry, we condensed the various ceremonies into one event. It was exhausting rushing from one type of ceremony to the next and I remember thinking, I can't wait for all this to be over so that we can just be alone. At the time I was living in Senegal, and so I put in a request to work from home so Hassan and I could be together in Cameroon. Suddenly we were living together for the first time and really getting to know each other better. Everything was perfect until I got pregnant, and then our issues with intimacy started. Pregnancy didn't change how I saw myself but I think it changed how my husband saw me. I think he felt strange about having sex with a pregnant woman, and so as my belly grew, our sex life faded away. At first I tried to initiate sex a couple of times but he just wouldn't respond.

After I had the baby I also tried to initiate sex a couple of times but again he was unresponsive. Gradually we settled into a routine where we had sex every couple of months and that didn't work for me at all. Whenever I would make a move on him, he would say, "Why are you trying so hard? It has to happen organically." After our baby was a year old, I decided to move back to Senegal. My husband and I agreed that would be a better country for our child to grow up in. Senegal has more amenities, like playgrounds, nurseries, and beaches, and I missed working in an office and having my usual support network. Even though I am Cameroonian, I hadn't spent much time there as an adult and so didn't have social networks there beyond my family. The original plan was that after a year or so my husband would move here to join me and the baby but that hasn't happened. Sometimes he comes over for a visit but we don't have sex. I tried to initiate cybersex once or twice but it just wasn't the same. We also started to experience a lot of conflict in our relationship, which made our sex life even worse. Falling pregnant again was a complete surprise because in the space of a year we had sex three times.

One of the things I am learning now is that in Islam lack of sex is also grounds for divorce. It is written in the Koran that sexual pleasure is a requirement for marriage. Our relationship was initially based on intimacy, and now, ten years down the line, there is nothing physical between us. I am in my thirties and I don't understand why my sex life has dwindled to a stop even though I'm in a monogamous marriage. It just doesn't make any sense to me. It's now May 2020, and the last time I was physically intimate with my husband was in February 2019.

The majority of women I interviewed for this book were complete strangers. Keisha is one of the few women whom I not only knew already, but consider a close friend. She lives in Canada and we initially met about six years ago when she visited Ghana for the first time. I remember thinking how beautiful she was, and what a great sense of style she had. Truth be told, I had a bit of a crush on her.

A few years ago, Keisha and I both found ourselves in London and went out to dinner with a mutual friend of ours who happens to be a highly respected African feminist activist. We ended up talking about sexuality and at one point in time our friend said, "You can't say you're a queer woman if you have never been in an open relationship with another queer woman." Although Keisha has long identified as pansexual and queer, that moment had her questioning whether she was truly queer, and whether there was any truth to that assertion. We concluded there wasn't. Queerness is a political identity. It's an expansive practice and a way of life that embraces the diversity of humans. And yes, while the sexual choices and relationships we engage in can be an important and deliberate part of how one expresses their queer identity, it's not the sum total.

In 2019, I traveled with thirty-four-year-old Keisha to her home in the Caribbean to mark Carnival, an event that on one hand celebrates the resistance of enslaved Africans, and on the other is a celebration of bodies and sexualities. I have always thought of Keisha as an extremely confident, sex-positive woman, and being in her home country with her made it easy to understand why she is the woman she is.

During J'Ouvert, people smear themselves with black oil and walk, dance, and run down the streets of Grenada. Keisha explained to me that it is one of her favorite Carnival events because it marks a dissolution of social class, and signals the moments when enslaved people broke free of their chains. There is no need to wear fancy clothing when you are going to end up covered with oil, and so people show up dressed in outfits that they know they are probably not going to be able to wear again. Some people carry broken chains and handcuffs as a visual reminder of their ancestors. In that moment it was easy to see how the politics that have shaped Grenada have influenced Keisha to be the feminist activist she is today. The other days of Carnival were a celebration of life and survival. I wore a variety of bright, skimpy outfits and danced down the streets surrounded by women of all shapes and sizes in the teeniest of costumes. It was an important affirmation that indeed all bodies are beautiful and desirable, and that's a message that I constantly remind myself of.

KEISHA

.

AS A CHILD, I spent a lot of time with my grandparents who lived in Perdmontemps, a part of town which was considered rough. The name of the neighborhood originates from the French phrase *perd mon temps*, a legacy of Grenada's colonial past. The name implies a "waste of time," and people from that part of town were considered as such: wastrels, wild, and the kind of people who spent their time gallivanting aimlessly. In other parts of town you might wake up to the sound of roosters crowing, but in Perdmontemps you are more likely to hear someone scream something like, "Wha de muddacunt yuh doin' dey?"

My grandparents were strict Catholics and considered themselves superior to their neighbors. I wasn't allowed to mingle with others in the community and the little girl I often saw playing by herself next door was not allowed to come into the yard of our home to play. From her house, we could often hear her parents screaming and cussing. I had no other way of getting to know her because she went to the local school, while I went to an elite school in a different part of town. As far as my grandparents were concerned, there was no way that Chandra and I were going to be friends. Girls like her could lead me down a wayward path. But then one day, my grandmother agreed that Chandra could come over to play. We were running around playing hide-and-seek when she suddenly pushed me against the wall and kissed me. That was the last day Chandra was allowed to come over. To this day I have no idea if my grandparents saw what happened or not.

My friends and I always took over the back row of seats on the school bus. In our crew was Tonya, who used to live in the US. She would tell us about the things that she saw her older sister do with her boyfriend. At her parties we always played mummy and daddy, and one day on our way home from school she told us, "Let's play a game. Who can put a pencil inside her wee wee thing?" and so we all did. This must have been when we were about seven or eight years old.

At the age of eleven I had my first boyfriend. I remember telling my mum about him, and she seemed okay with it because he was from a good family. He was the first guy I French-kissed. I broke up with him one day because the night before I had dreamed that he was going to end the relationship. By the time I became a teenager, my friends and I had developed this elaborate system of covering for one another, and so if I needed to hang out with my boyfriend after 6 p.m., for example, I would tell my mum that I was with one of them, and they would know what to say if she called their house looking for me. One night our system failed. I had gone to confirmation classes after school, and afterwards went for a walk along Grand Anse Beach with a guy who was also confirming his faith as a Catholic. It was a clear night, and the skies were lit up with what felt like thousands of stars. We walked hand in hand to the sound and smells of the ocean. We had miles of white-sand beach to ourselves, and we spent ages talking, kissing, and making out. I had completely forgotten my mum's usual routine when I had to come home on my own after school. As soon as dusk started to fall, she would walk down to the main road and wait for me. After dark, she didn't like me walking alone down the smaller side roads that would take me home.

Back on the beach Kevin had dropped down on his knees and asked me to be his girlfriend. A few minutes earlier he had asked if we could date and I had insisted that he do it on bended knee. By the time I got home all the parents had called one another and it was clear that I hadn't been at the home of any of my friends. When my parents asked me where I had gone, I told them, "You guys have been stressing me out so I went to the beach to pray." That night my dad got out his belt for the first time in years. At school the next day Kevin came up to me and said, "I heard you got licks."

By the time I turned seventeen, I had become an extremely horny teenager. All I had ever done with guys was kiss, dry grind, and occasionally get fingered. Over and over again. Some days, I felt that I could explode from sheer frustration. This was around the same time that I was prepping to take my A levels, and so my friends and I would often go to the university on the southern side of the island to study. One time, the junior cricket team for the Caribbean was staying on campus because they were training, and so all my friends and I paired up with the different players. My match was Derek, a guy from Trinidad. He had light-brown skin and close-cropped hair, and looked like the sportsman that he was. He wasn't overly muscular; you could just tell that he spent time working out and taking care of his body. Derek was a few years older, and more confident than most of the other guys I had been with at the time. He also knew how to make me laugh. I kept our routine the same as all my previous boyfriends—kiss, dry grind, and make out. Derek tried to persuade me to go all the way with him, and although I wanted to, I also felt unsure because I didn't know him that well.

I called my best friend Stefan who was living in Canada at the time and said to him, "I really, really, REALLY need to have sex. I feel like I'm just gonna legit combust," and he said, "Okay, I'm going to be home for the summer. We can hang out, and we can do it." When he came home we would go to parties together and make out in his mum's car. On two separate occasions he tried to put it in but it wouldn't fit. He said, "It's not working. We need a bed." He started to ask his mum if I could come over. She was clearly suspicious and would ask, "Why do you keep asking for Keisha to come over?" Finally one day she agreed that I could visit, and so Stefan came to pick me up after school. I wore a red-striped top and my favorite light-blue bell-bottom jeans. When we got to his house we went to his room and started watching a film, *The Usual Suspects*. That was always the drill: watch a film and at some point in time start making out. Halfway through the film we started kissing and touching each other, then our clothes came off and he started to go down on me. That felt really good. By then we were both completely relaxed and laughing a lot. Then he slid inside me and I started screaming. His siblings were next door and so he put his pillow over my head: "Keisha, you have to stop making so much noise." "I can't, it fucking hurts." I fell from the bed and somehow dragged the curtains down with me. When it was all over the windows were completely fogged over and we were both sweating buckets. Just then we heard his mum's car pull in and so we scrambled to get our clothes on. We went into the kitchen to say hi to his mum and I was convinced she knew what we had been up to because I was walking with my legs apart.

A year later I moved to Canada and started attending Carleton University, the same place where Stefan was studying. I spent a lot of time hanging out with him and his friends, but we never dated, although I was in love with him. To this day we're still friends.

In Canada my first roommate was a bisexual woman. I remember feeling puzzled when she told me that she was attracted to women because she also had a boyfriend. Our conversations helped me realize that all types of relationships are possible. At the time I still considered myself to be straight, and was still trying to be a good Catholic girl. It took another five to six years before I started to acknowledge my desire for women. By then I had become an activist and was involved in a lot of student organizing. I found myself drawn to women in activist circles. I thought they were so smart and wanted to spend more time in their company. I would often catch myself dreaming about kissing women, and I remember thinking, Whoa, it's white women that I'm attracted to. How disturbing. Now, I think that was because a lot of the other organizers I was working with at the time were white.

I didn't do anything about my desires. I was waiting for other people to make the first move. Around this same time I started working for a sex shop called Venus Envy. I had to learn about the various products we had in the store—all types of sex toys, massage oils, chest binders . . . In our quiet moments we also had to read this guidebook that we also sold in-store, and we were expected to eventually work our way up to leading workshops that covered topics like making sex pleasurable, managing vaginismus, and using chest binders. Even for Canada the shop was very radical for its time because of its focus on trans and gender nonconforming people, and being in that environment allowed me the freedom to come into my queer self.

One night there was a party at my university and this Ethiopian woman everyone knew was queer started to pay a lot of attention to me. She bought me drink after drink. It was clear to me that she had some intentions towards me and I got excited. Afterwards we went back to my place and had sex. She was the first woman I ever slept with. In hindsight I didn't treat her really well. I was a real pillow princess and everything was done for my pleasure. I made no effort to take care of her needs. Afterwards I asked her to sleep on the couch because she was too drunk to go home, and I didn't want to share my bed with anyone. Now I wish I had treated her differently. If I could go back in time I would make sure that the interaction we had was more reciprocal. At the very least I would have shared my bed with her and offered to make her breakfast in the morning. This was the period when I had really started to flirt with girls. The scene would usually be at a party on campus, there would be lots of alcohol, and I would start coming on to other women. I think I fancied myself as some sort of player.

After I finished university I moved to Toronto. One of the friends I made was a girl called Njoki. In some ways she was my opposite. I love to play with makeup, and Njoki barely wears any. It was like she knew that she looked so good that she didn't need it. She also had this sensual vibe about her, and this flirtatious energy. At the beginning I couldn't tell if she liked me or not. We were both in relationships at the time, and our boyfriends were also close and so we would often end up at the same parties. One day we found ourselves alone in the kitchen at a house party. I said to her, "You look really good." She said to me, "You look really good too," and we both reached for each other and started kissing. A similar thing happened when we next saw each other at an event. A few months later we were with a group of friends in a restaurant when I suddenly had this strong desire to be with her. I grabbed her hand, and we both went downstairs to the bathroom. When we got in we were instantly all over each other, kissing and fingering each other. We were in there for ages and people started banging on the door. By the time we came out a long line had formed outside, and we walked away with our heads held high.

Soon afterwards Njoki decided to move back to Kenya. I was prepared for that but I wasn't ready when she called me one night to ask if she could come over. I panicked and said no. In a previous conversation she had told me that she hated the fact that alcohol was involved every time we had hooked up, and so I knew that if she came over, we would have to do this sober. That thought scared me because she was still one of the first women I had ever been involved with sexually.

On her last night in Toronto, Njoki invited me and another friend over to help her pack. The boyfriend she had recently broken up with was also there, and while we were sitting in the living room packing, he was wearing a path in the carpet by constantly pacing up and down, walking from the bedroom door and across to the kitchen. Time and time again. You could practically see his brain working overtime as he paced. At any moment I was expecting him to take out his dick and wave it all over the room. I knew that Njoki had previously told him about our relationship. Eventually he left, and afterwards Njoki walked me to the bus stop. It was going to be her last night as a Canadian resident. We kissed briefly and I said, "I'll really miss you."

A year later some other friends and I went to Kenya to visit Njoki. On our first night we all went out clubbing, and when we came back she and I had sex. The following morning she woke up feeling guilty because she was seeing someone at the time. That really hurt my feelings. I didn't like the guy she was in a relationship with, partly because of the stories she herself had told me about him, and partly because I was jealous. I also didn't understand why things had to be different; we had never let a man get between us previously. I needed to get away and so traveled to Zanzibar for a few days, but the beauty of the island made no difference to my mood. I came back more distraught than ever before. I was constantly crying and emotional. My friends were so worried that they staged an intervention. That was when Njoki told me how much I had hurt her feelings in Canada. We decided that what was most important was our friendship, and we wanted to preserve that.

A few years later I went back to Kenya. I was expecting to stay with Njoki because she had a two-bedroom flat, but she told me that her new boyfriend did not want me to stay over, and the relationship was so new that she didn't want to rock the boat. It felt odd to me that in spite of that she joined me and two other girlfriends for a safari road trip. In the room that we shared at the Masai Mara, I wondered what she had told her man about this trip. Did he know we were going to be sharing a room together? One day she was changing in the room, and unlike previous occasions on that trip wasn't making an effort to hide her body. I could see her full breasts and her pregnant bump, which was another reminder of her relationship. I wondered if she was trying to show that she felt comfortable being naked around me even though the dynamics of the relationship had changed. I still felt attracted to her so left the room and had a smoke.

Today I feel like my best sex life is being lived in my imagination. I'm a lot more free in my mind than I am in my body. I dream and fantasize a lot but I don't necessarily create the kind of experiences that would allow me to enjoy the feelings that I think about. I want to be able to let go a lot more. One of my favorite moments was going dancing during a trip to Ghana. Usually when I go to a dance class I can feel how rigid I am. I move, but in my mind I am calculating all the steps. That night the music moved through my body. I was in total sync with my dance partner, Dave. I had only met him that night, but we danced throughout, and afterwards we went to the beach. We walked along the shore and it felt magical. I didn't care that the tips of my previously white dress were now brown with dirt. I didn't care that my leather sandals were now soaked with salt water. When we got back to the hotel I remembered that I'd made a prior date that I had forgotten about. I didn't care about that either.

At the age of twenty-two I felt like the last virgin amongst my group of friends. I didn't have the expanded definition of sex that I have now. I considered myself a virgin because I hadn't had penetrative sex with a man. What had kept me from having sex were the messages I had absorbed about young women and girls who had sex. Popular shows on Ghanaian TV had a common script. A young, fast girl falls pregnant, she has to leave school to raise her child, and as a result her life is destroyed. I saw this happen in real life. One of the girls in my boarding school fell pregnant, left school to have the baby, and, in a departure from the TV shows I watched, returned to school a few months later. Plot twist: the subsequent gossiping and finger-pointing drove her back out of school. I often wonder what course her life took.

How can we let go of the scripts we're given as children? How can our "rational" minds let go of beliefs that no longer serve us? How do we go from believing that sex before marriage is a sin to living our best sex lives? These are all questions that my interview with Bibi, a thirty-five-year-old Nigerian woman who identifies as cisgender and straight, raised for me.

BIBI

·

ZACH CAME TO meet me at the taxi stand and we took a motorbike to where he was staying. It was one of those big, fancy expat houses in Cotonou. I remember thinking, Wow, it's so good to see you, to be around you, spend time with you. We went out for dinner, and when we got back we both fell asleep. We woke up in the middle of the night and started chatting. Chatting turned to kissing. We started with closed-mouth kisses, then open-mouthed kisses. I remember falling off the twin bed—we laughed, pushed the beds together again, rolled over to one side, and continued kissing. He started to touch my boobs, stroke my clit, and started going in and out with his fingers. I had gotten an IUD before leaving for Nigeria, and when he was going in and out it started to hurt, almost like he was hitting the IUD.

"Stop."

He kept going. I got more and more turned on. He reached out for a condom and continued to kiss me. He tried to put his penis inside me, and it wouldn't go in.

I couldn't turn my brain off.

Shit, what's happening, why is this not working?
What's going on?
Is this still the right thing to do no matter what?
It's not like he is my boyfriend, we're just friends.
What are you doing?

This was one of my fears. I just wanted it to happen, I wanted it to go in, get it over and done with. He was someone I really cared about. I was really turned on and thinking, Let's go. Let's do this. But my vagina was like "sorry dude." I didn't want to say anything but I had to.

"This is my first time, I'm feeling a bit worried and scared . . ."

"What do you need? We'll take it slow, we'll take it easy, we'll make it good."

I'm grateful that my first experience was with him. I wanted to feel normal, and for it to feel okay, and it did. It had taken me years to get here but finally, at the age of thirty-two, I had technically gone all the way. I had managed to do this in spite of all the voices in my head, in spite of the repression, in spite of a sense of shame.

I grew up as a Christian in Nigeria, but when I moved to the US at seventeen I became more Christian. I joined a church, got baptized, and joined a discipleship group. Sin was a conversation in our everyday discussions— the avoidance of sin, and not doing sinful things, which included thinking about sex. We were told, "You don't want lust in your heart." In a strange way, it heightened my awareness of sex, but I knew it was something that I could not do until I got married. I had never had sex before, so for me it wasn't a big deal—I wanted my virginity to be a gift when I got married. We were told that sex was one of the perks of marriage. I did not want to go to hell, and really wanted to get closer to Jesus, but some of the women who had been sexually active before joining the church struggled. I remember one of the girls in the church telling me: "If I need to pee, I'm gonna go right away. Because when I hold it and finally pee, it gives me a similar release."

I remember thinking: Whatever you need to do to keep your salvation, girl, that's what you do.

Subsequently I went to a women's college that was progressive in certain ways, but I never paid attention to any of the conversations around sex because I was still really religious. I went through college and never kissed anyone. Around the same time there were changes happening in the church. It had been so strict and people were having difficulties. There was a sermon, which will stay with me forever, and the preacher said:

"Sex is not necessarily the enemy, it is a natural thing; however, as Christians you are not allowed to have it until you're married. It's one of the perks of marriage. Once you're married you can do it all the time." So I thought, Sex is the gift I'm going to get if I hold out.

What I struggled with when I was in grad school was that all my amazing, interesting, and cool friends would not go to heaven unless I preached to them so that they could have a change of heart and become Christians. That was really hard for me to swallow, and I started to question that, and when you question one thing, you start to question other things as well.

By the time I was thirty, I had started to think: This is stupid, I just need to find someone I am attracted to and just do this thing. By now I had talked about sex with friends a lot, and read about it, but there were always these voices in my head:

This is a moment of no return.
Once you have had sex it is done.
You can go to hell for this.
You are now officially a scarlet woman.
You have broken one of the laws of God and that's not sexy.

I would be making out with a guy and my mind would go: Oh shit, what are you doing? You just met this guy at a bar. Another time, mid-makeout, I blurted: "I am a virgin!"

We both froze for a pause.

"So do you want to do this?" he asked.

"I don't know."

It was almost like I wanted the decision taken out of my hands so I'd be like, It just happened to me, but once I had the chance to think I poured cold water over any such thoughts.

Which is why it was such a big deal when Zach and I finally had sex. He was a white boy from Minnesota. We liked each other for a long time. We had similar interests: music, art, books, anything Africa related. We could talk about everything but we couldn't talk about the fact that we liked each other. When I decided to move from the US to Nigeria, he came over to help me pack. He spoke about how much our friendship meant to him. I was touched but that also scared the shit out of me. I thought moving to Nigeria would increase the likelihood of me meeting and dating a Nigerian man, which is ironic because I am now dating a white guy.

I have always avoided getting into relationships because I did not want to get hurt or have my heart broken. I saw what it did to people around me, and I didn't want that. I don't know where I learned to be afraid, but the way fear manifested itself in my life was the fear of putting your heart in someone's hands. That sense of stripping yourself and being intimate with someone and then they use *that* against you. I had a fear of loving someone in spite of needing to protect myself. I had a fear of caring for someone and yet being unable to reach them. That really scares me.

It is not easy for me to cum. It takes a combination of factors. I am trying to learn to get out of my head. My brain is so busy when I'm having sex, and I feel really nervous. It's a kind of female performance anxiety. I still have a sense of shyness. I feel like I don't know a lot and I haven't figured out how to communicate what I want and need. I watch for people's reactions: Are they going to get me? Am I going to ruin the moment?

Sex feels like the one area in my life where I am not confident. That makes me sad. I am an adult in so many ways apart from this. For a long time I shielded myself from relationships and intimacy . . . this sharing of yourself with another person, being willing to let someone into your heart, letting this person have some modicum of power over you. Realizing that vulnerability is not the worst thing that could happen to me as a woman. I keep asking myself, What is it going to take to develop the confidence to have the kind of sex I want to have with my partner?

I met Tom, another white man, while I was in DC. We worked for the same organization until he moved to Uganda to take up a different role, but we stayed in touch even after I was back in Nigeria. By then he had moved to Congo, and when I turned thirty-four, he called to wish me a happy birthday. We chatted for a while and then he said: "I need to get out of Congo."

I said, "I'm broke as shit but I love traveling."

We started to look at options. We decided on Morocco; it was four hours from Lagos to Casablanca, and we could split the cost of the trip and share a hotel room. I had decided that 2015 was my year of being open and saying yes. I remember thinking to myself, Nothing will happen. I had also just started seeing someone in Nigeria. I arrived at the airport in Morocco before he did. His plane landed and he started walking towards me: Oh shit, he is really attractive, why would I even think I wouldn't be attracted to him?

We caught the train to Marrakesh, had dinner, and went to bed. The next day we explored the city. It was Ramadan so most restaurants were not serving alcohol. I remember wanting a glass of wine; we were passing by this riad and I saw this couple drinking and I said, "Oh my god, wine, let's go eat there." We ate, drank, talked, and laughed. We went back to the room, and sat side by side on the bed looking on my iPad for things to do the next day. He wanted to go to Fez, go through the mountains; I was fine with wherever he wanted to go. We were sitting close to each other. At some point in time he sat behind me, I leaned against him, and he started massaging my neck. When he touched my boobs, I remember thinking, whatever . . . then he started kissing my neck, and then someone turned, I can't remember who but we started kissing, and kept kissing. While our lips were still locked together he lifted me up, leaned me against the wall and continued to kiss me. He started to say:

"Your boobs are amazing."

"Your body . . ."

"God . . ."

I felt so attractive and wanted, I could hear myself moan and then I started to think of Ramadan: Please God don't let us get arrested. What will I tell my mother?

He went down on me, and continued to talk:

"Your vagina is amazing, it is beautiful, and the taste of it is so good, I don't want to stop."

In my head I am thinking, Na wash, but best wash ever.

I felt a twinge of guilt when I remembered the guy I had been spending time with in Nigeria but I reminded myself, It is 2015, the year of being open and saying yes.

We were in Morocco for seven days. It was a dream vacation. We spent the time holding hands, kissing, having leisurely sex, eating good food, and seeing beautiful things. I had to leave earlier and at the airport I felt sad to be leaving Morocco, leaving him . . . I remember thinking, Why can't we go home together?

There are some people you meet, and you think, Oh, you must have an interesting story to tell. I first met Ebony* in a club—she was wearing a sheer black negligee set, which was in line with the "pajama" theme for the night. She's the kind of person anyone would notice in a crowd. She has long, thick, free-formed locs, a striking face, and a modelesque body. I watched her wine on the guy she was with. Their erotic dance moves caught the eye of many people in the club. They made a good-looking couple, and I could practically see the sexual chemistry sizzle.

Subsequently I learned more about Ebony. She is a nomadic South African creative in her mid-thirties who travels all over the world for her art. She identifies as sexually fluid, and that sexual chemistry that I could see in the club between her and the man she was with? In real life it's been more of a drizzle.

Ebony and I have both had relationships with men who identified as Rastafarians and for that reason were reluctant to perform cunnilingus on us. We both persuaded our partners to give "going down" a try, and ultimately decided that no oral was better than reluctant oral. That's one of the things I have learned when it comes to sex. If your partner is not keen to try a sexual act, don't keep trying to persuade them to change their mind. Acts of sex always need to be enthusiastically performed.

EBONY

▪

I THINK OF myself as a nomad. I'm happiest when I travel, and experience new cultures and people. I've built a global life for myself and rarely spend longer than three weeks at home. That is unusual behavior for a South African; as a people we tend to be more inward facing.

I find that it's hard to really get to know people when you are constantly traveling, and so I tend not to have as much sex as I would like. I also know that a traditional committed relationship would not work for me, and I am not interested in having children. I don't want to feel tied down in any way unless the person I'm with is just like me, willing and able to travel the world at a whim.

I have a lot of sex with myself. I own several toys, and I always pick one or two to travel with. Over time, I've learned that I need to be careful not to pack any toys in my hand luggage. There was one time that I got stopped at Dubai airport. The immigration guy who was dressed in a long white traditional outfit pulled me to the side and demanded that I open my case. He pointed to my dildo, asked me to remove it, and said, "What is that?" I told him what it was. "You can't bring it here. It's not allowed." I ended up having to leave my toy in a bin. So far the United Arab Emirates has been the only country where I have been unable to find a sex toy to buy. Yet it was the country where I experienced the most sexual harassment. I felt particularly targeted as a Black woman. Emirati men seemed to view Black women as objects, easily available for sex. Men constantly tried to grope me in the mall or would solicit me while I was sitting at the bar of my hotel. I ended up purchasing a burka and wearing that throughout my stay. I felt free in it because I could wear nothing underneath.

It took me a while to realize that traditional monogamous relationships were not for me. I've been engaged three times. The first time was to a woman. I was still very young at the time, and although we were in love it was too hard to fight for our love. On paper, South Africa has one of the most progressive LGBTQI legislations. The reality is different. We were constantly told that we were unAfrican and evil. Lesbian women were constantly killed and raped. Other lesbian women we knew were told by their family that they would rather they had HIV than be queer. I wasn't strong enough to deal with all of that and the relationship ended.

Have you heard that Nick Holder song "No more dating DJs"? It goes: "No more dating DJs, MCs, producers, hip-hop critics, radio hosts, et cetera." I think they forgot to add "Rastas, spiritual types, hoteps, etcetera."

I spent three years in a relationship with a Rastafarian man who never sucked my pussy because reggae musicians and the so-called custodians of Rasta culture would say things like, "Fire bun man who suck pussy." Men who went down on women were also derided as batty. I think that if eating your girl's coochy makes you gay that's okay because then we can all be gay together. There's nothing wrong with being gay. How can you allow other people's perception to govern what you do in your personal life? That's the one period in my life when I allowed other people's beliefs to limit me. Eventually I persuaded my man to go down on me but he was racked with guilt every time he went down south. He felt like I was swaying him from the one true path. It's no fun when someone thinks they are going to go straight to hell every time they go down on you.

When I left that relationship I started a group for women to learn about living sensually in harmony with their true selves. I was particularly interested in the connections between sexuality and spirituality because I wanted to work mainly with Rasta women. I wanted my sisters to know that sexuality is not evil, and that there are ways to align your sexuality and spirituality. I wanted these women to get to know themselves, and to figure out what their boundaries were, and sometimes to encourage them to veer out of their comfort zones. All my Rasta women friends have between three and six children. I would ask, "Are you enjoying this process of making children or are you just getting high, having sex, and making babies?" "How can you start to talk about the things that you would like to experience in the bedroom?" "How can you introduce that to your man?" "And if you can't, how can you self-please?"

That period was when I had really gotten into self-pleasure, and so I had become an advocate for the cause. It was also around the same time when there was this craze around yoni balls. After childbirth, many of my friends were interested in figuring out how to tighten their pelvic muscles, and so I started producing yoni balls out of precious stones like jade and rose quartz. It took me a while to realize that these things don't work for everybody. Some women's bodies literally rejected the balls. Their vaginas would push them right out. Initially I thought the women were doing something wrong. Maybe they hadn't bonded with the crystal. Or they didn't clear the crystal and set clear intentions. Then it began to feel too much like packaging a type of "sexy spirituality" and now I no longer endorse yoni balls. It's the same way I feel about how Black consciousness has been commercialized in South Africa. It's a Black Power T-shirt, Afro earrings, a Steve Biko top, a Kwame Nkrumah cap, or a Marcus Garvey hat. It's just a commodity. You wear your conscious-ness or you perform your consciousness in these popular ways. That's how I ended up feeling about the yoni balls because you can work out your pelvic muscles without crystal balls. Just Kegel exercises.

The last relationship I was in completely ended the myth of monogamy for me. I had just gotten engaged to Dave and we were driving to Durban to celebrate. His phone was hooked up to the Bluetooth system in the car and every so often the music would be interrupted by the sound of ringing, and a robotic voice saying, "Primrose calling." Now under normal circumstances Dave always picks up his phone around me but on this drive he kept stead-fastly ignoring it. Eventually I snapped, picked up his phone, and unlocked it because I knew his pin code. I checked his messages from Primrose and there it was. She was pregnant. Not only had he been cheating on me but he had also risked my life by sleeping with another woman without protection. I demanded that he drop me off by the side of the highway although I was more than one hundred kilometers from home. After that experience I decided that was the end of monogamy for me, and now I've been polyamorous for the past six years. I hear life begins at forty, and so I know that in the future I may make a different choice, but for now this works for me. If I do ever end up with another man, I'll make sure he's older and has already gone through his midlife crisis.

I'm currently in a relationship that I need to extricate myself from. A few years ago I was at a music festival in Spain and I heard some good dancehall playing. I came out to dance and saw this tall, dark-skinned man. That's my weakness—melanin. We had so much fun dancing together and decided that we would hang out throughout the festival. At festivals everyone showers in the open so I saw his body. I told him, "Hmmm, you have a big dick," he was like, "Hmmm, you have big boobs."

Have you ever had sex in a tent at a festival? I've never sweated so much in my life. I was dripping wet, we were sliding all over each other, and we could hear people outside the tent, which meant they could also hear us. Afterwards we kept in touch and a few months later I went to visit him in Germany. He's a qualified aerospace engineer but works as a bartender. That's something I don't get. Why doesn't he leave Germany and take his skills somewhere else? He could easily find work in another country if he put in the effort. Recently we've been together because we both traveled to Ghana for the Year of Return. We've been here for a month and we've only had sex twice. One time I whipped out my toys and he visibly got uncomfortable. To make matters worse his best friend is always around, and sometimes sleeps in the same room as us. I came here to live my best life but now I feel trapped, and for me that's a sign that I need to make a drastic change. I've learned to ask myself every day, Are you happy today? And if the answer is no I make a change.

Out of all the women I interviewed, Elizabeth is the one I have known the longest. I can't remember the year we met, but what I do recall are some of the memories we've shared. Like the time we went out clubbing and my friend Paulette and I carried Liz and her wheelchair down a long, winding staircase to Floridita, a Latin bar and salsa club in Soho, London. Liz was in my crew. We called our collective "For Sisters." We were a group of African Diaspora women who would meet regularly for meals and drinks to network, share experiences, and support one another.

At the age of nineteen I moved back to London. Although I was born in the city, I had no roots there. In 1980, my mum, facing the prospect of raising two children alone in a cold land, decided to return to Ghana, and in 1997, I made the return journey to start university in London. In the readings I had to do for my Cultural Studies degree I discovered the works of Black feminists, primarily African American women like bell hooks, Alice Walker, and Patricia Hill Collins. I started to think more deeply about my own gendered experiences. I "remembered" that my earliest consensual sexual relationships had been with girls in my boarding school. I started to wonder what that meant. Had I been a lesbian in school? Was I now straight? I still hadn't had penetrative sex with a man. Was I still a virgin?

In our "For Sisters" gatherings we talked mainly about our career and business dreams. We knew that as Black women the odds were stacked against us succeeding in the corporate world. What we failed to recognize at the time was that in the future world of dating we would be dealt an unfair card as well. On one hand exoticized as

*overly sexualized, and on the other hand undesired as partners. There
has been lots of research that shows that Black women are the least
likely to be chosen for dates on apps.*

*My friend Elizabeth is a forty-four-year-old heterosexual woman
of Nigerian and Scottish heritage. Her light skin and long hair are
considered stereotypically desirable characteristics in Black women.
Liz is also a Black woman who uses a wheelchair and navigates
dating in online spaces. Her experience of online dating ranges from
being exoticized because of her disability to being ghosted because she
uses a wheelchair. My conversation with Liz challenged me to consider
my own participation in ableism, and to see my own internal
contradiction more clearly. How can I truly consider myself a body-
positive person when I have never felt sexually attracted to a person
with a visible disability? Why have I only ever had sex with other
able-bodied people?*

ELIZABETH

·

I STILL REGRET not marrying my first love, especially in today's era of online dating, where men are so quick to move on to the next available woman. We met when I was seventeen and he was five years older; we started to spend all our time together and he quickly became my best friend. I was seeing someone else at the time. He got jealous. He started seeing someone else too, and I thought, Why are you with her? At the same time I didn't see him as boyfriend material. I just wasn't drawn to him physically. He was tall, with average looks. He wouldn't turn any heads if he walked into the room, but women were attracted to him. He was super smart, which is what I liked about him. He tutored me in physics, chemistry, and math, although I didn't really need the extra lessons. It was a way for us to spend time with each other. After about an hour of tutoring, we would just spend the rest of the day hanging out. I used to call him Mr. Encyclopedia because he had all of these random pieces of information stored in his brain, like when particular porn stars died and what the cause of death was. I was an avid reader and so would sometimes quiz him about things I'd read, and he always already knew all about them. Even now he's the blueprint for the kind of man I want to be with. Someone smart and easy to talk to.

One day out of the blue my mum told me that we were moving to London. It was such a shock. I had been born in Lagos and had barely ever left the city. My whole universe was there, my friends, family . . . Lagos was home and now we were leaving in a month's time because my parents were breaking up. All this time Tunde had been telling me how much he liked me but I had completely friend-zoned him. Now that I knew I was leaving the country, I started to feel really conflicted. I had become interested in him in a romantic sense but

I didn't want to do anything when I didn't know if we would ever see each other again. The last month together became really intense. We started to spend even more time together. We would kiss and make out but never went past that. He said to me, "I've been telling you for the past year how I felt and you never reciprocated. Now you're leaving, and you're telling me that you like me too?"

I was so lonely when we moved to London. I had no friends and knew absolutely no one apart from the people I had traveled there with—my mum, my sister, and my niece. Tunde and I would write long letters to each other. It was really like sending each other our diaries because we would note down what had happened every day for about a week and then send it in the mail. It was the nineties, so letters took a long time to arrive, and by the time you sent yours, you always knew there was probably another one already on its way to you. We also used to record ourselves speaking to each other on cassette tapes and send them to each other through people who were traveling back and forth from London to Lagos. During my first year in London I saved any spare money I had, including my grant, and then when school broke up for the summer, I bought a ticket home to Lagos. I wanted to see Tunde.

It was magical. It felt like we had never been apart. I spent a month in Lagos. That was when we had sex for the first time. After that we started to date. Back in London I would save all my money to buy phone cards. His family didn't have a phone at home, so I would call his cousin who lived next door and tell them I'd call back in thirty minutes. In that time they would run over and get him so we could speak. The phone cards always ran out so quickly. You could chat for about twenty minutes and then you'd be out of credit. After the first year it became more difficult to maintain the relationship. I had also gotten more settled into life at my university and was starting to make friends. I felt like we were growing apart but Tunde didn't feel the same. He asked me to marry him. I was hesitant. From what I had observed in Nigeria, marriage wasn't very attractive. Husbands constantly cheated on their wives and a lot of marriages were ending in divorce. I told him I wanted to wait until I had finished university. A year before I finished he told me we needed to start planning our wedding. I had to tell him that I'd changed my mind. I heard from friends that that really messed with his head. He became a player and started dating lots of women in Lagos. He was broken until he met a particular woman who put him back together. They got married but I didn't know that for ages. Even when we reunited in Lagos several years down the line, it took a while for him to tell me that he was married.

With all the men I've dated, I've always been their first girlfriend who is a wheelchair user. For some of them, they may have had a girlfriend who broke her leg and had to use a crutch or chair for a few months, but they've never been with anyone who was disabled. I remember one of my exes had dated someone who was deaf, but that was an exception; all the men I have been with have never been with anyone who has a physical disability. So for the men in my life being with me is a new experience.

Sometimes it can be awkward. They are not sure what to do. They wonder how much movement I have. They are not sure whether they can move me around, and I'm always like, "Do your thing, take control, be assertive. Move me how you want to move me. Tell me what you want me to do. Don't have any hang-ups or assume I'm going to feel uncomfortable in any scenario." I really can't stand passive men who wait for me to make the first move. I just think, Oh please, this is not going to work. I have a strong personality, and so I need someone who can match that strength. We can still have that back-and-forth where we switch roles, I can take control and be the dominant one, but I'll get bored if I always have to be the lead. With some men it's fine; their attitude is, "Screw it, I'm just going to do what I normally do. I'm going to be dominant and possessive. I'm not going to treat her any differently from other women." That kind of confidence is a turn-on for me. And then with other men they are like, "I'm not sure, is this okay? Are you all right with this?" In my head I'm thinking, Please just stop talking, you're breaking the flow, just do it.

I do a lot of online dating and so I make sure to tell people before we meet that I'm in a wheelchair. I get different reactions. Some people say, "This is not for me," and that's the last I'll hear from them. With those that keep on chatting, they'll very often ask, "So can you have sex?" Why is that even a question? Do men think people with disabilities are asexual? That they have no sexual feelings or desires? If someone wants to have sex, regardless of their disability, they will find a way. If desire is there, and someone is willing, there is always a way to have sex. I always jokingly tell men, "The only thing I can't do is stand up and have sex. Besides, when is the last time you had sex standing up? What position do you usually have sex in?" Most people have sex on a bed or on some sort of surface. I'm fine just so long as you don't expect me to stand up against a wall. If you can hold me against the wall, which I've also experienced, then that totally works too.

On the flip side, I've also met some men via dating apps who are really turned on by the idea of being with a woman in a wheelchair. There was one guy I had been chatting with, we were already really attracted to each other, and then I told him I was in a chair; he then became even more intense and said, "Now I really need to have you." That felt creepy, it was like I had become some kind of fetish for him. With some other guys, sleeping with a woman in a wheelchair is like ticking a box. I've slept with a blonde, I've slept with a Black woman, I've slept with a woman in a chair.

Then there are those folks I meet in real life. Maybe we meet at an event. We get chatting, and then they say something along these lines: "I'm so intrigued by you. I want to know what it's like to have sex with you." Part of that is because I'm in a wheelchair. They are not interested in getting to know me as a person. If an element of that attraction is about the chair and I'm just an object of curiosity to them, it's really off-putting. If a guy is drawn to me and wants to have sex with me, that's fine. I'm not some kind of circus freak. What happens once we've had sex and you've satisfied your curiosity?

The worst are those men who have some sort of God complex. Those who think they have a healing dick. I've had men tell me, "If I have sex with you, you'll be able to walk." This has happened twice now. Granted, one of those experiences was when I was much younger, even before I met Tunde. It's like they think they have the magic stick. What's going to happen? You insert it, and then I'm magically healed?

Since my last relationship ended about a year ago, I haven't had much of a sex life. I don't want to waste my time with someone if I don't see a shared future. I'm at a stage where I'm now looking for something long-term. I like having someone special in my life. That person you know you can always hang out with, talk to, and have sex with. All relationships have a natural expiration date. The people I know who got married in their twenties are now getting divorced. My hope is that if I get married now, by the time we reach our expiration date we'd just be too old to bother to end things and so will stay together.

Recently I've gone back on Bumble. I've spoken to a few people but only been on one date. I find that nowadays I'm very detached on dating apps. You start talking to a guy, he's showing interest, sending you good morning messages, asking how's your day going, sending good night messages, all of that, and then one day it fizzles out because he's on to the next. Other times people get really intense very quickly and want to meet up but everybody's busy in London and it can be impossible to align your schedules. When that happens, you suddenly stop getting all the messages because they are off to the next one. Initially I used to feel bad when these things happened because you get into a routine where you are talking to this person on a regular basis and then they disappear. Or you have just one date and their interest fizzles out. It sucks when that's someone you want to know. It's okay when it's my interest fizzling out. I know men also have these experiences on dating apps. There are some men I've met who I've friend-zoned so they've shared some of their experiences with me. There are women on dating apps who just want to be taken out for a nice meal or just shown a good time. There are a lot of men on their case and so they don't want to commit. It works both ways. There are just so many options and dating apps out there.

One of the things I do appreciate is when men are open and honest about what they want on a dating app. I like it when a man says he's looking for something casual and not interested in being committed. That way I know not to waste my time. The worst is you start chatting with a guy, he seems serious, and then a few weeks later he says, "I'm not really ready to commit, let's go with the flow." Yeah right, you just want to flow into my panties. On the flip side you also get the men who are just way too serious. There was one guy I went on a date with, and he said, "I'm looking to be married by the end of the year." I thought, Do you know that we are in August? That was a bit extreme, although I appreciate people who are intentional about their dating. At least I know then that person is dating with a sense of purpose and looking to have a long-term relationship, although sometimes those people can also be too much. That level of intensity can be off-putting. It's okay if by some miracle you feel exactly the same, but it's never the guys I want who say after one date, "I really like you." That's still always a shock to me when that happens. You don't know me, you don't even know my last name, and you want to be committed to me? It's emotionally draining.

A few years ago I went back to Lagos on vacation. I decided to go to Tunde's family home, which was only a few streets away from a friend's house. When his mum saw me she just screamed my name. I had always gotten along with her. She told me Tunde had moved out and gave me his number. When I called he knew instantly who I was but still asked, "Who is this?" I later on found out that his wife had been there when I called, and when she heard him mention my name, she said, "Abi, your girlfriend is back," and he jokingly told her, "Yes, she's back, it's time for you to leave." I didn't know all of this at the time. I didn't know he was married. When I saw him I just thought to myself, You made a huge mistake, but he actually vocalized it. He told me, "You messed up."

That bond between us was still there. When we're together it's like no one else exists. We forget that there are other people in the room. People look at us as if to say, "What's going on?" and then we say, "Oh no, we are only friends." Initially he hid his marriage from me, and then I ran into some mutual friends who then said, "Tunde's wedding was so great," and I was slightly shell-shocked. We had been spending every day of my vacation together. He told me that he hadn't known how to tell me that he was married and had a child because once we reunited all the old feelings he had for me came back.

Fortunately we hadn't been together physically. That period put a strain on his marriage. His wife thought he was going to leave her. He told me, "I can't even touch her. I don't want to have sex with her." He was conflicted. We continued to see each other every day for the month and a half I spent in Lagos, and when I came back to London we would chat all the time. That really messed with my head. Eventually I told him, "This has got to stop. We need to put some space between us. This is not healthy. You're married and have a child." Otherwise I knew it would only be a matter of time before we acted on our feelings and I would have felt really guilty. I know he would have felt even worse. So we decided to put some distance between us, not talk as often, and just maintain a friendship. We're still close. We speak every now and then.

Naisha and I were connecting for the first time via Zoom and the thought that kept crossing my mind was, *Oh my god, she's stunning.* A friend had introduced us after asking what my definition of African was. "Would you consider including a white African woman in your book?" I was adamant that I wouldn't. There were lots of books written about the sexualities, desires, and fantasies of white women (think of Lisa Taddeo's Three Women, *for instance*) but none centering on the diversity of Black African women. "Would you consider including an Asian woman?" she asked. "It depends if she also identifies as African," was my response. I'm always down for some Black and Brown solidarity.

It was a joy to speak to Naisha. She is a thirty-four-year-old South African woman of Asian descent. She is the only woman I interviewed who went from identifying as bisexual in her early teens to concluding in later years that at her core she is a straight woman on the queer spectrum. My trajectory has been very much the opposite. In my early teens I had little to no understanding of human sexuality. I didn't think much about the sexual interactions that I had with girls in my boarding school, and I certainly did not recognize myself as bisexual. It wasn't until my twenties that I started to understand sexuality as a spectrum, and finally started to identify as bisexual.

NAISHA

•

OVER THE PAST five to six years, I have come to the realization that I am straight, although I started identifying as bisexual during my teenage years in South Africa. This awareness came slowly to me, and at the cost of hurting a number of women I was in relationships with. I was living in Berlin when my seven-year-old marriage ended. I had convinced my husband to move there with me from London, although at the time it was clear that our relationship was already on the rocks. Six to nine months later the inevitable happened. Subsequently, I learned about polyamory and thought the concept was really cool and began having multiple relationships. At one point in time I was with two men and one woman. I felt very happy. My relationship with the woman was going fairly well except that she hated polyamorous relationships. I also didn't feel as strongly towards her as I did towards the men in my life at the time. What I did enjoy was the quality time we spent together. I liked being her friend and doing couple-type things with her.

I've been told that I give off a queer vibe. In bars women often come up to me and say, "I don't think you're straight." Even when I insist, "I'm straight, I have a boyfriend," I'm told, "I don't think you are." I'm not a hundred percent straight. I have had lots of queer experiences but I've never fallen in love with a woman. Often I feel like women don't listen to me when I tell them that I am straight. In Berlin, one of my friends is a queer DJ and so I go to lots of queer parties in the Latina scene. The music is usually reggaeton and there's more of a Caribbean vibe. The crowd is often filled with women and a few men. I love listening to good music, and I love to dance so that's my scene. I feel way more sexual in those environments. Those are also the kind of places where you can easily meet people that you may have a casual hookup with.

One time I was hanging out at the club with this woman I thought was straight. We were with a group of friends and everyone was dancing and drinking. Suddenly she started kissing me, and I went along with it. At some point in time I said to her, "I usually just hook up with guys nowadays. I'm pretty much straight." And she said, "Me too." I thought, Cool, this is really not a big deal then. Over the next few weeks she and I continued to hang out. Every time I was sober I would say, "I'm actually so straight," and she would say, "Me too." I liked that I had someone to hold at night, someone to wake up next to, and someone to go out for breakfast with. It wasn't necessarily about being sexual for me, but more because it felt good. I kept trying to dial back the sexual part of the relationship with no luck. I started to express the fact that I didn't want us to hook up and she'd say, "Just come out for a drink," and at some point in time in the evening would start kissing me. I would just go along with it, but I started feeling that my wishes were not being respected. When you've hooked up with someone before, they tend to think that there's no reason for you not to hook up with them again unless you're in an exclusive relationship. That's been my experience with both men and women. Eventually I started to avoid this woman. She had only been in Berlin temporarily, and wanted to meet up one last time before leaving the city. That meetup never happened.

My lesbian circle of friends describe me as exhausting. They say, "She doesn't know what she is," or, "She'll kiss the girl but is really nuts." I started to feel more like I was an arsehole man who says things like, "I'm happy with the way things are right now," only because they don't want to commit to a relationship. The reality is that my relationships with women have never worked. They will usually last for about two months and eventually I'll get distracted by a man. Part of what I've hated about my lesbian relationships is that I'm always cast as the more masculine person because of my size. I'm five foot eleven and I've been the taller one in all but one of my relationships with women. The truth is I like being the woman in a heterosexual relationship. My current circle of friends are also mainly women who identify as straight, although I've kissed or had sex with one or two of them. They are also more interested in men even though they have had relationships with women. For now I'm choosing to identify as straight because I am not truly queer and I feel that I have caused more hurt and pain by identifying as such.

As a teenager I had crushes on both boys and girls. This was way before I had any physical experiences with any person of either gender. I also grew into the height I am now at the age of twelve, so I was far from petite. I was tall and had big boobs, which I hated. I felt uncomfortable with my body and started to adopt more of a masculine façade. I realize now that I was trying to shield myself from the violence that girls and women experience in South Africa. I turned twelve in 1994, the same year that Nelson Mandela came into power. A lot of things changed in South Africa at the time. My parents were activists and my mum was a feminist, and so from childhood I was exposed to a lot of people from different types of backgrounds. I think that's how I developed an openness in terms of who I'm attracted to. A lot of my mum's friends, for instance, identified as queer or lesbian.

I've always been a bit of a chameleon, both sexually and racially. I went to private school on a bursary from the age of nine and was exposed to people from many different racial backgrounds. Although I felt attracted to people from different races, I also had a sense that it was somehow wrong. Most of my childhood relationships were with people who were white, Black, or Cape Colored. I remember that at some point in time I made it my mission to kiss someone of every race. I am of Indian heritage, and at the age of seventeen I went to Durban, a city in South Africa with the highest population of Indians. When my cousin took me clubbing that night my one goal was to kiss an Indian person. I succeeded in that but to date I haven't had sex or a relationship with an Indian person. My two major relationships have been with a white English man whom I married, and my most recent partner was a Black South African man.

I met my ex-husband at twenty-four while I was in London on a work visa. We met three weeks before I was due to return home to South Africa. My plans had been to start traveling around the world and to make a living by teaching English. All that changed after we started our relationship. I applied for a six-month extension on my visa so that I could stay on in the UK. When that ran out we moved to South Africa together, and after a year got married. I think everything went topsy-turvy partly because all we originally wanted was to live in the same country. Our differences soon started to show up. He was from a working-class family in North Yorkshire; his family were conservatives, and very organized in terms of how they lived their lives, a trait which I originally admired because it was so different from how my chaotic left-wing activist family lived. In October they would create Christmas gift lists and everyone would get the gift they had on the list or receive a £10 or £20 gift voucher. It took me a while to realize that the unspoken rule was that you would have to send a thank-you card back, and if you didn't you just got the cold treatment.

When we got together I hadn't thought about how important family was, and we hadn't had any conversations about our future plans. I wanted to travel and explore new places while he got more and more like his family as time went on. He used to be open-minded and flexible when we'd met, both age twenty-four, but a few years down the line he became rigid and controlling. He wanted to put down roots. He wanted us to buy a house and to have children. We ended up doing things that felt excessively grown-up to me. By the age of twenty-eight we had what seemed like the perfect home aesthetically but I kept looking at other people's lives and thinking it would be more fun to be like them. I tried to focus on the positive sides of our relationship. We both liked cooking, we had some great friends, and I could ignore how bad our sex life had gotten. He had erectile dysfunction and so having sex could be an extremely frustrating experience. My solution was to avoid sex. We would have sex once a month or so even though I've always had a high sex drive. Somehow we kept the relationship going for seven years, and then when I got the job offer in Berlin I persuaded him to move there with me.

I traveled home to South Africa in 2016 and met Jabu at a concert. At the time I had only come home for a short visit, but a few months later I moved back home permanently and the two of us got together. The connection I felt with Jabu is one that I have never felt with anyone else. He's funny, we have great chemistry, and he's also way taller than I am. Sex with him has been the best

I've ever had mainly because he was willing to learn about my body. When we initially got together I felt like the more experienced partner as he's six years younger than I am, and I was his first serious long-term relationship. There's a lot of love between us, and when it came to sex we had lots of good conversation, and so I was able to openly express my needs and desires to him. Sex was fun, and we both orgasmed all the time. Of course it took us a while to get to that stage, and at the beginning things were a bit slow, but because he was keen to learn, it got really good. We both also have high sex drives. In some of my previous relationships I felt that I usually wanted to have sex more often, or the other person was at a different pace sexually.

One of the difficulties we had in our relationship was that I felt he was emotionally distant. I feel like this is a pattern for me. I tend to be drawn to people who have their emotional walls up. We also had very different ways of showing our love towards one another. He prizes loyalty and consistency, and I show my love in more active ways—by cooking, buying little gifts, and planning weekend getaways. He didn't do things like that. He spent all of his time working, and I felt squeezed into off-peak hours. Like he would hang out with me on a Monday night, and the rest of the week I didn't feel like a priority. There was a time that we broke up for about four months. We were no longer in a relationship but still hooked up once a month or so. Eventually we got back together.

One day we'd gone to a party together, and I was pretty drunk. Someone I had hooked up with during our breakup touched my back in a rather intimate way and later Jabu quizzed me about that. He wanted to know if I had slept with the man who had touched my back at the party. I had. The guy was someone who was in the same social circle as Jabu and so he got really upset because he considered the guy a friend. He felt I had betrayed him in some way even though we hadn't been together when I had hooked up with the other guy. He was also upset that I hadn't told him originally about being with that guy. We've been trying to work on our relationship and he says his goal is to forgive me but he can't seem to get the thought of me and the other guy out of his head.

He constantly feels unhappy and can't seem to move on. He told me that he feels like he doesn't know who he can trust. I think he's being overly dramatic. It's not like he and the other guy were super close, and we were not together at the time. I think our relationship is over for good.

I had been visiting Toni in Montreal, Canada, when she asked me if I wanted to go away on a girls' trip. I said yes. Toni had been chatting with this woman who lived in the States, and she had invited her, and a bunch of other queer women, to come over for the weekend. We crossed the border and in a few hours arrived in New Hampshire. As we got closer to our destination, I couldn't help but notice large US flags prominently displayed outside a number of houses. Overt signs of patriotism and nationalism make me nervous, but that feeling dissipated once we arrived at our location. Our host was Charlotte, an academic who had recently moved to take up a job at a nearby university. Naike*, whom I had previously met in Montreal, had also come down for the weekend, with her partner and two children. Also in our party was Alex, the designated driver during the trip from Canada to the States.

Charlotte had only recently moved, and with the exception of her bed, none of her furniture had been delivered. By early evening the kids were tucked in, and the rest of us sat on the floor in the living room drinking wine out of plastic cups. As midnight approached, we started to unfurl the sleeping bags we had traveled with. Naike and her partner went to one far end of the room and got cozy. I could see Antoinette and Charlotte making eyes at each other, and then Alex piped up. "Don't worry, we can see that the two of you want to be together. Nana, you don't mind sleeping with me, do you?" I wasn't sure if I wanted to bunk up with Alex but I also didn't want to be the spoilsport that would prevent my friend from getting some, and so I said, "Of course not." I stretched out my sleeping bag next to Alex's and shortly afterwards someone switched off the lights.

"Come closer," Alex said, and I shuffled a bit closer to her such that I was now a little spoon to her big spoon. A few minutes passed by, and in those moments I could sense the building of sexual tension. "Can I touch you?" whispered Alex. I said a quiet, "Yes." "I can't hear you, what did you say?" I was conscious of my friend on the far end of the room, and of Naike and her partner giggling at the other end of the room. I wasn't sure if they could hear me. I said yes a bit louder.

In the morning I got to chat with Naike, who is a thirty-five-year-old Haitian woman, about her relationship. I was curious to learn what life was like for a queer couple raising two young children. At the time I was struck by the possibility of two women raising a family together. I knew lots of single queer women, and lots of partnered queer women, but hadn't yet met any queer folks who were actively parenting together.

NAIKE

.

IN HAITI, VODOU is recognized as a national religion. The divinity of sexuality is close to the divinity of death, which is regarded in high esteem. On the Day of the Dead, usually celebrated in November each year, people do not go to school. If you walk the streets you see people fall into trances, and at night, you hear Vodou ceremonies taking place all over the country. In Vodou there are divinities and deities that reflect the spectrum of human experience. Sexuality has its own gods, goddesses, and in-between-gender goddesses. Sexuality is vulgar, but not in the Western sense. Vulgar is blunt, courageous, verbal, and sexual. Physicality and the moving of bodies in dance is very sexual. Being able to do these vulgar, sexual dances, even in high society, is regarded as culture, and Haitians are proud of their culture. In one way or the other, Vodou permeates all aspects of the culture, even among conservative Christian families and high socioeconomic groups.

This was the backdrop to growing up Haitian before the internet. There was closeness to the land. My grandparents would take me to the countryside and I would see people bathing in rivers; people with their fingers and toes in the earth, working the land. This experience of shamelessly seeing Black bodies, of feeling the spirit of labor, of proximity to earth, has shaped how I look at my own Black body. I was about nine years old when I first touched myself. I thought this was a special thing that only I could do. I had the most powerful orgasms of my life in early childhood, and I could feel how powerful my body was.

Mica lived next door to us; he came from a good family. My mother and the community of aunts that raised me trusted him. I felt safe with him too even though he was only fifteen years old, the same age that I was. He was cute: the kind of cute you see on television. He would play his guitar, carry me on his back, take me to the beach. He made me feel good about myself. He could see something in me that I could not yet see in myself. He would touch me, finger me, and eat my pussy with a passion. It took a week of preparation before we both lost our virginity together. He had a perfect tiny penis. Mica and I stayed together for four years.

At eighteen I moved to Montreal to attend university, and broke Mica's heart a year later when I fell in love with someone else, who happened to be a woman. I had always loved women. As teenagers, when we played mum and dad, I always assumed the role of a dad and would do anything the girls wanted. The woman I met in Canada was seven years older than I was. She was prettier than I was. She had her shit together. I did everything she wanted me to. I did her homework, I bought her things, I even shoplifted so I could give her more gifts. One day we were on the bus heading to the movie theater, which was several stops away from my house. No physical words passed between us, but when we got to my stop we both got off the bus. I had never walked three blocks so fast before. We opened the door, our lips found each other right by the door, and there we stayed. Time whirred by in a blur of plea-sure. I have no concrete memories; it was like a smoke-filled dream. Learning each other's bodies, our lips clung to each together, and we twisted and turned our legs so that our clits could rub against each other. I screamed, and screamed, and screamed as I came.

My friends and I typically spent winters sitting in studio-like apartments puffing on weed. We would do some ecstasy, drink some alcohol, and listen to Bob Marley. One of us would start a game, or turn to another and start kissing, or start to peel off the other's layers, and we would end up in a mix of limbs and bodies. At the time it always seemed like fun, but afterwards I felt like something had been taken away from me, I felt drained of my essence.

I kept waiting for her to want me. She never considered me a girlfriend. I was someone she would see in between fucking guys. It took a year for me to leave but ten years to heal. I swore, I will never be with a woman again. With men I knew I was never totally theirs—I was a good fuck and I could wield that like a weapon—but with girls I had no defense.

It was with my second male lover that I realized that sex with men drained my spiritual powers. He was a friend of my first boyfriend, he had wanted me for years, and when he approached me, I was weak and my self-esteem was broken. He taught me about the importance of intentionally preparing for sex: flirt the entire day, hold eye contact, roll up a spliff. Inside me he would circle his hips, he would pick up the rhythm, and then break it. I confused pleasure with love. He was draining my power, my inner power, my goddess power.

I knew at the age of thirteen that I wanted children. I had grown up raising children. Bathing them, changing their diapers, making them burp. It was like I was cultivating motherhood within me. And then at twenty-four I met Zion, the man I knew I wanted to father my children. He was the perfect thing to do to get back at my family for the years of feeling less beautiful, too dark, and unwanted by my dad's Black-white family where Black babies are born with blond hair. My mother—who was Senegalese Black—and I were protected only by my grandmother, who loved this child of her favorite son: her chocolate-covered grandbaby. Zion was not Haitian, he was not rich, he was not even well educated. He was smart, an activist, and a Black nationalist. I would go to these spoken word events just to listen to him perform poetry. I said to him, "I want to have your babies." We met in September, by May I was pregnant, and in January I gave birth to my little girl.

Zion tried unsuccessfully to control me, but my mother had modeled an alternate way of life. When my dad left to become a Buddhist monk, she negotiated her pleasure with blunt pride, and focused on creating wealth for herself and her children. I remember that when I was fifteen years old she told me something I have never forgotten: "Whatever you are doing, unless you have experienced it super slow you haven't tasted anything." I didn't taste anything with Zion. I would edit his poetry, wash his locs, massage the pain out of his body, and yet he never saw me.

I changed when I fell pregnant with my son, our second child. It was a hard pregnancy and I started to rebel. I said to him one night: "I am not well, we need to talk about this. This is not working for me. You really need to listen to me." Tears traveled down my face as I spoke to him but all I got in response was silence. When I turned over to look at him he was asleep. One day I said to him, "I'm leaving." I don't think he believed me. I was calm. There had been no fight, no confrontation. That was when he started being nice to me for the very first time. He bought me flowers, he took some photographs of the children that he framed and gave to me. He told other people he loved me and expected them to pass the message on to me. He never said, "Don't go."

When my son was three months old, I went to a spa, and while waiting for my massage, I took my eyes off my book and saw this gift of a man: rich Black in complexion, sparkling teeth, an abundance of eyelashes, and as if that wasn't enough hair, locs that fell strong and heavy down his back. He saw me looking at him, and started chatting with me. I realized I knew his sister. A year later I left the father of my children, and I called her:

"What's your brother's number?"

"Antoine is a bad boy."

"I don't care."

I said to Antoine, "I need someone to help me separate from my partner, and it needs to be light and easy," and it was; the breakup was very easy for me. When the relationship with Antoine ended I met Jean-Claude, the last man I will probably ever sleep with. He was the kind of guy who meditated and was in touch with his spirit, which was beautiful, but his huge penis made sex uncomfortable, and he was not one of those guys that you could have good lesbian sex with, and so I said to myself, Maybe you should just go home.

Home is being closer to myself with someone. Someone I can share a deeper sense of self with, without fear, and without judgment. I started seeing women in activist circles. Most of the women who would approach me were white: I got involved with a circus girl from Portugal; a woman from Mexico who took what she wanted from me, and then went back to her relationship; an Italian who wanted to be my world and meet my kids, but I didn't allow just anyone to do so. I craved a relationship with a Black woman but didn't feel a sense of connection with anyone I met. I took to the internet, paid up to join a dating site, and selected my criteria. And then I saw her profile. She said she was a practicing Muslim, and was looking for a relationship with a woman. There was no picture on her profile but I was curious. I sent her a message: "I would like to get to know you more if you're interested. Here's my number."

When she called me we spoke for four hours. I felt I had known her forever. It felt like we had been brought up in the same town, eating the same food, attending the same schools. At the end of the call I said to her, "I know we met on a dating site, but I think we should try being friends, I don't want to lose you." She wasn't part of my typical activist world. She was just this beauty-filled human that I shared heritage with. I didn't have to explain myself or my culture to her. Finally, in cold Canada, I had found a warm connection.

On one of our early dates we went to the movies. I like *cinéma de répertoire*, alternative movies. While sitting in the darkened room with my date, I started to squirm: Why did I pick this film? I should have chosen a Hollywood movie, she's not going to enjoy this. I was frantic to remedy the situation and blurted: "Do you want to come to my house?" We spent Friday night to Sunday night making love. We ordered in food, and ate in bed with plastic forks. There were no labels on our relationship. We just were. Eventually she met my children, we moved in together, and she supported me in caring for my children. They called her Auntie.

Then things changed. Now she says she wants to get married. She wants us to be monogamous. Monogamy is a violent word: it's her way of trying to control me. The desire to be intimate with people is ultimately down to the individual because our bodies and existence are ours. When I am really into someone, I get a kind of tunnel vision; they are the only one I can see. There is that inexplicable connection but that is not the only way to be. I believe in the cosmic celestial: an intense fiery connection. It is a possibility, an opportunity, a state of wonder. In the context of well-being and safety, monogamy can thrive, but it comes from within; it is not an imposition by others. Anything that is imposed has the potential to strike a chord of resistance. I was monogamous because I didn't have to be—I break free when people try to hold me down, box me up, and place little labels on me.

I am tired of contorting myself twenty thousand ways to please her. One would think she is my mother with all these conditions that she sets, but in reality I am the one who mothers and takes care of her. I love women politically so I don't want to dump her, replace her, or consider her disposable. Before I met her my friends would say to me: "You Black woman searcher, what are you looking for?" and I said, "I want to meet someone like myself." Most people would say, "That is the most fucked-up thing I ever heard." But I know what I mean. I know how I love. I want to meet someone like me. I want someone who can love me to the standard that I love. I need to be able to share my truths and for my truths to be received with humor. I want to share my anger, my rage, my disappointments, my dark side, my desire to die sometimes, my desire for another woman. I need these truths to be received with humor, with goofiness, without this need to control me or my creativity. I want to meet someone like myself, and recognize her as a familiar.

As a baby feminist I had no comprehension of the importance of sex workers' rights. I had read Andrea Dworkin and Catharine MacKinnon and concluded that women who worked in the porn industry were all being trafficked and exploited. When I watched porn I always felt guilty, like I was complicit in the oppression of women (and maybe I was). At nineteen I didn't have the more nuanced understanding of sex work that I have today.

My understanding of sex work started to shift when I attended an International AIDS Conference held in Mexico. At the time I had just started working for the African Women's Development Fund (the first grantmaking foundation established on the African continent by African women), and my then boss had decided that I would accompany her on the trip to Mexico. I was struck by the large numbers of sex workers attending the event, and the prominence they had in the conference. I remember attending a panel led by sex workers and asking a question that today makes me cringe: "Why would anyone want to be a sex worker?"

On the way back to the hotel one evening I asked my boss the same question. She explained to me that a woman could find herself in particular circumstances and determine that the best option for her was to do sex work. That answer allowed me to open my mind to the possibility of considering sex work as a valid form of work. As I continued in my feminist activism and interacted in more feminist spaces I started to meet more and more sex workers who helped me expand my understanding of sex workers' rights even more. I met women like Philester,* who blew apart all my previous misconceptions of who *a sex worker is. Philester is a thirty-two-year-old Kenyan woman. She is also a sex worker, a mother of three, and the coordinator of the Kenya Sex Workers Alliance (KESWA).*

The following story includes experiences of child rape and sexual assault.

PHILESTER

·

I MET BILLY soon after I turned eighteen. I was working in a club in Mombasa at the time. He was that client who kept coming back time and time again. One day he asked me if we could go out on a date. We went on several dates and I started to fall in love with him. He made me feel special. He treated me like a woman. He was kind, gentle, and easy to talk to. I thought he understood me, and who I was as a person. After a couple of months we moved in together. Soon afterwards his job transferred him to Tanzania, and our relationship became a long-distance one. Throughout our relationship, I had kept my job as a sex worker. When Billy returned from his posting, he moved to the capital, Nairobi, and I went over to visit him. That's when I fell pregnant with my second child, a girl. I moved back in with him, and we resumed our relationship. Everything was going well. I had a healthy baby girl, and went back to work. Billy wasn't happy about that. While I was working he would come to the same hotspot, and pick up women from there. Out of all the places he could go to, why did he have to come to the same place where he knew I'd be working? Our relationship started to fall apart. We were arguing with each other all the time. We would have these loud shouting matches. I knew it wasn't healthy for me or my baby girl so I left.

And then there was Esther. We met when a client booked me for a group sex session. She had also been booked by the same client. He wanted us to first have sex with each other, and then with him. Afterwards she and I exchanged contacts, and we started chatting. She said to me, "I enjoyed having sex with you. Do you think that is something we could continue to do?" We started dating and fell in love. We worked from different hotspots but both lived in the capital so would take turns visiting each other. Her personality was extremely different from mine. Whereas I am this hyperactive, extroverted person, she was quiet and composed. We made an agreement that I could have sex with as many men as I wanted, but I couldn't have sex with women. In time that began to feel like a restriction. I had lots of women clients who often contacted me wanting repeat services. Many of them also referred me to their friends. The majority of my women clients wanted to explore and experience having sex with a woman. Sometimes they heard stories from other women, and wanted to experiment. Sometimes a friend would tell them, "I had sex with this woman. She's a sex worker. Here's her contact." The relationship started to affect my business and so I decided to hit the pause button.

One day I went clubbing with my friends. We were not there to work, we were there to party. I'm sitting at the bar downing some shots and then in walks my ex, Billy. I hadn't seen or heard from him in three years. He came over to me and said, "It's been ages."

"Yes, it has been ages, you haven't even come over to see your daughter."

"I was transferred to work in Rwanda. I only got back two weeks ago."

We chatted some more, and then he asked, "Are you working today?" I needed the cash, so said yes, and we left the club together. Afterwards he asked if he could come over and see his daughter, and I agreed. I've always had a soft spot for him, so within two weeks we had moved from a business relationship to a personal one. I thought this time things would be different. He knew who I was, nothing had changed on my side. He started telling me how he felt jealous when I was with other men and asked me to choose between him and my job. I chose my job. My job has always been there for me. My job has never mistreated me. I love my job. Once I made my choice Billy became violent. He started beating me. He became psychologically violent. He got into my head. I started to feel small and like I was nothing. He told me that no other man would want me because I am HIV positive. He himself was HIV negative and so that cut particularly deep because I had been open with him about my status. I started drinking heavily and became an alcoholic. Every day felt like a struggle. The more I sank into a depressive stupor, the more Billy felt like the man. One day I found him in a club with another woman. I left quietly but when he got home I started shouting and screaming. He started beating me, and at one point in time he pushed me so hard that I fell and my head hit the side of the bed. I woke up eight hours later in the hospital. I later found out that my nanny had come in, found me lying unconscious on the floor, and told Billy that they needed to take me to the hospital. When I woke up I had no memory of what had occurred. Once I was back home Billy stopped abusing me physically but the emotional violence continued.

When I turned seven years old my mum had a mental breakdown and was placed in an asylum. She was a single parent, and my siblings and I got divided up between her sisters. I was sent off to a different town, Malindi, where my auntie lived with her taxi-driver husband. He raped me every day while she was at work. After I turned thirteen I decided to run away. I joined a group of girls whose mission was to secure a white man who could look after them. These girls all lived together in one room and they allowed me to join them. After a few months I realized I was pregnant. The girls took me to see this woman who they said would help me have an abortion. She took one look at me and said I was too young, and my body so tiny that I would die if she tried to abort the fetus using the traditional methods. Instead she told me to stay and give birth, and then afterwards they would sell the baby. I had nowhere else to go and so I stayed. After four months I went into labor and had the baby. I heard the child cry but I didn't even get to see it before it was taken away. I don't even know whether I had a boy or a girl. To this day I have never forgotten that cry I heard.

The woman told me later that she had sold the baby and was keeping the money because she had looked after me for four months. She continued to take care of me for a little while longer until I healed and then I left and went back on the streets. I started to save the money I made and enrolled in a boarding school for girls. I paid for the first year of school by myself and during the holidays I came back on the streets to earn more money. That's when I met a white man. He told me to stop working on the streets and asked me to move in with him, and so I did. When it was time for me to go back to school he paid for my fees. When school broke up for the holidays I came back to the flat we shared and found a letter he had left for me. He said he'd had to go back home, and that the rent had been paid for another two months. He left an email address but never responded to any of the emails I sent. After two months I had to move out of the flat. I had no money because he'd told me that he was going to come back. I hadn't gone out to work, and had no funds to pay my school fees. So at fifteen or sixteen years old, I went back into sex work full time. I got pregnant again and when I was seven months along I went to a clinic. They ran a whole range of tests on me. The nurse told me directly, "Your results are not good. You're HIV positive."

There was no counseling offered to help me deal with this news that they had just given me. However, they told me that it was possible for me to have a child that was HIV negative. I knew other sex workers who were HIV positive and so I reached out to one of my friends who was living positively, and she advised me to do everything the doctors said. I started going to the clinic regularly. I wanted my child to live free of HIV and all other diseases. I delivered a healthy baby boy, and after two months started working. By then I was eighteen, so I was finally old enough to make a choice about the kind of work that I wanted to do. I decided that there was no point in trying to find another job. I loved my job. I had a community of sex worker friends and clients who were there for me, and who I could talk to when I needed. That was when I actually made the choice to be a sex worker.

One night I was in a club when a man came in. I initially thought he was a potential client but later he introduced himself. His name was Jimmy and he worked for the International Centre for Reproductive Health (ICRH). He told me that they were looking for girls like me who could be peer educators and that if I was interested in learning more I should come to this particular clinic where they were going to be the following day. Since I wanted to learn more about living with HIV I decided to go. At the clinic they asked me a whole range of questions to figure out if I was a sex worker. I was open and honest with them, and they selected me as one of forty people to be trained as peer educators. ICRH decided to go further by selecting leaders for each zone they worked in; at the time I lived in Chaani, a slum-like village within Mombasa. I went through another interview process and was successfully selected as the zonal lead for sex workers in Chaani. I thrived as a sex worker leader, and in that role got the opportunity to learn a lot.

There was a conference of sex workers held in South Africa that I attended. There I met other sex worker activists, and got to learn about the struggles that sex workers in other countries faced. It was clear to me that we had similar challenges. At the conference we had talked about the need to build a regional network of African sex workers, and when I and other Kenyan sex workers returned home we decided that we needed to start building a movement of sex workers. That led to the creation of KESWA, which was led nationally by Daughtie Ogutu.

At the local level, I decided to start a support group for sex workers living with HIV. We called our group the Chaani Hostess Club and created very simple structures to manage our affairs. As a group, we wanted to learn more about HIV, we wanted access to new information about living with the virus, and we wanted to be part of a movement of activists who were living with HIV. At the time the National AIDS Council of Kenya had what was called TOWA (Total War Against HIV and AIDS) funding to support local groups, and our group was able to benefit from their support. I started to network more within the sex worker activist community and got introduced to other human rights groups, like UHAI, which also ended up supporting my local group. In time, there was a vacancy at KESWA when Daughtie, their coordinator, moved on to another position. I applied for the job and, alongside John Mathenge, was selected as a coordinator. John later stepped down to head an organization he had founded for male sex workers and I became the sole coordinator of KESWA, a position that I have now held since August 2013.

I feel proud of the many achievements of Kenyan sex workers during this period. We speak up now on the many issues that affect us. We're better organized, and as a result are able to channel more human and financial resources into our work. Our understanding of sex work is politicized, and we have been able to create greater awareness of sex workers' rights. Increasingly, more people who are not sex workers speak up for sex workers' rights. My job as a coordinator of a national organization keeps me busy, and sometimes for a period of, say, two months I may have no space to actually take on any sex work. Yet I can't let down my clients—they call me, they email me, and I don't want to disappoint them. I recognize that I am a coordinator because I am a sex worker, and so that doesn't take the place of sex work in my life. I still go to my favorite hotspots, and I still maintain great relationships with my hotspot family. I miss them when I stay away too long. These are the people I have worked with for so long, and I consider them family.

My leadership journey was also what gave me the strength to leave Billy. There was a time when I was participating in a leadership institute for sex workers supported by Open Society. As part of that program we had a group counseling session and lots of people shared the difficult experiences they were going through. I realized that I wasn't the only person going through difficult times and that I needed to stop feeling sorry for myself. I started healing from the inside out, and in time gained strength to leave that relationship once and for all.

Over the past two years my relationship with my mother has improved, although she's still not happy that I am a sex worker, and thinks I might have taken a different path if she had been there to raise me herself. I don't talk to her about my work but I have been open with my son. At the age of ten I told him about my HIV status, and when he turned thirteen I told him that he might read about me on social media, and hear people say different things about the community I belong to. My son is intent on being a pastor and his response was to say, "Mom, you know me, I'm venturing into becoming a pastor. It's not because there are no pastors in Kenya or there are no pastors in the area where we come from. It's because I want to become a different pastor. A pastor who listens to people, a pastor who tries to understand people within their situations, and a pastor who appreciates people for who they are. I'm giving them an opportunity to know who God is. And that's the reason why I force you to go to church with me every day, so that you can have an understanding of the God that I want to serve. It's not the God that judges you."

My son became religious at a young age, and when he turned six he started insisting that I go with him to church. I made this one of my priorities, and every Sunday, whether I was tired or not, I made sure to go with him to church. I grew up Muslim but I now identify as a Christian. I believe in God, I believe in praying, and I believe that my relationship with God is a personal one.

Recently, my son was selected as Mr. Teen Kenya in a national competition. As part of that process he was asked what he would do if he was chosen as the winner. He said, "I don't know what you people know, but I come from a very controversial family. My mother is a single mother, she is also a sex worker, and she lives with HIV. The surprising news is that I am a pastor. But me becoming who I am and she being who she is doesn't make her any less my mother. This is me assuring you that if I win, I will not treat people differently. I will allow people to be who they are, believe in themselves, and always do the right thing." I was in tears as I listened to him speak.

I had really wanted to interview Krystal in person. At the time we were introduced, she lived in London, the city that I consider my second home. A month ahead of my scheduled trip to the UK, borders around the world closed, so I contacted Krystal to ask if we could meet via Zoom instead. That's when I learned that she had recently moved to Berlin. On my screen was a curvy black woman with long box braids. She wore a robe that kept falling off her shoulder to reveal a slip of a negligee. She looked like a woman living her best, indulgent life. I usually start my conversations by asking people how they identify in terms of their gender and sexuality. I also ask people to tell me where they're from. For some of my interlocutors, these are easy enough questions that break the ice, yet simultaneously these are questions that get to the heart of deeply felt issues. Krystal is a thirty-four-year-old Black British woman of Jamaican and Zimbabwean heritage. She described herself to me as a Black transsexual woman, whose sexual orientation is functionally pansexual but is socially conditioned to prefer straight cis men.

If you occupy the same spaces on Twitter that I do—Black, feminist #Afrifem—you will often see on your timeline tweets about Black trans women who have lost their lives due to transphobia. In speaking with Krystal, a Black trans sex worker, I learned about how she has to navigate her life knowing that the normative world can be an unsafe place for most trans women.

The following story includes experiences of rape and sexual assault.

KRYSTAL

·

MY ATTRACTION TO straight cis men is the bane of my life. It's a curse. They don't care about me. They don't care about my writing, my politics, my thoughts, my intellect, or the fact that I just saw a Palestinian film. They don't care about my full humanity. All they see is the jiggling of my tits and my bum. To them, I'm the modern-day Hottentot Venus. That's all that's going on. That has nothing to do with me. That's not something I can control. I have no intention of tricking any man into liking me. There's nothing of value in that for me. On the contrary, the more knowledge they have of my transness, the better for me. If they know, they can come into my life and start paying for things. They can pay me for sex work, they can buy me groceries or jewelry, they can transfer funds into my account. It is only when you are transparent that you get the material benefits of your objectification. Because men run the world they feel that they are able to control all the spaces that I inhabit, and in that terrain, I am a sexual object. When I walk around in leggings and a vest men see that as an invitation.

After my transition the world became a very different place for me. Men came on to me in different public places. I was chatted up while shopping for groceries in supermarkets or when riding the bus. Men came on to me in the daytime. They catcalled me in the streets. I was whistled at. I can't deny that being objectified in that way felt affirming. I felt desirable. That was liberating. The men who were coming on to me felt less guilty about being attracted to me. It wasn't that I wasn't objectified before, but this time it was different. Earlier, men would point out my body with intentional violence. They were angry that they found my body arousing. The sentiment was, "How dare you wear that outfit?" "What are you doing?" Once I transitioned and became more conformist in my gender representation, I was less queer and transgressive. I wasn't seen as dangerous. The world is still a dangerous place for me but I am not immediately regarded as dangerous. In a sense the violence hasn't changed. It's mutated. It's changed shape. I went from being a faggot to a whore.

Before my transition I was socially and sexually involved in the gay male scene in London, although I always felt like an interloper. It was constantly made clear to me that I didn't belong there. People pointed out things about my body, my shape, and how I carried myself. At the time I was experimenting with my gender presentation. I would wear sports clothing, and underneath I would have on women's underwear. I would go to gay male spaces and look for the bisexual men who would be turned on by my femininity. In those spaces I was never anyone's first choice. The white men who dominated those spaces would be looking for the BBC and Mandingos, and my energy was the exact opposite of that. So the men I ended up having relationships with were both fluid in their sexuality and in their arousal. It always felt like I was on the fringes of the scene. In that world I was cast more as the entertainer. I had all the charisma of a drag queen but without the spectacle. For a brief period I flirted with drag but it wasn't for me. I didn't want roses and a stage. My femininity was not a spectacle. All I wanted to do was to manifest the divine feminine through my body and be in the world every day as myself. That wasn't available to me for many years.

It makes me emotional to see trans kids like Zaya Wade being able to exist in the world as who they are with the full support and love of their families. If I had been left alone as a child that's who I would have been. Simply a trans child. Being in nursery was a blissful time. I wore dresses, played with dolls and other girls. The bullying started in primary school, but at the time I had an imaginary friend, Madina, and I had discovered a love of words so would disappear into the universe of Enid Blyton, or be lost in Sweet Valley High or the Baby-Sitters Club.

In secondary school the bullying got a lot worse, and also became sexual. Boys would beat me up, but they would also grope and grind their bodies into me. The general consensus in school was that "Krystal is gay." That alone was taken as justification for the way I was being treated. No one asked, "Why are these boys grinding their groin into Krystal in the middle of the high street?" On the contrary, I was the one always seen as the troublemaker because I was the gendered other. Teachers would see me being beaten up in the corridors of school and do nothing. Instead they would ask me, "Krystal, why are you always friends with girls?" I remember my year eleven prom, just before I left school. I wore this ridiculously camp silver suit. We had gone out on a boat for prom and sailed along the Thames. When we got back I was walking down the plank to get off the boat, and our teacher said to me, "Mind your heels, Krystal." He said it in such a way that it was obvious that he had been bottling his feelings up for the five years that he had been my teacher, and now that his salary was no longer in question, he could make this really clunky joke for no one's benefit but his own.

In sixth form my world changed. I went to St Martin's, a white middle-class school. Those left-wing bourgeois kids loved me. They were gagging: "I always wanted to get a friend like you," "Oh my god, you are so wonderful." The violence immediately came to a halt and instead I was tokenized. By then I was sixteen years old. My parents could see that I wasn't becoming masculine in the way they had expected me to. They could feel me withdrawing but had no idea the extent to which I was rebelling and having wild sexual encounters. At the age of fourteen I had fallen in love with a Greek boy and we had been having a clandestine sexual relationship. From that same age I had also started having sexual relationships with older white men. I can see now that I was too young for all those sexual experiences, but there was nothing anyone could have told me at the time. I thought I was grown. This continued through university. I was mainly involved with men who were on the down low, and later with bisexual men. They had to be people who were aroused by my softness and femininity. In the spaces of these men I could experiment. I could be a girl for the night. At the time I hadn't told anyone that I was trans but people could feel it. My best friend was one of those people, as well as random people I would meet at parties. They would tell me, "It's not too late, you can turn back."

I didn't declare myself as trans until my late twenties, when I went into rehab to get over my addiction to alcohol and drugs. Before, I would just talk around the issue. I would say, "I am different." A lot has changed over the past five to ten years. At least in more liberal and radical spaces we are beginning to ask people what their pronouns are. When I was in secondary school there was no language around transness, even though I remember watching films like *The Crying Game* with my mum, and later watched *Boys Don't Cry*, about Brandon Teena. That was also the era of RuPaul, and my mum thought they were delightful. My mum raised me to be a particular kind of girl even against her own knowledge. She was far from transphobic. She was diagnosed with Alzheimer's in 2009, and had no language around gender identity and transness. She was a proud Jamaican woman, and I was her firstborn, so I've always wanted to make her feel proud of me. I wanted to be respected as a woman.

My gender isn't about putting a wig on. To be trans I needed to have my feminism respected, to have my career respected, to present as the woman I saw myself as. I didn't fully come into myself until I could wear the Marks & Spencer dress, until I had laser treatment and surgeries. Until I could do my hair and makeup. I did not want to be perceived as a transvestite, cross-dresser, or drag queen. That is not who I was. I wanted to make my mother proud. I wanted to make other Black women proud. Going to therapy in my late twenties, and finally getting sober, gave me the confidence to finally live as myself. That was when I read Janet Mock's *Redefining Realness*, and found Black trans women like Kat Blaque and groups like the T Time Network. That gave me the language that enabled me to name myself, and a vision for my own life. I had never wanted that much for myself. My self-esteem was so low, my expectations for my life were even lower. As time went on, I started to learn more about how the stories of trans people had been suppressed through the ages. Understanding that history helped me understand my own past and youthful wildness.

Although I still face transphobia now, at least I have confidence within myself. I have hustled a career for myself as a freelance journalist. I have bylines in the likes of *Harper's Bazaar* and *Vogue*. I have literally pulled myself up by my bootstraps, but I also have a lot of class privilege, even though my own background is lower middle-class. My mum worked in local government and my dad was a secondary school teacher who came to the UK from Zimbabwe. I went to university and I'm hella bougie and, through my education and experiences, have had a lot of access to straight white men. The men I have been in relationships with have paid for my writing courses, my rent; they paid for me to go to rehab, took me on holidays, and bought me food. All that has been materially beneficial to my life, and helped me get where I am now.

At the same time, I don't want to say to another Black trans girl, "Girl, you need to do this." There's nothing progressive in saying you just need to suck the right dick, or you just need to find the right white man. It's not reparations. If you have to put in the labor of sex, boost their ego, and perform emotional labor, that's not reparations. That's really difficult work. I am fatigued so I know how much work it is. The admin, the promotion, the reputation management, the need to constantly schmooze and network. It's a lot. For a long time I tried to keep the sex work I did a secret. I tried so hard to find a job that I thought was worthy of me. I have a French degree. I have worked in education and hospitality. I would have loved to work at one of the major galleries, publishers, charities, or retailers. I've applied for those jobs. I've applied for hundreds of jobs. I've applied for jobs where the pay is £10 an hour and jobs where the pay is £35,000 a year. Those white liberal folks are simply not interested in hiring me. They do not want me, a Black trans woman. Even in those circumstances where I've been given an interview, I could see the disdain written on their faces. I moved from London to Portsmouth to Brighton, and my experiences were the same. The truth is, the life of being a writer/activist was not paying the bills. I was constantly borrowing £20 from my sister. I will do anything to continue to focus on my passion, which is to write, document, and archive. Eventually I decided to move to Berlin to do sex work. Here there are ready-made communities for me. There are recovery groups for trans sex workers, for example. There are also bookshops, places to brunch, and lots of public parks. Since I only recently moved here, I'm considered newly exotic, and so that's been great for work too. I have written more in the five weeks that I have spent here than in my last six months in the UK.

With every man I meet I ask myself, Is this the man that is going to kill me? He could be saying anything under the sun, "Sweetness, what's your name?" or "You're a really pretty woman," and my mind will go to the headlines of the number of trans girls who have been killed. In my mind, every man I meet is a potential murderer, and so I am very careful about the way in which I disclose who I am to them. If I meet a man on the street, for example, that's a social situation, that's not a client. If I meet a man in, say, an African food shop next to my salon, I have to be aware that I may not be able to go back to that salon the following month to have my hair braided. I don't tell people I have met on the street that I am trans until I have them on the phone. If I think the man is a viable sexual partner with some potential for a future relationship, then I will tell him in our first phone call or text exchange. Sometimes I will give people my Instagram handle or I will say, "I am a transsexual woman, is that okay with you? If you're not attracted to me that is absolutely fine."

Usually what follows is a conversation. Men will usually ask questions like, "Do you have a dick or a pussy?" "How long has it been since you transitioned?" "You're transsexual? What does that mean?"

Then they will list off the sexual acts that are, or are not, on the table. If I don't come off as grateful, or if I come across as acting like I am too good for them, or speaking in a way that indicates that my class level is higher than theirs, or they feel that I think too much of myself, then they start to denigrate me. That happens roughly thirty percent of the time. The rest of the time, I just end up having sex with those men. If I meet a man and do not tell him that I am trans, then that's a sign to me that I am not interested in him, and I don't want him to have the knowledge of me being trans as a card that he could potentially hold over me. If at any point in the future a man becomes angry with me, he could tell everyone about me, and potentially endanger my life.

I tend to meet my clients online via porn sites, and the first thing that anyone sees on my profiles is the word TRANSSEXUAL in big bold caps, but sometimes men don't read, they just look at the pictures and call. I'm always very clear about the type of transsexual that I am, the kind of sex that I am offering, and what my availability is. I charge for particular sex acts and my time. Men make all sorts of promises that they can't deliver. They say, "I'm going to go two-three rounds," or "You won't be able to walk after I'm done with you." Then they come round and it's over in seven minutes. For a sex worker that is great. You paid for this amount of time, you've not been able to fulfill what you said you were going to do, but the money is already in my pocket.

For the past couple of years I've had two partners in the UK. I am polyamorous and they both know about each other, although they have never met. One is a middle-class man, and the other is a working-class man. Previously all my formal romantic relationships were with white middle-class men and frankly that was because I wanted to be able to gold-dig myself into a position where I could feel secure. Then I got burned. I was raped by a man who is definitely upper middle-class during my days on the chemsex scene fueled by crystal meth, GHB, or methadone. This man was a lifelong Labor voter and had a great professional reputation. These men are not the holy grail. I also didn't like the level of pretension that exists in left-wing bourgeois circles. They may have read bell hooks and Frantz Fanon but they still treat you in a particular way. Judith Butler cannot maketh the man.

At the end of the day, I found that the men with whom I had the more honest relationships were working-class men, and the men with whom I had the most emotional relationships were Black men. We watch the same shows, we eat the same food. They bring me cartons of Rubicon, or guava or mangoes. They call me up and say, "I'm coming over, I got some food," and they arrive sucking on some oxtail. Being with Black men has been important for my healing. When I was younger I was considered super smart. I was reading the recommendations from Oprah's Book Club from the age of thirteen. I would give advice to young Black men and tell them to dream and to believe in themselves. Then those men masculinized and didn't hang out with me anymore because they didn't want to be with someone as queer as I am. I missed those men that I knew in the streets of Edmonton and Tottenham, and now as adults we've found each other again.

Estelle and I were introduced by a mutual writer friend. I remember our first meeting. It was in a coffee shop in Accra, Ghana, where we chatted easily for an hour about our mutual love of books. Over the years we continued to meet in other spaces. In Kaduna, Nigeria. In London, UK. Our connection was sparked by a shared love of words, and then became so much more. We started to reveal more and more of our innermost selves to each other. Estelle would ask me about my experiences of marriage and divorce, and would share with me the questions she had about her relationship. We would often talk about our shared interest in exploring polyamory. I studied coaching and so in general I prefer to avoid giving people advice, but in my friendship with Estelle I found myself breaking that cardinal rule. "Follow your heart" I would say to her. "If you're not happy in your marriage there is no reason to stay." Estelle stayed in her marriage much longer than I would have liked her to—which is a good thing. Ultimately she did not listen to me, she listened to herself.

Estelle is a twenty-eight-year-old Black cis woman of mixed African and Arab heritage whose ancestors came from Ghana, Sierra Leone, Lebanon, Egypt, and Spain. She is British and lives in the UK. She's recently come to recognize herself as pansexual.

The following story includes experiences of rape and sexual assault.

ESTELLE

.

AFTER NINE YEARS of being in a relationship with Olamide, including being married for two years, I've come to realize that I need to leave in order to claim myself for me. Leaving will mean carving out time and space to listen to my inner voice and figure out what *I* want. Ending this relationship is going to cause me a lot of pain. I'm going to lose this man who has been in my life since I was twenty years old. I am going to lose my relationships with his family, particularly his mum and sisters, with whom I am very close. Yet I cannot stay. Staying will mean rendering myself invisible. Staying will mean continuing to kill a part of myself. I am choosing to walk away from a secure, loving relationship. I am walking away from my best friend. He has done nothing wrong, yet for many years there has been a voice within me whispering, "Leave."

That voice has gotten stronger as I have worked on loving myself, listening to my body, and truly understanding my own desires. I have learned that these things matter. My sexual orientation matters. It matters that I am polyamorous. I have a heart that is expansive and can love over and over again. I can have an infinite number of connections with multiple people. I can no longer deny who I am because staying in this marriage will mean doing exactly that. I thought I could leave those parts of myself dormant, which is why I agreed to get married. I believed that our marriage could survive anything until I realized that for it to survive, I would have to sacrifice who I was. Now I have given myself permission to leave. I don't want to resent my partner. I can't impose an open marriage on him when he believes in lifetime monogamy. I don't want us to live a life that is about what *he* wants rather than what *we* want. I also don't want him to be alone on this life journey called marriage, and so out of love I need to step away.

I never felt that I could be myself while I was growing up. I grew up between Ghana and the UK, and from a young age I was desired by boys and men who saw me as beautiful because of my light skin and facial features. I was always told, "You have good hair." It didn't matter that I grew up hating myself because I wanted to look more African, as I felt that would make me a whole person rather than someone who didn't know whether they were Arab or African. I was also sexually abused at a young age. I remember describing myself as a prostitute at the age of eight because I was now performing on others those acts that had been done to me.

I couldn't be myself, even with boys my own age. I had to perform in particular ways for them to even want to play childhood games with me, and so I learned really early on that I had to act in a certain way around boys and men. I've always felt that I need to be alert in public spaces, especially around Black boys and men. Someone always comes up to talk to me. Someone always wants something from me. Sometimes I try to make myself smaller in public so no one notices me. Other times I make myself more noticeable. I went through a phase of blow-drying my hair straight all the time. I did that occasionally when I wanted attention. Even though I've never felt beautiful, I knew that people perceived me as such by Western beauty standards. I rarely wanted attention. The majority of the time I didn't want to be seen. I wanted to be invisible. I didn't find much pleasure in the attention I got from men and boys. I just wanted to be safe.

Olamide and I met at university. We were both the same age when we met—twenty years old. He knew instantly that he wanted to be with me, and very intentionally would make sure he was always in those spaces where I was. He kept asking me to date him and for the first five or six months I said no, although we began spending a lot of time together. After a while it seemed silly to keep saying no. We spent so much time in each other's presence that my friends didn't understand why we weren't officially dating. Eventually I said yes to being in a relationship with him. I can see now that if I had known what I know now—that "no" is a complete sentence—things may have ended up differently. Once we made things official, Olamide wrote to all his ex-girlfriends and told them that he had started a new relationship and could no longer stay in touch with them. I hadn't known he was going to do this. I felt a bit uncomfortable, but that was his way of signaling to me that he was willing to cut everyone out of his life and focus on our relationship. He was always so sure about us. He has always been clear that he wants to give me the world, and to be a provider. There was a security that I felt in my relationship with Olamide that I hadn't felt growing up. Our relationship has been a very peaceful one. There has been no drama, which is really important to me. We have always supported and championed each other. We've given each other space to make mistakes. We've also had a very independent relationship, which has allowed each of us to explore and grow.

I don't think Olamide fully realizes it, but he's been a huge part of the reason why I now have the strength to listen to my own inner voice. I consider him my best friend. I've always been open with him. He's always known about my attractions to other people, for example. So even now, as we're facing the end of our relationship, he's been really understanding. He hasn't tried to blame me or shame me. He said, "Okay, I get it. You have been saying this for years." I always spoke to him about my growing understanding of my sexuality, and recognizing that I'm polyamorous. I've also had multiple crushes throughout our relationship. Sometimes I've told him about some of the people I'm crushing on. Other times it's obvious because of my reaction when I see someone that I am attracted to. I might just go, "Oh my God," and in that moment it's like I have forgotten that my life partner is there and that he has emotions and feelings. That has been difficult for him to deal with.

There was a point in time while we were engaged that we broke up. There was someone I had a deep connection with yet I knew that I wasn't going to be with that person in the long run. I needed to release that deep love that I was feeling for someone else, and that was emotional work that I couldn't do while engaged to someone else. So I broke off the engagement because I needed to understand how I could have deep feelings for two different people at the same time. I was heartbroken because I was releasing someone I loved, yet I was also in a celebratory mode because I was embarking on a journey with someone else. That was when I figured out, oh, the heart is really expansive. I can hold space for this person that I'm releasing and I can also hold space for this other partner that I'm currently with. That doesn't make me a bad person. It doesn't mean that I'm giving half of myself to one person, and half to another person. I'm giving my full self to both people. It was freeing to give myself permission to recognize how much capacity for love our heart has.

I have always known deep down that I am attracted to both women and men, but previously, I never gave myself permission to fully acknowledge that to myself. That's because I didn't feel like I could act on my desires. I grew up in a deeply Christian household and I internalized homophobia. I felt that I didn't want my actions to bring shame on my family. It was only in 2019 that I finally allowed myself to acknowledge that my desires, fantasies, and attractions were legitimate. Most of the time the people I have crushes on are women, but I also began to recognize myself as pansexual when I found myself attracted to people who are trans, or cis gay men, for example. I realized that what's important to me is the connection I feel to a person. I feel drawn to a person's soul and not their bodily containers.

Recently my desire to be with a woman has intensified. I have been fantasizing about sex with women while in bed with Olamide. That made me panic. Initially I felt, There's something wrong with you, and then another part of me said, You've been in this relationship for nine years now, maybe you need to start listening to your body. And there was still another part of me that said, Is that a good enough reason to leave this stable, secure relationship?

One of my fears is around starting a sexual relationship with other people. It will mean opening boxes that I have long closed. At a young age my sexual agency was stolen from me through a series of sexual assaults and rape. I will need to explain to any new partners that there are certain sexual acts that I do not enjoy. I don't like to be fingered, for example. In my late teens someone I considered a close friend raped me. We went to the same university, and used to hang out all the time. Often he would come to my room and we would watch movies together. I never thought he had any ulterior motives. One day he forced himself on me. Nothing I did or said stopped him. It was a very violent act and one of the traumatic memories I have from that time is of being fingered. Since then I haven't been able to enjoy that act. I don't even insert my fingers in myself when I masturbate. I can't even bring myself to think of it. I'm hoping to get over that but I also know that these things take time. Maybe in the future I'll be able to practice with someone when it feels safe and natural. I don't want to rush but it's something I want to enjoy again. I hate that someone has robbed me of finding pleasure in that act.

The journey to reclaim my sexuality has been a long one. I am working hard not to allow the traumatic experiences from my past to define how I experience my sex life. By listening to my body, I now know what consent feels like. It's taken me several years to get here. Olamide was the first person that I had consensual sex with. When we first started having sex I would just lie there. I can see that during the first two years of our relationship I wasn't enthusiastically consenting to sex. I was physically intimate with him not because I wanted to, but because I felt like I had to. It felt like I was outside my body watching someone else have sex. He was aware that something was wrong because he couldn't connect with me.

In the third year of our relationship I walked away from the church. For most of my life, the church had formed my sense of self and how I viewed the world. Leaving allowed me to start over from a blank slate. I no longer felt like I wanted to fight the desires of my flesh. I decided that I really wanted to listen to what my flesh wanted and desired, and not cast it as carnal, hedonistic, or demonic. I started to recognize my desires as natural, and that's when I began to enjoy sex with Olamide. The change took him unawares; he later told me that he once called his friend and said, "I think Estelle is cheating on me because our sex life has changed." I'm grateful to him for staying with me throughout the difficult first years of our relationship. He didn't have to stay with me but he chose to do so.

I've now gotten to a stage where I can really enjoy and engage in sexual behavior and attitudes that I feel are fulfilling and enriching to me as a human being, and I'm grateful for that part of my journey. I can now center pleasure and the erotic in my life. I am equal parts excited and scared about having sex with new partners. I worry that I might regress to that time when I didn't enjoy sex. I worry that I might be triggered to those times when I did not consent to sex. When you have been with someone for a long time there's comfort and security. You don't have to explain the sexual acts that you like, or don't like, because you've already had those conversations. Will I have to explain to every new partner that I do not like to be fingered and why? How does one have that conversation, and do I need to have this conversation every single time with a new partner? These are the issues that I am going to have to navigate, and it scares me. I don't think the other side is going to be any greener when I step away from my marriage. I am choosing to walk a much harder path, one that is unpredictable.

The other fear I have is of the pain that is to come. The pain I will feel from undoing someone from my life. Olamide has been integral to my own growth and healing. I know it will take a lot out of me to fully release him. I don't think that there is anything that can prepare me for the sense of loss that I am going to experience. The thought of a future without Olamide in my life is a scary one. For so long he has been my safe place and my rock. I try to remind myself of how much I have to gain by working through the pain. I have to remind myself that I am finally claiming myself for me. I don't even know what my final self will be like eventually, but allowing myself to go on that journey of self-discovery is going to be my biggest reward. I hope to arrive at a place where I feel super clear about who I am. I think breaking my heart open will allow me to expand. A broken heart gives you more ground to learn and play. It means you're shedding old skin, and that can ultimately be a good thing if you allow it to teach you. If you choose to remain stuck in pain you won't progress. But if you allow your intuition to lead you, and you trust your inner voice, ultimately things will work for your own good.

In December 2016 I visited Rwanda for the first time. I was on holiday. My generous hostess made sure I had a good time, and took us on a trip outside the capital. I have fond memories of swimming in Lake Kivu, making sure to document that moment for the Gram. We were staying in a hotel, and from our veranda I could see the country's border with the Democratic Republic of Congo (DRC), a country I have previously visited for work. In DRC, I heard women share testimonies of the horrific sexual abuse and violence experienced during the years of conflict, as well as in peacetime. I also visited hospitals that cared for survivors of sexual violence, some of whom were as young as two and three.

Once we were back in the capital, Kigali, my hostess invited a group of Rwandese women to meet me and to spend an evening chatting about sex and sexualities. That was when I first met Bingi, a twenty-one-year-old Rwandese woman who identifies as heterosexual. The following day we met up in a nearby restaurant and she told me about a passionate all-consuming love with a man she still thinks about to this day.

It is easy to recognize the big acts of violence that emerge from war and conflict. It is much harder to recognize smaller acts of violence that chip away at a woman's self-esteem and confidence. Bingi's story is a reminder that sometimes you need to walk away from love to save yourself.

BINGI

.

I ENJOY HAVING sex. When I'm in bed with someone I like to explore, experiment, and push my boundaries. You know that feeling you get from reading a good book? That's what sex does for me. Sex saved me from depression. It helped me escape. I needed to get out of my home, and get my family out of my head. Sex was my escape. I would always find a way to see my guy and just be in bed with him. That's all I wanted to do. I would go to his house at, say, 4 p.m. and not leave till 4 a.m. All we did was get high, make love, then repeat. We could go for twelve rounds. I was eighteen at the time.

Paul was the love of my life. Before we met, my friend told me about him. She was in love with him. She thought he was so smart and handsome. She used to tell me that he and I would get on. He had friends who told him the same thing about me. At the time he lived in a different country, and so he sent me a message on Facebook. We started chatting and then sometime in 2012 he came to Rwanda. We planned a meetup. When I got to his house he was looking scruffy; he apologized and said he had been smoking weed all day. From then on we saw each other every day. We would just hang out and smoke weed together. He had a whole bunch of different girls he was seeing at the time. I was also seeing someone else but Paul didn't like him.

I started to develop feelings for Paul but I didn't know how to express how I felt because he had become my best friend. Then he started to act differently towards me. He became more affectionate in a way that wasn't friendly. Sometimes he would stand behind me and hold me closely. It felt very intimate. I acted normally but I loved it. Paul was a rapper and a singer so we spent a lot of time in the studio. One day he walked me home after a session and later sent me two very long text messages saying that he really liked me, and it was not as a sister. He said, "I think I'm falling in love with you, and I would love for us to have a relationship." I knew I wanted a relationship with him too but I felt unsure. I had just ended a relationship. Initially I said to him, "Let's not rush it," but then after a while I said, "I'm feeling you too, let's go for it."

It took seven months before we first had sex. He kept saying, "I don't want us to do this now because you are too excited." We would start making out and then he would stop me and say, "You're too excited right now, I don't want it to happen like this." One day we were just chilling in bed and he said, "I'm ready." Just like that. I had been ready for four months and he'd kept saying I needed to wait until he was ready. During that period we had done everything else. We would kiss, he would touch me with his fingers, he would go down on me, I would go down on him. I was a virgin so I didn't know what to do. He would tell me, "This is what I like, use your tongue like this, go fast now, go slow now." One time I was sucking his dick and his mum called. He told me, "Don't stop, I'm going to talk to my mum." He and his mum are best friends. So there I am, going down on him, and he's on the phone with his mum. At some point in time I burst out laughing and he said, "Girl, don't talk with your mouth full." That's the funniest memory I have of us. I heard his mum say, "Are you at the gym or something?" And then he said, "Yeah, Mum, I'm at my house and doing some exercise."

Our first time together was a beautiful experience. He had a big dick. The most beautiful dick I have ever seen in my life, even to this day. It was long and big. It was the perfect size for my vagina. Maybe it's because he was my first. I've been with about nine other guys since him, and some of them were more skilled, but for me he's still the gold standard. He just knew what to do. He knew how to be rough and gentle at the same time.

We were together on and off for about three years. At some point in time he went through a depression and started doing crack. I was in a very bad state at the time. I was still trying to heal from losing my dad, who had passed away in 2011. My relationship with Paul became toxic. I recognize now that I was addicted to him. It was like we were a drug for each other. We always needed to be together. And then Paul started to become emotionally abusive. We would be in public with friends and he would say things like, "Shut up, woman, I'm talking." Or I would be at his house and he would say, "I don't want you in my house right now." I would break up with him, and then he would start pursuing me even harder than before. He would say things like, "I get in crazy places and I take it out on you because you are the only person who matters to me." I started to realize that I cared more for him than I did for myself. It became clear that if I stayed with him he would continue on that path, and I would keep forgiving him because I loved him so much. And that's when I realized I needed to prioritize myself. I said to him, "This love is not going to work if I'm loving you more than me. If I'm loving the relationship more than myself. I have to prioritize my own happiness, my own goals."

Since Paul, I haven't had a relationship where I have been as deeply connected with someone else. I know Paul is the man I want to spend the rest of my life with but I can't. I don't think he is willing to change, and so if I had stayed with him I would have gone back to loving him more than myself. Our breakup really affected me. I was so lonely. It still feels like I lost a piece of myself. I was in a dark place for a long time after the breakup. I didn't even see the point in living but I managed to get away from that feeling. One day I woke up and thought, I think I'm over him, and started dating other people. I made sure to keep busy and tried not to see him. It's still difficult because even now when I bump into him I think, Shit, what happened?

After Paul I dated this other guy, but he was so boring. He had a small dick and was not good in bed. He is the kind of guy who just wants you to do everything. He just lies in bed and wants you on top of him. He would come really quickly too! I started to fake it with him. In spite of everything I thought he was a nice guy. He would play the piano for me and sing to me for hours. I thought, Let me just make him happy. Eventually, I broke up with him because I couldn't continue to fake it. After that I became bolder. I started to meet guys at events I would go to or through introductions from friends. Sometimes I would walk up to a guy and say, "You know what, I think we could be a great match, I'll just be over there if you want to come and chat with me." And then a few minutes later the guy would inevitably come over and say something along these lines: "I think you're interesting." With those men, I was only interested physically.

That's how I met Bamboo. Sex with Bamboo felt like making art. I didn't even have feelings for him but I felt like I was painting when we had sex. He wasn't too rough and he wasn't too soft. It was like we recognized each other through sex. I didn't have to say shit. He didn't have to say shit like, "Where did you learn how to do that?" After spending one night with him I never saw him again. I remember that when I first met Bamboo, I thought he was such a beautiful man. He was also a tease. We'd be at a party or a club and he'd be kissing another girl but looking right at me. I would say to him, "Why are you teasing me like this? Take me home." He would say, "Not yet, right now I am just enjoying doing things to you." Sometimes we would both be at the same event, and he would come over to say hi and grab my arse. This went on for about six months. I used to run into him all the time but after we had sex I never saw him again. I'm not upset about that. I wasn't trying to have a relationship with him.

Around the time we hooked up I lost my phone and so we couldn't be in contact. We would just see each other at events and talk for a long time. Technically, he was a better lover than Paul, and I wasn't even in love with the guy. He was the best I ever had. The night we hooked up we had this competition to see who would get drunk first. Earlier on I had been outside the club smoking, talking to my cousin, and then I saw Bamboo walk out of the venue. I went over to him to say hey and he said, "I think tonight is the night." He said he wanted to buy me a drink, so we took three shots each. I said to him, "Why are you trying to get me drunk," and he said, "Let's see who says stop first." So we had beer and shots. At some point he took my hand and said, "Let's get out of here," and he took me to this house that was still under construction. The only furniture was a couch. It was perfect. We had sex on that couch and it felt so much better than any bed. There were no curtains so I was worried about someone walking by and seeing us. My older cousin lived in that same area, and I was concerned that he might see me walk out of the house.

My best friend told me that I go out with the same type of guys. There's a little piece of Paul in all of them. I thought about it and it's true. The men I've been with are not everyday people. They are smart about their shit, and they are aware of what is going on around them. They all get high. They're very mature. They're deep. You can't tell what they are thinking about. They are good in bed. That's what attracts me.

Sex can help you figure out the type of person you are. Sex has definitely helped me know myself. The guys I have been with and the ways we have had sex have helped me figure out the kind of woman I am and know the type of man I want in my life. It's helped me know the extent to which I am willing to please my man. It's pushed my buttons as a person, and helped me to evolve.

PART 2: FREEDOM

WHEN MY MARRIAGE ENDED, I DECIDED THAT I WANTED TO DO THE
thing that had always been denied to me as a young girl. I wanted to sow my
wild oats. I moved continents and went back home to Ghana, but returned
without the fears of my childhood. The fear of men sleeping with you and
telling all their friends: "Dat chick, I chop am."

There was Abraham: he would be remembered for giving me vaginal
orgasms twice in one night as we fucked in his car while parked in the compound of his home. We constantly came up with new things to try. I'd send
him a text: "I'm going to drive to your house naked. I will be there at 9 p.m.
Make sure you open the gate naked." It was all fun and games until a friend
innocently showed me a picture of her out on a double date with another
friend. And there was Abraham, arms around another woman. Is she prettier
than I am? I asked myself. At least she is fatter than I am, I thought. "That's
the guy I've been seeing," I told my friend. Her mouth opened in an O.

And then there was Kandi. This time I was doing this with my eyes wide
open. I wanted to have sex with a woman as an adult woman. I didn't want to
fumble in grotty bathrooms, or touch soft lips while hidden underneath sleeping cloths as I had done in boarding school. I want to experience what sex

with another woman is really like, I said to myself. After hooking up with girls throughout university in the UK, Kandi was doing her best to stay on the straight and narrow in Ghana. But our eyes lingered a bit too long on each other, and there was a certain knowingness in the curve of our lips when we smiled at each other. We ended up in her flat one evening after going out to a show at which her boyfriend was DJing. "Sit on my face," she said, and I did. I fell for Kandi, but she only ever saw me as a friend. She would tell me about other women she liked, and then one day she told me about another woman she had had sex with. I think by then she had forgotten we had been sleeping together.

I stopped counting the number of people I had sex with. There's no point counting when you struggle to remember names, and your body count is more than the digits on your fingers. I see certain people and remember, OMG, I fucked him once. Some people stand out:

Maya paid for me to stay in the Hilton Garden Inn near Macy's in New York, and I had an open relationship with her for close to a year until I started chatting with Peter, whom I had never met before, but who was planning to move to Ghana. I agreed to date Peter based on the intensity of our Gchats, but in person I didn't feel that same intensity around him, and I broke up with him while he stared at me with pools in his eyes.

The artist who said, "I need you to go deeper," while I rode him in the back of my car.

The songwriter who made me eggs for breakfast when we woke up in the house which he shared with his family.

"It's like watching Black love," my friend declared as she watched her lover go in and out in between my thighs in the candlelit suite they had specially booked for the occasion.

For the most part my lovers were younger men. They would happily take a trotro to mine no matter what time of the day it was. They would dive between my thighs and stay there as long as was needed. They would tell me what they wanted to do to me, and do it over and over again. For the most part they wanted me to cum, and took pleasure in my pleasure.

This period of sowing my wild oats was important for me. It was a deliberate act to be a "bad girl," to learn to have pleasurable sex, to allow myself the space to experiment and figure out who I am. Sexual freedom doesn't look the same for everyone. For some, it is ultimately choosing to be celibate, or accepting that they are asexual.

A huge part of sexual freedom for me is embodied. Loving my body as it is has been a journey, and so I feel most free when I am at home in my body, lounging naked on my bed, stripped of all pretenses, my boobies freely rolling to wherever they choose to land, my belly relaxed and soft, my thighs apart, my hands wherever they may choose to lie. With no one around me, I am my most free self. I also feel free in community; when I am with my feminist sisters, when I can speak my truths without fear of being judged, questioned, or canceled.

When we think of freedom it is easy to imagine that it is a far-off, distant place, but in reality, we can all be free in the here and now. We achieve freedom when we let go of the weight of societal expectations, and when we find our people—those who love us, care for us, and hold us up when we start slipping.

The women featured in this section show that there are many ways to be free in sexual relationships. It's no accident that the vast majority of women featured are from the lesbian, bisexual, and trans community, and/or practice polyamory. These are women who have resisted societal norms of compulsory heterosexuality and monogamy, and have searched both within and without for other ways of practicing love. In my conversation with Fatou of Senegal, she kept reiterating how she would always say to new partners, "I am a free woman." This was a constant refrain because new lovers would often try and reshape her into something she was not, would demand monogamy when they knew she was polyamorous. For Alexis, freedom came with the wisdom and experience of age, as well as meeting a partner in her sixties who, like her, is comfortable playing with masculinity and femininity. For Gabriela, diving deeper into a spiritual practice brought her to a place where she could create relationships that were freer.

Freedom is not a destination that one arrives at and can choose to stay there forever and ever. Freedom is a constant state of being, an energy and a state that we need to nurture and protect. Freedom is a safe home that one can return to over and over again.

I initially met Fatou* in 2016, when we attended a Pan-African gathering of feminists in Harare, Zimbabwe. One evening I co-led a discussion on sex and sexuality. It was designed to be a fun, interactive session. Women shared their personal stories, and my co-facilitator passed around different types of sex toys for people to touch and feel. The next day a woman approached me. She wanted to share her experiences with me. She spoke French, a language I have formally studied but only speak at a very basic level. Fatou stepped in to be our interpreter.

I learned that the woman who had approached me was a Senegalese woman who had been married at a young age to an older man. She and her husband had subsequently moved to Mauritania, a country that she described to me as discriminatory towards Black people. I was keen to learn more, and so I quickly told her about my book project and asked if I could interview her subsequently. She said yes, but we never managed to have that extended conversation.

In 2018 I traveled to Dakar, Senegal, for work and reconnected with Fatou. I asked her if I could interview her for my book and she said yes. We went to the beach and lay on some sun loungers, and I hit the record button on my phone. Over the years I have maintained close contact with Fatou and I consider her one of my inspirations for how to live a solo polyamorous life. From a young age Fatou has negotiated life in Senegal, a fairly conservative Muslim-majority country, as a bisexual woman with multiple partners. At the time of interview, she was sixty years old.

FATOU

■

ASAD AND I got together while we were both married to other people. We were all friends and then I fell in love with him. I think he loved me too but I didn't know that initially, and thought my feelings were one-sided. I've always been the kind of person to go after anyone I fancy. It doesn't matter whether they are a man or woman. One day, Asad came to our house after he had been out for a run; he was sweating and looked so good. He sat on the floor with his back against the wall. I sat right opposite him, and spread my legs apart. I wasn't wearing any panties. He later said to me that he wanted to taste me when he saw how I was made. That was more than thirty years ago.

We keep breaking up and coming back together. We've broken up at least seven times for different reasons. There is never any acrimony. Sometimes we break up because he says he wants to try again with his wife for the sake of the children, and I always say, "That's fine." Usually there is somebody else I am eyeing and I want to try that person too, and so it works out. The first time we had sex it was a disaster. We were in his house and because he was married I was very nervous. After we had been making out for a while I pushed him off me and said, "Leave me alone," and walked away. He later told me that really upset him. The second time was a very different experience. We went away together, and had privacy. I wasn't nervous, I trusted him, and he put a lot of effort into pleasing me. He's never stopped putting in his best efforts. He calls me a chicken. When a chicken has sex it's over very quickly. I get satisfied and orgasm really easily.

I will never get married again. I think the institution of marriage has been set up to trick women. They tell you that once you get married the guy takes care of you, but that's not true. Many women lose all the privileges of a free woman when they get married and what they gain is nothing compared to what they lose.

My ex-husband and I were friends before we became lovers. We met because we were both members of a communist organization. We had that in common, but we were very different when it came to sex. I am very cerebral when it comes to sex. I like to read about sex, talk about sex, tell stories about sex. My ex didn't like that. He was religious and so thought that was not right. When I told him that I wasn't having the type of orgasms I thought I deserved he said, "No, this is only in the books, it never happens like that in real life."

After a while, I decided that I didn't want to stay married and asked for a divorce. I told him, "I am no longer in love with you and I want my freedom." He told his brother, who was a huge influence in his life, and his brother said I only wanted his money. I said to him, "You don't have to give me even one franc. I want a divorce," and it was only then he was willing to go to the judge to say that we wanted to divorce amicably. At the time my mum did not know about the divorce; none of our extended family did apart from his brother. After all these years my daughter says he's still in love with me because he never married again. We had two children together, a boy and a girl, so we will always be connected through them. Even Asad, my lover, thinks my ex is still in love with me. When he wants to tease me he says, "You should go back to your husband."

Before my ex and I got married, I got pregnant. He insisted that I get an abortion. He said, "I cannot come to your family and tell them you're pregnant. Your mum won't be happy." I felt very bad about the abortion. I saw it as a failure. I didn't understand. We loved each other, we wanted to be together, and so if by chance I was pregnant, why did we need to wait till we were married so I could have a baby? Why did I need to have an abortion? I saw no logic in that. We were going to get married anyway. I said to him, "Let's go ahead and have a baby, and people will know we had that baby." He said no. I felt very bad and the conditions under which I had the abortion were terrible. Abortions are illegal in Senegal and everyone involved, including the person undergoing the abortion, the doctor, or whoever is carrying out the procedure and anyone who even knows about the abortion, is regarded as an accomplice. So, for example, if a man knew his daughter was going to have an abortion and he took her to the doctor the three of them could go to prison. That is still the case to this day.

I don't even know if the guy who did my abortion was a real doctor. There was no way to check. He lived in one of those big compounds in the medina and he did the abortion in a small wooden hut. He inserted something inside me. It was sharp and it hurt a lot. I'm not sure what it was, I didn't look, but I started to bleed after I left. I was supposed to come back later so he could confirm if the abortion had worked. I asked my brother to accompany me, although he didn't know what I was doing. My brother waited outside the hut for me. Inside, the man pinned me to the bed and forcibly had sex with me. When I left, he said, "You should come back," but I never went back.

I didn't know what to do or where to go, I was so distressed. I didn't tell anyone what had happened in that hut. Not even my brother or my future husband, who was the one who had arranged for me to go to that place. I felt so ashamed. I asked myself, Why didn't you yell? There were lots of people there. I thought I should have yelled even if that would have led to something bad happening to me or my brother. Why didn't I do it? I felt so helpless. I've never told anyone this story before. This is the first time I'm speaking about it. I knew that if I went to the police they would say, "You are not supposed to have an abortion." After that I started to protect the people around me. If one of my friends needed to have an abortion, I would make sure I was next door and that they knew what to do if something went wrong. I would say, "If you need me just yell my name, I am just sitting outside the door."

I've always loved women. I love women's bodies, I enjoy their company, I love women just the way they are. I also think women can be complicated, and for this reason I haven't had a lot of women friends. My first homosexual relationship was when I was a teenager. She was a girl in my neighborhood who was a tomboy just like me. Our relationship felt very natural. She dated young men just like I did. We started having sex without making a fuss about it, and while both of us were still in other relationships. We were just two young bisexual girls. Neither of us were the jealous type and that was a great comfort.

Our mums tried to separate us. They thought we were a bad influence on each other. We were both very stubborn. She had a motorcycle and we would go out dancing at night, which used to enrage our mothers. One time she tried to organize a threesome but it was a disaster. I think her guy hadn't taken her seriously when she had discussed it with him. The three of us were in the room and he told her to leave, and that he wanted to talk to me. When she left he started to lecture me. He said, "Why are you doing this? It isn't right." I was confused and angry and had lots of mixed feelings. I started to cry and said, "You have no right to tell me what to do and who to do it with. If you want to talk to someone, talk to your girlfriend." I was eighteen at the time. That put me off threesomes for life. Twosomes are complicated but threesomes are three times more complicated.

Freedom has always been important to me. In all my relationships I would always try other men. Sometimes women too, but not that many because I think relationships with women tend to become the most complicated ones. I found that most women were possessive and would not understand that I love them but still want to sleep with someone else. When it comes to possessiveness I think women are more fierce than men are. I never hid who I am, but whenever I initially told a new lover about being attracted to someone else they would think I was joking. I would just keep saying to them, "I am a free woman."

I started most relationships while still in a relationship with someone else, but that same person would turn around and demand that I be faithful to them. I would just say, "When you met me I was with someone else and you knew about that," so I would just go for what I wanted. Sometimes we could talk about it, other times it became a lot of drama, and sometimes people would say, "I cannot be in a relationship like this," and would leave when I got attracted to someone else, but I never lied about my feelings. Never! That was important to me. I don't want to lie about being free, and even my kids and sisters knew what kind of woman I was. Sometimes my sisters would say, "It's against religion." My kids grew up with me, so although I didn't speak to them directly about polyamory, I lived my life and they saw it. Even if it was clear to them that this is not what every woman is like.

I think I am how I am because of my father, although we never talked about sex. He was a free man. He was very open about his multiple relationships even though my mum didn't like it. I admired my father for being who he was, for being different. He lived his life on the fringes. He was a doctor, and here in Senegal, medical doctors are considered part of the elite, but that wasn't him. He always made friends with people on the margins, mainly artists. He liked to live a simple life, spend time in the village, which is exactly how I am. I am not a city person. I am not sophisticated, and I think I got that from my father.

When I was younger one of my male cousins said, "If a man is attracted to you it's because they have something homosexual within them." When I was younger I didn't look like a woman. I didn't dress like a woman, I didn't talk like a woman, I didn't behave like a woman, but I've never been confused about being a woman. I am a woman who doesn't want to behave like a woman just because that's what convention says we must do. As a child, my two younger brothers were my best friends, and my eldest sister hated me. She was critical of me, always saying, "You should not go out with that person, you should not behave like this, people are talking." She never leaves me alone, even now. When we meet at the airport to go on a trip together and I'm dressed in a way that she doesn't like, she will go into her suitcase and give me something else to wear. She'll say, "How can you travel from country to country dressed like this? Wear this dress, change your shoes." One time I was carrying a plastic bag on a trip and she reached into her suitcase and gave me what she considered a proper bag for a traveling woman. She's like that even now.

I have changed as I've grown older. I used to be willing and open to having sex with other men. In the past I could be in a relationship with two men at the same time, but now I feel tired. I am a lazy lover. I got tired of trying things with new men, and sometimes doing things I don't like, such as men who are very physical. I'm not very physical, I'm tender and gentle, so trying a new man who was too physical for me put me off being more open to new experiences. Asad is a Speedy Gonzales, and I'm a very easy-to-please woman. *Une femme facile* in the sense that it's easy to make me reach orgasm. I think we are still together because I am not very demanding sexually and still very open. I am not the kind of woman who is jealous, who will be mad because he is sleeping with other women.

I know Asad sleeps with other women, and I sleep with other women too. In the past we've broken up because we had STDs, minor ones, and whenever that happened, he would blame me, and say, "You are the one who sleeps around," and I would say, "What about your women? Even conventional women sleep with other people, they just don't talk about it." I thought that was so crazy. How could he say I sleep around but his other women don't? Was he in their underwear everywhere they went? I've never done an HIV test and I hope I am not positive. I don't think I will ever get tested. I was lucky because sleeping around with people who also sleep around can be very dangerous. Sometimes we use protection but not always. When I meet people initially I use protection but the rest of the time we don't, and so I think I am lucky, or maybe I am HIV positive and I just don't know. I've had really dangerous behaviors.

I have slept with about fifty people. Some people just once, some people for a month, some people for a year, some people for several years. I was not counting. Some people will call me a whore, but that's something I have always been ready to hear. When they called me a whore I didn't take it negatively. It came from people who were making love with you and wanted you to stay with them. When you reject monogamy they call you a whore. Even if they knew that is how you were, they expected you to change. I would say this has nothing to do with love, this is just the way I am.

My interview with Helen Banda nearly didn't happen. She had written to me via Facebook, my least favorite platform, and I only discovered her message months after she had initially reached out.

Hello. It's great to see African women like yourself trailblazing for the rest of us. I heard you are writing a book about African women and sexuality, and you are interviewing women who live a sexually liberated lifestyle. I am a married polyamorous, pansexual African woman. I am an African woman, born and raised in Zambia . . . I moved to the USA for college. I have lived here ever since. I have been married to a midwestern white American male for eleven years. We have three children, and we are a very close family. Our closeness is precipitated by our oldest daughter, who has special needs and is medically fragile. Death is never too far from my mind . . . It took a lot of courage to open up our marriage, especially since I was the one who pushed for it. It has been a very rich journey of self-discovery and acceptance. I feel there is so much the world needs to learn about embracing one's sexuality and identity. We are not openly polyamorous, nor am I openly pansexual, but I'd love to get out of this confining closet. If you have time to talk some more, please feel free to reach out.

The minute I saw this message I tried to call Helen via Messenger, but she didn't pick up. I frantically sent her a text message, which she thankfully responded to. A few days later we spent several hours chatting via WhatsApp.

Helen is a thirty-nine-year-old cisgender woman whose journey to polyamory is one that I feel especially inspired by. In spite of the rigors of work, motherhood, and caring for a child with special needs, she's found a way to explore polyamory and the world of kink, and now recognizes her sexual orientation as pansexual. Helen's story shows that with the right partner, it is possible to successfully renegotiate the terms of one's marriage. Traditional heterosexual motherhood and marriage doesn't necessarily signal the end of experimentation and the journey to discover one's sexuality.

I was married once and during that period in my life I felt societal pressure to conform to a particular model of "wifedom." I remember having lunch with a woman I had just met and she reacted in shock when she learned I was married because, "You seem so free." My personal experience of marriage, including the hundreds of marriages that I have witnessed, is that overwhelmingly it is restrictive for women. It was a joy to speak to a woman who was able to openly communicate with her husband about her sexual needs and desire, and who had an equitable approach to childcare to ensure that each of them had space and time to explore their sexuality.

HELEN BANDA

·

ONE DAY, ONE of the moms in the neighborhood playgroup said to me, "My husband and I are swingers and we're looking for people to explore with. Do you know anyone in the lifestyle?" I looked directly in her eyes, and consciously arranged my face to appear calm and nonjudgmental. My husband and I had talked about opening up our marriage several times but I didn't know any people who were swingers. "No, I don't know any people who do that," I said. She went on to tell me about swingers' clubs where couples could go and swap partners. We ended up chatting for hours. I got home so late that my husband was already in bed. I woke him up and said, "I need to tell you about this conversation that I just had."

I have always known that I was attracted to women as well as men. My husband had said to me, "If you're out and you meet a woman you fancy, go ahead and explore, just tell me about it." I had given him that same pass but in ten years of marriage neither of us had taken that option. On the contrary, I had lost myself to motherhood and focused my energy on our three children, especially our firstborn, who has special needs.

My husband and I decided to open up our marriage. We joined a swingers' site online and started visiting some clubs and met a few people that way. We took a five-day trip to Canada and went to an adult social club in Toronto where I kissed a girl for the first time. We started going to these meetup groups called munches where people meet for lunch in a restaurant and chat about the polyamorous lifestyle. These conversations were helpful in figuring out exactly what you were looking for, whether that was polyamory, swinging, or something in between. There were discussions on how to establish boundaries in your multiple relationships. I learned a lot through these events. People would often recommend books we could read, or podcasts we could listen to, and we'd get lots of advice. Initially my husband and I tried to go to these munches together but we realized that it was more efficient for us to take turns so that we didn't have to pay for babysitting. One day I went to a meetup after work, and as the conversations started, I realized it was a kink-centered polyamory munch. I was a bit freaked out because I thought, OMG, these are kinky people, but at the same time everyone looked so vanilla and ordinary. Plus we were all sitting in a regular restaurant, and it was clear that most people already knew each other.

Some folks started talking about this website called Fetlife and so I asked, "What's that all about?" When they explained, my reaction was, "What the heck?" The man sitting next to me said,

"I run a BDSM munch on the other side of town."

"You mean you beat people?"

"Only if they want me to."

"How could you?"

"It's all consensual."

I wasn't quite sure what to make of it all. Everybody was so nice and ordinary. Later that evening another guy came up to me and said, "Hello, you are really beautiful. That's my girlfriend over there." He was pointing to another woman who was seated further down the table, and then he said, "You need to come to my Halloween party. It's going to be in my private dungeon."

"Ummm. I'll have to check with my husband first."

"Bring your husband, come and have fun. You'll need to join Fetlife in order to get the details for the party."

Right there and then someone took my phone and helped me set up a Fetlife profile, and then I RSVP'd to the party. I thought to myself, you know what, you only live once. I can't say I've lived on this earth but never went to a dungeon when I was given the opportunity to go.

When I RSVP'd to the party I was told that it was a potluck and to indicate what dish I would bring. We were also encouraged to dress up with the Halloween theme in mind. Neither my husband nor I do themed dress codes and so

I wore an evening dress, and he wore more ordinary clothes. We had all sorts of exit plans in case things got too weird. I told him, "Carry me out if I see something strange and faint." When we arrived at the venue we had to pay a cover charge and sign a waiver that basically said we were there voluntarily and were responsible for our own safety. In the kitchen there was lots of food. People wearing Halloween costumes milled through the two living spaces in the house, stopping every now and then to chat. We ended up in a conversation with a lesbian couple, and I told them, "This is all very new to us." They started to tell us about the kink world and the importance of vetting and of safe play. One of the wives offered to show us the dungeon.

To get to the dungeon you had to leave the house and cross the road. On the outside it looked like a huge garage. In a former life it had been a workshop, which the owner had converted. Once you entered there were a series of hooks where you could hang up your coat. Inside, the first thing I saw was the marketplace. There were tables set up with all sorts of supplies like riding crops and vibrators but there were no vendors. All the items were individually priced and there was a jar on the table so all you had to do was pick your item and put your money in the jar. We climbed upstairs and saw a room that looked more private. Our guide told us, "A lot of people like to play with rope here." I wondered what that was all about.

We came back downstairs and went to the main space in the dungeon. There were several different stations. There was a crossbar for the flogging station. There was another station that had huge rings hanging down and there was a woman who was doing all these acrobatic moves inside the rings while someone took her photograph. There were tables that looked like ordinary massage tables. There were spaces for electric play—I had no idea that was even a thing. There was a station that had something that looked like a saddle. There was a section filled with comfy seats. All kinds of people were there. Some walked around naked, while others were fully clothed. There was an older man walking around who looked to me like someone who could be a sixty-year-old CEO of a bank. He was wearing one of those formal dresses that I see women like Madeline Albright wearing. He wore white heels and carried a structured handbag. No one batted an eyelid at him. It felt very much like people could be themselves in this space. There was no alcohol in the dungeon. I was told that in a space where consent is paramount, it's important that people are not intoxicated.

Our guide whispered as she spoke to us. "You have to be quiet in the dungeon. People are working on scenes and need to stay focused. It's important not to distract anyone. If you want to do a scene with someone you have to talk to them beforehand. You can't just walk into a scene and ask to join."

She explained other rules to us. "You will be kicked out of the dungeon if you violate consent. You have to preserve people's anonymity. You can't see someone on the street and say, 'Hey Jake, it was great seeing you at the dungeon last night.' Don't interfere in someone's scene unless you have been invited to do so. Tell a dungeon monitor if someone is harassing you and refuses to stop."

We continued to walk around the dungeon taking everything in. I saw this older man in a booth looking simultaneously tired and happy. There were two younger women with him rubbing his shoulders and whispering to him. They were all giggling and laughing together. In another booth there was a woman who I had seen on the saddle earlier; she and the guy who had been with her were now hugging. I asked, "What's going on here?"

"This is another important part of kink. Once you finish a scene there's aftercare. Whoever is domming has to make sure the sub is in a good place because in a scene you get all these hormones that fill you with euphoria, and you can crash if the person in the scene just walks away from you. Even the domme might need some aftercare to help them come down from the high."

I thought that was the most beautiful thing. I learned that the euphoria from a scene could last for even a week, and so sometimes, whoever had been the domme would continue to check in with the sub to make sure they were easing off that high. Otherwise the sudden disconnection could cause a visceral reaction, which is described as "sub space" or "down space." Just imagine how people feel when they are withdrawing from a drug and that can give you a good idea of what it's like to be in sub space.

There was this scene I saw that stuck with me. There was a woman lying on what looked like a massage bed and there was a guy wearing rounded metal-tipped gloves who was running his hands over her body. I asked my guide, "What is going on over here?" and she said, "Oh, he's just giving her a massage." That answer didn't satisfy me. This was no ordinary massage. And so later when I saw the woman wandering through the dungeon on her own I went up to her.

"Excuse me, I am new here. I am curious to know what that guy was doing to you."

"Come on, let's go ask him."

She pulled on my arm and I followed her to the guy she had been in the scene with earlier. He was wearing puppy ears on his head, and on his neck he had a dog collar that had a bone hanging off it. His chest was encased in a leather harness and on his feet he wore furry boots that went all the way up to his knees. He was in the middle of putting on briefs when we stopped in front of him.

"She's asking about your gloves," said the woman who had been in the scene earlier. I piped up. "I'm curious, I've never seen that before." The woman wandered away as my husband remained nearby.

"I can do a scene with you if you want, but I'm just about to finish another one."

"That's okay. We were just about to leave anyway," I said while indicating my husband.

"If you like I can try it on your shoulder so you see what it's like." I nodded while he slid his hand into his glove. He glided the tips of the glove over my shoulder.

"That feels amazing." I tried to get my husband involved. "You should try this. It feels really good." He shook his head and remained slightly at a distance.

"Can I get your contact information?" I said to the man with the glove.

"It's on Fet."

I took his Fet details and nodded to my husband, indicating that I was ready to leave.

"What do you think of my underwear? Should I wear the orange or the black one?"

I turned back to look at the man with the glove.

"Definitely the orange one."

In the car I immediately looked up his Fet handle and messaged him. We met up and now he is one of my partners.

When my husband and I started exploring the lifestyle we would try to do activities that centered around couple play, but that didn't really work out. Sometimes we would meet up with a couple, for instance, and it would be clear to us that the woman wasn't a hundred percent into it. So we decided to explore individually, which was also much better for our childcare arrangements. This individual exploration also helped me realize that I am more polyamorous than I am a swinger. I'm not opposed to swinging at all. I just prefer to have consistent play partners. In the past year I've dated way more people than my husband has. I'm aware that he's been keeping score, and has some issues with competitiveness and jealousy. I have had more relationships than he has because it's also much easier for me to find partners. He's a kind, considerate, geeky type of man, but not someone who is super charming or who finds it easy to come on to other women in a bar, for instance.

For the most part, I tend to meet people on ordinary dating websites. My online profiles clearly state that I am ethically nonmonogamous. There is just one person that I met in real life and started dating. We met while I was on a business trip. She lives in Atlanta, a thirteen-hour drive from me, and so we ended up in a long-distance relationship for several months. We are very similar in terms of our drive, ambition, and views on life. We are also both open-minded, love to travel, and are married. She's very much in love with her husband, as am I. In many ways it was a close-to-perfect relationship except for the distance. Both of us like to be able to spend time with our partners and it was difficult for us to see each other regularly. We both felt that we wanted to be with people we could see more often. Then she met someone else who lived near her and started to spend more time with that person. I knew that closeness and intimacy were what she needed. It was the same thing that I wanted and so

I told her, "I don't think you have the capacity to juggle all of this, and I don't think that I do either." It was an amicable breakup and we're still friends.

Most of my exploration has been with Puppy, the guy with the glove who I met at the dungeon. Our relationship has been mostly sexual and kinky, which is also because of where he is in his life right now. He just turned thirty and so is about ten years younger than I am. He also has no children, and doesn't really understand my responsibilities and needs as a parent. Hanging out with him is a form of escapism. I can message him and say, "What are you up to?" and then go over, watch Netflix, spend the night, and come home in time to take the children to school. He also comes over from time to time so we do fun stuff like kayaking. When Puppy and I first started seeing each other, his girlfriend recommended that I take a kink 101 class. I'd registered for the class but I was nervous about going on my own, and my husband wasn't interested, plus he also needed to babysit.

One time we went to this munch that was about how to deal with jealousy in a polyamorous relationship. We were seated behind this couple and ended up chatting with them a lot. The husband seemed uncomfortable throughout the entire discussion and so I got the impression that jealousy was definitely an issue for him. A few days after the munch, the woman and I met up for a coffee. I told her about my experience at the dungeon and she said, "My husband is kinky but I'm not." I told her how fascinated I had been by the glove, which is apparently a kink. A few days before the workshop I texted my new friend and asked if there was any way her husband, John, could accompany me to the event. On the day he showed up at my house to pick me up. We were both nervous. Neither of us had been to anything like this before.

At the workshop we discussed consent, safety, and the importance of knowing who you are playing with, as well as the different types of play. There were also different stations set up where you could check out different demonstrations and experiences if you felt so inclined. John and I started walking around. We stopped at a demo station for wax play and learned about the concept behind wax play, the various types of wax, and the range in heat and temperatures. A demonstration was done on someone but I didn't think wax play was for me.

A lot of the demo stations had people all around them so eventually we wandered over to the one station that was free. It was the rope station. The woman there told us about rope safety, the kind of discussions you should have before getting into a rope scene, deciding whether you are doing a full suspension or partial suspension, and the importance of knowing where blood vessels are so you don't overly tighten those areas. She started to show us how to do some basic knots and I thrust out my hand and said, "Here, you can demonstrate on me." She showed John some knots and he started tying up my hands. She would correct him as he went along. "No, do it this way." He kept practicing and she started to show him how to do a basic tie around the chest area. He started to wrap the rope around me and in an instant something changed. We both started breathing heavily. I could practically feel the blood pumping through my veins. That was a surprise. Neither of us had any previous experiences with rope play. After that I said, "Right, we're going to go to every station." We went to the paddle section but that didn't do much for me. We went to the flogging area and again I offered to be demonstrated on. Every time they flogged my leg I giggled. I was told it had that effect on some people. Afterwards John said to me, "Watching you get flogged was such a turn-on." I replied, "Good for you!"

John and I ended up dating for about four months. When his wife was out of town, I would spend the night at their place. She would text me and say, "I set the room up for you. Let me know if you need anything." They also came over for dinner with their children, who got on very well with our children. In many ways it was the kind of relationship we had been looking for, but John and his wife were not in a good place. She wanted a divorce and he wasn't taking that very well. Eventually they broke up. I still text both of them from time to time. My husband chats more with John's wife than I do, often meeting up with her for coffee. They are platonic friends and have never been sexually involved.

It's really important to me that my relationships are ethical. There was one person I had to end things with for that reason. He is a lieutenant colonel in the army and travels to my state once a month. We met via an app and in our chats he told me how close he and his wife were. They had both been in the military and were a very physical couple. Their idea of fun was to go on runs together. They had no children and were the most important people in each other's life. He shared with me how his wife's health had deteriorated over a few years, and as a result she now had a really low libido.

On his next visit to my state he checked us both into a hotel. The sex was amazing. Afterwards I asked him, "How aware is your wife that you're pursuing other sexual relationships?" He said, "She's okay with it but not exactly aware." I quizzed him further. It turned out that his wife had said that she would prefer for him to hire a sex worker but he hadn't wanted to. He told me, "I want a more intimate relationship. It won't stop me loving my wife." I completely understood where he was coming from and I told him so. I also insisted that he would have to tell his wife and seek her consent before we could continue seeing each other. I told him he could give my number to his wife if she wanted to speak to me. I wanted her to know that I wouldn't try and steal her husband and wasn't a threat to their relationship in any way. For me it's really important that I bring joy into my partner's life. I want to be a positive influence, not a negative one. A month later he called me to tell me he was coming into town and had booked a hotel for us. Later he rang back to say he couldn't make it anymore. That was our last interaction and so I presumed that conversation with his wife didn't go well.

It's partly because of this experience that I said to James when we met that I wanted to meet his wife. We met at a social club that I had gone to with my husband because he had a date, but men could only get into the venue if they were with a woman. James is Nigerian and so I was wary. So far I haven't wanted other Africans to know about my lifestyle because I'm concerned that people, particularly women, will be hostile towards me. I don't care much about how that will affect me personally but I am concerned about any potential impact on my children. Generally, I haven't met a lot of Africans in the lifestyle. At the social clubs there are usually a few African men but my experience is that we usually don't have the same philosophy around sexual liberation and sex positivity. The men have come across more as opportunists who think the women on the scene are easy. I haven't felt that they have any respect for women who are embracing their sexuality. African culture says women should not be sexually forward, but men love sexually forward women. The difference is that while they would date such a woman, they wouldn't marry her, and so there is a difference because they don't respect you. As a sexually liberated woman I am more than my vagina and I have found it hard to meet African men who view me as such.

So I was skeptical when I met James. I wanted to meet his wife so we could all be clear on our various roles. She told me about a previous relationship he had been in that hadn't worked out because the other woman, who was also African, wasn't in the lifestyle and acted more like a traditional second wife. She felt we were more what they were looking for. At the moment we are all just getting to know each other. I recently had drinks with her, and prior to that I went out for lunch with James. In a few days we are all supposed to be having dim sum together. I don't know what will happen with that relationship, whether I'll end up being with James alone, with James and his wife, or whether both sets of couples will end up together. At this stage there's a lot of ambiguity, which is fine. We haven't put a label on it and we're just going to see how things work out.

Opening up our marriage has made a huge difference to the relationship my husband and I have. I'll always love him but I have no expectations that he or anyone else can meet all my needs. Most people demand that one person be everything to them. The perfect lover, the provider, the protector. I think that's asking too much of any one individual. I can't be all that to my husband either. I can be his best friend, I can one hundred percent be his emotional support. If shit hits the fan, I'm there for him, but I know that if I got into a fight he'd be the first one to run away. On the flip side, if I'm sick, he's there with a pillow and offers to make me soup, and that's great.

Over the past year I've been on a journey of discovery. I've realized that polyamory is natural to me. I now know that I am not only bisexual, but pansexual, kinky, and polyamorous. I met a gender nonconforming person, for instance, and we had a great sexual encounter. I wonder what else I don't know about myself yet. There are a couple of things I do know. I'm a sexual person, I love to explore, and I want more than one partner. I also want another girlfriend. I want people who will understand my life and become part of my support system. I want meaningful relationships, and I am open to those turning into love.

I love to eat, and one of my favorite things to do is to invite people I find fascinating home for a meal. There is a magic that happens when you gather the right people in a soothing ambience, with delicious food and drinks. Inviting people to my home has been one of the ways I have deepened my relationships with people I previously knew peripherally—like Ozioma, a creative whose work I admired and had followed over the years. One of the really great things about being an African feminist is how interconnected the community is, and so I was thrilled when Ozioma reached out to me one day to say that she was visiting Ghana with her partner. Over dinner I was struck by the fact that these two were the oldest African queer elders I knew. Although I had only just met Alexis,* Ozioma's partner, I thought she had a beautiful spirit and was an easy conversationalist. She is also a writer and so I suspected that she would be generous in sharing with a younger writer, and I was right.

Alexis was born in Harlem, New York, and was seventy-one years old when I interviewed her. She identifies as a Black queer feminist. She is Afro-Caribbean, the maternal side of her family originating from the Caribbean islands while her paternal heritage can be traced back to North Carolina in the US. In this story she shares about the joys of finding love in her sixties, the importance of self-pleasure, and the role that the erotic, and a love of food, plays in her love life with her partner. This was one of the conversations that I found the most affirming as I start to grapple mentally with the implications of growing older.

ALEXIS

.

SOMETIMES I FEEL very alive when I wake up in the morning. I'll usually touch myself while my partner is snoring loudly next to me. There is something very exciting about doing that. I think self-pleasure is very important.

I have a good erotic life. My partner and I like to indulge in what we call "debauchery." One night we were drunk and going full tilt at it, it was amazing, and so we made an agreement that it was okay to have debauchery in our lives. Black people are not often invited to identify themselves as "hedonistic" or deeply in our bodies. Our sexualities are often pathologized, and so we came to the agreement that nothing we do is related to pathology. Some nights or afternoons (my partner doesn't feel very sexual in the morning) we make ourselves feel good by having drinks and food, and that leads to having sex and making love. I'm very explicit during sex. I engage in what people call dirty talking. It turns me on and I think it turns her on too. I know this because I get results. We also make use of our hands and have a box of sex toys; we often add new toys to our collection. Usually, we take turns pleasing each other. Just last night, my partner was saying to me that we need to find something new to do sexually. I'm pretty sure she was suggesting that we experiment with tying each other up. We've talked about this before, and are both excited by the idea.

We are both in our seventies and have had many lovers over time, so we know our bodies in ways that we didn't fully know them in the past. We're willing to engage in sexual acts that interest us, we can talk about, and say yes I'd like to try this but not that. For example, my partner made it clear to me that she doesn't want me to ask her to do anything that will have her on her knees for a long time because she has bad knees, and that will cause her discomfort, which will interrupt her pleasure.

It takes energy to have the kind of sex we like to have, so if we have sex once a week that's great. If we have sex every two weeks that's great too. It's not about quantity for us. It's really about the quality of the loving we can share as self-identified women.

My erotic life has to do with intimacy in the bedroom, but it is also part of a larger reality that has to do with living together, feeding each other, listening to and talking to each other. What we do outside the bedroom is also a part of our bodily experience. Often we can be turned on just by talking to each other.

We have been together for four years now. I was instantly attracted to her when we met. At the time I had just come out of what I thought was a terrible relationship with another woman and I was pretty much done. I wasn't trying to get with anyone else. I said to myself, "I don't want to see another woman, I don't want to smell another woman, I don't want to touch another woman," and then I met the woman I am with now. A mutual friend introduced us, thinking that we were intellectually compatible. I don't think she thought anything romantic would happen between us. At the time, I had a new book out, so my partner, who is also a writer, was meant to interview me for a publication she was connected to. That feature never happened.

At the time I lived in New York and she lived in Florida, so she invited me to come over for a long weekend. I was a bit reticent, but she told me that it would be all right and she would make sure that I was comfortable. When we initially met, one of the first things she told me was that she didn't cook. I was like, "What the heck, how does this person not cook?" I like to cook and I also like to eat. But it turns out that she just doesn't like to cook for herself. She made this amazing meal the first weekend I visited her home. That really freaked me out because I wasn't ready for the food that she made. I wasn't ready to have any home-cooked food since she had told me that she didn't cook. That was also the weekend that we had our first sexual encounter with each other. It felt very easy and familiar. At the end of the weekend, I flew back home, and the following Monday she traveled to Haiti for two months. We talked every day while she was there. The distance gave us time to think, and it also allowed us to miss each other. Both in terms of missing each other's bodies, but also the comfort of being with each other. It's amazing to be in your sixties and meet someone that you absolutely fall in love with.

I have learned over time that relationships require work. When you're younger, you have a sense of love as being magical and so relationships happen in that particular space of magic, and it's easy to feel that's all one needs, but now I know that relationships require work, and constant work. The desire that is in the relationship also needs to be nurtured, and thought about, and reentered and reimagined. I think we don't have that information when we go into relationships at a younger age. My partner and I have a number of agreements. We have an agreement that we will only let a certain amount of time go by when we are mad at each other. We can spend the day being pissed off but we can't spend the night being pissed off, so within hours of that quarrel we have to come together. That too is part of the work. It's about taking the hurt or anger and working through that to get to a place of transformation, whether that's understanding or an agreement to disagree.

The other part is doing a lot of listening. When you're with someone who is also in their seventh decade you have to really understand that the ways they participate in life are in many ways very set and relate to years of living before they met you. They also have stuff you're not going to be able to change—not that you should want to—so part of the work is really having to do the listening. Another big part is recognizing difference. We often go to relationships thinking that we're going to become one with the other person, but that is just not a good idea. People don't become one, people become themselves, and so part of the work is to understand that the other person is also evolving into themselves, just as you are also evolving into yourself, and that evolution is very often not the same. It may be similar on Tuesday but very different on Friday. It might look the same Wednesday morning at breakfast, but Wednesday night it looks like something else. Recognizing difference in the context of one's self, and one's body, while living together with someone else is very important.

One of the things that really turns me on about my current partner is that she's really smart. Sometimes it's annoying how smart she is. She thinks she knows everything, because she does know a lot. I am turned on by her intelligence. It's really sexy. I find myself watching her mouth when she talks. It's not just what she says, or how she says it, but the use of her mouth is very sexy. I often find myself watching her eat or watching her drink. I learn a lot from her and that's a turn-on even when I don't feel like listening. Her mind is sexy, and when I'm stuck in my own world, I know I have someone who has a mind and uses it. She is really good at asking me the kinds of questions that open my work even more and I find that exciting. I believe I do the same for her because she's told me that she likes talking to me, because I am always pushing her work forward and pushing her out of the comfort zone of her own creative and spiritual work. And so I think in relationships between women (although I can't speak for other women), because we have grown up in these cultures that devalue us as women, irrespective of where those cultures are, it's really important for us to uplift each other's intellectual, creative, and spiritual energies. My partner and I do that for each other. And we also struggle to do that for each other. It's not an easy thing to do.

In our relationship she does most of the cooking, although we both like to eat. We like to eat together. We love food. We keep saying we have to lose five pounds but at this point in life you just have to enjoy yourself. We understand food as a nurturing reality, and a way of exchanging information about each other, and each other's lives, because we come from different diasporic backgrounds. We have different cultural knowledges; you can say we come from different kitchens and so we're constantly exchanging knowledge with each other. For the most part, we tend to stay out of each other's way when the other is cooking. I can tell when my partner has cooked because there is always evidence of that on the floor. I am old-school, so I clean while I cook so there's no evidence of the process. With her there is always evidence, and her food is always delicious. She's especially good at cooking fish. Her people came from a fishing village in Nigeria; her paternal grandmother was a fisherwoman. It's always an amazing experience when I taste fish she's made. It's not a flavor or taste that you can get used to if your tongue is alive because each time you're tasting different ingredients. We do a lot of cooking at home; we also go out to eat a lot because we like to eat and we live in a city, New Orleans, which is known for its food culture—so it's really hard to lose those five pounds.

I evolved into my sexual orientation. I had sexual intimacies with men up until my thirties and I didn't like it as much as I liked being intimate with women, and so since then the bulk of my relationships have been with women. In my early thirties, I identified primarily as lesbian, and now I describe myself as a Black queer feminist woman. I embrace the term "queer" because I also understand identifying as a lesbian is not necessarily identifying the range of my sexual desires even in terms of my relationships with women. Part of what is really great about my current partner is that neither of us identify as masculine or feminine or what we call butch or femme. We see ourselves as operating within both of those realities and so we don't pick one in lieu of the other. Finally finding someone who can articulate that reality and feels the way that I do has been a great joy for my intimate life, because I can be on top but also be on the bottom. She can be on top but also be on the bottom. Part of how we communicate our sexual desires is with the different dildos and toys that we have, and also the different ways we play with masculinities and femininities both in the intimacy of the bedroom and also being around the house.

This sense of confidence in myself, even in terms of being comfortable with playing with masculinities and femininities, came with age. I know people who are twenty or thirty years younger than I am who already have that sense of themselves, and I am happy about that. I have been here longer, but I have had a longer road to travel in terms of the ways Black communities identify those of us who are also Black but don't identify as heterosexual. I hope in time all of those labels and terminologies fall away. I don't know if it will happen in my lifetime but I am hoping that there will be a day when people don't have to resist and articulate a sexuality based on its opposition to another. That there will be a moment where all sexualities are "normal" and there is no reason to think differently when you see two people who appear to be the same "gender" walking down the street arm in arm or holding hands. So for me, it has actually been living up until this moment to both be confident and also have the language and intellectual understanding of who I am.

We decided to get married because of the economic realities of living in this country. I had a previous partner who I had been with for twenty-two years. When she died in 2005, my rights as her long-term partner were not immediately protected. I had to get a lawyer to do that. My current partner and I have assets together and we didn't romanticize the marriage at all. We didn't have a wedding, for example. We went to a justice of the peace, dragged two friends with us as witnesses, and signed a piece of paper, and it was all over in about three minutes. We talk about our marriage day as opposed to a wedding day because we weren't interested in participating in all of that even though marriage in this country is now legal. We weren't interested in normative realities for same-sex marriages also. We were simply interested in having a practical understanding of what it means if something happens to me or to her. We don't want to have to get a lawyer to intercede. We already have this by virtue of signing a piece of paper.

I was born in Harlem in 1948. I was a teenager when the civil rights movement began in the 1960s. I was still living at home. I was one of eight children my mother raised by herself. None of the men she was with fathered their children. None of those men married her or took care of us. She was a woman on her own, on welfare, raising eight children. We grew up poor. That doesn't mean we didn't have anything to eat, but it meant that we were economically distressed and so all of the things other kids had were not necessarily available to us. My mother also insisted that when we turned thirteen we get jobs because that was our way of helping the family. When you got a job, you took your paycheck home, she took some of it, and you had a little left to do whatever you wanted to do. So I understood myself as Black, poor, and female very early on in life. I remember that when I was twelve years old, I looked at my mother one day and made a decision that I was not going to live like that. I was not going to have all these children, I was not going to have these men, and I was not going to be poor. I think that was partly a critique of her life, as well as a critique of the Blackness that was available to me as a woman.

Even so, I had the benefit of living in Harlem, so I could see all that historical Blackness around me. I remember going to see Malcolm X on the corner. I think it was 116th Street on Lenox Avenue in Harlem and I remember being totally freaked out because it was a crowd full of Black people, mainly Black men, and white police. I had never heard any Black person talk the way he did in front of white people so I was both terrified and completely in awe of this man. By the time the 1970s rolled around I had already been to Cornell University, which is an Ivy League university. After two years, I decided I was done. I felt that the Black revolution was coming any day, Black Power was on the rise, and I wanted to be with the people. I did not want to be with these white people, in this white institution, and so I dropped out, much to my mother's and my grandfather's disappointment. I came back to New York City and by then I knew I wanted to be a writer. I found a writing community in Harlem and published my first book when I was twenty-five. Virtually every book I have written has won an award. My work has generally been recognized as outsider literature, at the same time I have had a foot in and out of mainstream publishing. I've had a great life. I was the first North American writer to interview Nelson Mandela upon his release. I went back to school when I was in my forties, got a master's degree and a PhD, and taught for twenty-five years at the University of Buffalo before retiring in 2007.

I got pregnant once and had a miscarriage. I think that was the gods' way of letting me know, "Wrong guy, wrong time, don't do it." That was in my late twenties. In my late thirties I thought about having kids but I was never sure whether I wanted children or not. I have carved out a life in which I haven't given birth but I have people whom I have mothered and continue to mother. I have people who view me as a mother figure and I see them as my children. There's a place for all of us and I think that the notion of mothering gets extended when we think of the ways in which women mother and father across gender. My mother would always say to us when we would ask about our missing fathers, "I am your mother and your father." So I understood early in life that was a possibility, and that someone could mother and father you beyond their own gendered realities.

In many ways this book has been made possible by a vast network of African feminists, some of whom are my friends or acquaintances, and others whom I have never met before. Strangers shared my callouts with people they knew had fascinating life stories and friends suggested people I could interview. That's how I met Miss Deviant, a fifty-two-year-old Black lesbian from the UK. She invited me to interview her at home in South London, and we walked up the communal stairs that her male sub had cleaned the day before while wearing nothing but an apron. She told me that she had her sub clean the public areas of her flat only when her neighbors were away.

We sat in her living room and I sipped on peppermint tea while she told me about working in the sex industry, being part of the bondage, domination, and sado-masochism (BDSM) subculture, and how she had fallen in love with a younger woman after identifying as heterosexual for most of her life. She showed me pictures of herself at work. Usually dressed in tight black latex, smiling while she inflicts pain on her subs, who tend to be white men. Part of what I found fascinating in my conversation with Miss Deviant is how she used her role as a dominatrix to subvert traditional gender roles. Her subs tend to be rich, powerful white men who perform very little labor in their own homes, and so sometimes she deliberately assigns them to perform acts of service for their wives and partners.

MISS DEVIANT

■

IT WOULD BEGIN with a phone call.

"Your mistress is coming, you need to be prepared."

Click clack, click clack. I deliberately wore high heels because of the sound it would make on the wooden floors in his kitchen. His instructions were to be naked, kneeling on the kitchen floor, facing the door, head down low. He was forbidden to look at me. Nearby would be a mug of boiling hot water with two teaspoons in it. Sometimes I would put the teaspoons on his nipples. Other times I would walk around him, and leave. Sometimes I wouldn't turn up at all.

To amuse myself I would call him and ask him to wank with Brillo pads. The state of his cock later would tell me he did it. I fucked him up the arse. It was awesome. That is how I became Miss Deviant by name and nature.

I was adopted as a baby, I was sexually abused as a child, and from the age of eleven I was constantly propositioned in the streets. I remember thinking as a kid, What is on me? I had a very boyish frame, but maybe that was the attraction. In my teens I would confuse sex and love. I was wild. I would have sex with lots of boys. By the time I was sixteen I was homeless and living on the streets, running around the West End of London. At night I would queue up for a bed at Centrepoint, but the following day everyone would have to leave by 10 a.m. I got referred to Riverpoint, a sister project at Hammersmith, and from there I got a job as a chambermaid in a hotel at Earl's Court. I kept seeing massive bags of condoms when I cleaned the rooms. I couldn't figure it out. I had never thought of using condoms personally. I knew I should; after all, this was the eighties, and AIDS was everywhere. One time I was asked to help two long-term residents pack up to leave. They were chatting about business being bad and going back up north. "Have you got your own business?" I asked. "Nah love, we're toms."

At that time, I was earning twenty-five pounds a week. I sat on this information for a few days; it just kept playing over and over in my mind. I wasn't a virgin and they had told me that all they did was to walk around the street and get customers. I started to walk around, and it was like my eyes were open for the first time. Not all the girls were in miniskirts like you see in the films. This was reassuring because I was still quite boyish at this time. I decided I would have a go at this. One night I went out and walked the streets. I had no condoms, but this guy eventually picked me up and we went back to his room. He fucked me every which way for about two to three hours. I still remember his smell, and the contortedness of his face from the exertions of fucking me. It was vile. I'm not doing this again, I thought. When he finally finished with me I went back to my hotel room, and put the twenty-five pounds in my bedside drawer. After a few minutes I took it out and looked at it. I did that over and over again. I had earned an entire week of wages in a few hours.

I started to hang out with this West London crew—all the boys were pickpockets, and all the girls were prostitutes. I had a ponce but he did it with such aplomb and style. Pimps were organized, had several girls, and charged each girl an amount. Ponces would take everything you had. My guy was adamant: "You do not touch drugs. Don't do class A drugs." I was always in trouble with my ponce because I would go off raving with my friends. I don't know what saved me. He never beat me although he was renowned for beating girls.

One time one of my friends disappeared. I knew she was attached to an agency in Soho and I was worried about her so I went there and demanded, "Where is my friend?" They told me, "She's gone to Germany, we're looking for more girls, do you want to go?" A week later I was on a plane to Germany. I had never been outside the country before. At the airport, two guys walked up to me, said something in German, and then grabbed my bag. It wasn't until I was in their car that I thought, Uh-oh, this isn't such a good idea. We pulled up at a red-light district in Bremerhaven and who do I see but my mate in the window. We just screamed and ran towards each other. Germany blew my mind. In London I was constantly running from the police, always being nicked, being hauled before the courts. In Germany I was sitting in a window, registered to work, and had to go to the clap clinic once a week. A van would come round once a week and get all the girls who hadn't gone to the clinic. The shame! It was always the English girls having to get into the van.

After two years the normalcy of the situation started to get to me. It was very common to have the mother working behind the bar, the daughter doing admin, and the father being the general pimp in the area. At twenty-one I decided I had had enough and wanted to get out of the industry. I came back home. I couldn't find a job and started working in bars in Soho. There you didn't sell sex, you sold drinks, although you could make private arrangements if you wanted. It was one of those places where you would say to a man, "Buy me a cocktail, sir," and when his bill came it would be £300 even though you had only drunk a Coke. I just felt sorry for the guys. To a couple of guys, I would whisper, "Yeah, you just need to go, the guy is coming with the bill." I didn't last very long there, and started working in restaurants and legit bars until I met a friend who was working for the local government. That's how I drifted into social work—it is full of people who have been abused, and middle-class white women who want to help the little people.

I spent the whole of my twenties being fucked as opposed to me fucking whom I wanted to fuck. In my thirties it became really important to me to lead my sex life. I would say to guys, "If you let me take control you will have the best sex of your life," but I still wasn't managing to do this successfully. I was still passive during sex. I started to take a bit more control with husband number three, who was more open-minded. He liked anal sex, and having his bottom played with, but he was also dominant, and liked to tie me up.

At work I had a close male friend, and every Friday we would go to his for drinks. We called it "washing off the week." One night we were very drunk and he told me that he was a submissive and a masochist. I remember thinking, There is no way in hell that is for me. He said, "If you are not submissive and you're not a masochist what do you think you might be into?" I could literally feel a light bulb switch on. I got a really weird yummy feeling in my stomach. It was the same feeling I had had when I was seven or eight. I was a tomboy, and brought up in a very middle-class family surrounded by lots of books. The boys in particular had war books. I remember reading one of my brothers' books and there was a passage where someone had a flannel over his face, and water was being poured over the flannel so he had a sensation of being drowned. I remember reading that passage over and over again and it gave me that same tingly feeling in my stomach. I now know that it was waterboarding.

Still, it took me until my thirties to discover BDSM. My submissive and I started to get emotionally tied to each other. I considered leaving my husband, and then pulled myself together. My sub was hurt for a while, our friendship came to a halt temporarily, but now we're good friends again and often speak fondly of our summer of love. I drifted back into my marriage but felt unfulfilled. We had been together for ten years, and married for two. For the first time in my life I was settled and had lived in one place for twelve years; I had never experienced that before. As a child, I had been in care and moved around a lot. I started to feel trapped in the marriage. I was also doing drugs quite heavily by then; that was the catalyst that brought the marriage to an end.

In my forties there was a change of government, the Conservatives came into power, and there was a cut in social workers. I was applying for jobs and not getting any. I didn't believe in signing on for welfare, so I wondered what to do next. Should I try escorting? I was discussing this with my friend with whom I had the summer of love and he said, "Why don't you become a professional dominatrix?" I started to research on the internet, I advertised on dating sites as Ms. Bossy Boots, I made it clear in my profile that I was expecting remuneration and that I would boss men around. A guy messaged me and told me I was on the wrong website. He suggested I try Informed Consent, and so I did, and there lay before me the whole BDSM community.

I was in awe that there was a community, and by the range of that community. In BDSM there are no bounds, it is just your consent that stops you from doing whatever you want to do. There was a group for pro dommes; I went on that page and said, "I want to be a pro domme, is there anyone who can talk to me?" They were so scathing. Two people sent me good responses, one of whom was R, who I am still friends with today. She told me, "Don't become a dominatrix, incorporate domination into your natural personality; then you will become a domme that's you . . ." I am known as the smiling sadist—I can really hurt people while singing, dancing, and clapping. I thought, This is awesome, I can do this as me. I felt comfortable in the pro domme community—everybody came to the table as they were. I realized that I could use my sexual being without giving up my sexual being. I started doing sessions topless; I would allow guys to orally pleasure me although I didn't find it pleasurable.

My friend was horrified. He said, "I have been seeing pro dommes for years and they don't do that." I believe that as a pro domme you should be able to do what you like. I would do naked sessions, wearing just stockings, and would slap men if they got a hard-on. I started to change the way I dommed. I made it clear on my website that "I do not guarantee happy endings" but still seven out of ten guys would ask, "Can I have a happy ending?" I would say I cannot guarantee you a happy ending and they would say, "But I am paying you."

I had an awakening in the last three to four years about being a woman in this world. I realized that male submission is bullshit. Men can dip into it but when they go out into the world they are not advocating for equal pay. I have met a lot of male dommes and I find them very predatory. A lot of men call themselves dommes because it gives them access to women. I was at a party once, and a male domme tied up his female sub intricately and left her in the kitchen where she was struggling to get loose. People were around and laughing, I could see she was getting very frustrated. I recognize that could have been part of their play but I didn't like it. Her domme was not connected to her. He was talking to someone else in another room. I hate to see a male domme playing with a woman unless I feel a particular connection between them. In the BDSM world you do not interrupt people's scenes. You can get banned from parties for doing things like that.

A lot of pro dommes have female subs to sexually satisfy their clients. Towards the end of my pro domming days I decided I wanted a female sub for myself and not for anyone else. I was desperate to dominate a woman; I had flirted with women in clubs and the energy was different. I advertised for a female sub and E approached me. We exchanged a few messages on Fetlife, we met up, and I instantly fell in love. It was like hitting the jackpot. She had just gotten into kink herself. She is a beautiful Black woman, androgynous, slight build, shaved head, and rides a motorbike. She is seventeen years younger than I am. I think I have always been bisexual but prior to E I had never had full-on sex with a woman. Sex with E is fire. Until I met E, my sexual relationships with guys were all about them asking, "Did you cum, did you cum, did you cum?" It was so irritating. It wasn't about me cumming; it was about their male ego. E has given me sexual freedom. I am still finding my feet in terms of sex with her. She says that I'm pansexual, that I'm attracted to souls and personalities more than body types or gender.

Over the past two years with E, she has made me view women very differently, and myself very differently as a sexual being; she has rounded me up into being a more complete person. E wants to be of service to a mistress; I could give her that experience but it wouldn't be real, and I want her to find her feet in the BDSM community, so I introduced her to another mistress. They had some practice sessions and now E is going to serve her for real. The first time she went over she ended up staying later than she had intended to. I started feeling anxious: What is she doing? Jealousy crept in. When she rang me to say she was home, she sounded so excited, I was trying not to rain on her parade, but she could tell something was wrong. Eventually I explained to her how I felt, I asked for one or two days to process, and I felt better after a day. Now we are looking for a playmate for her.

There is always going to be a risk that she could fall in love with somebody else, and they could form an emotional attachment, and of course I would be devastated, but for all my experiences in life what I do know is that I would come out the other side. I think we would always be friends unless one of us fucks the other over. She is such an important woman in my life outside of our relationship. If she formed a relationship with someone else, I would have to separate myself for a little while to heal, but I like to think that with everything else I fucking got over in my life, I could get over this too.

I was all set to interview another woman from Costa Rica when I met Gabriela, a forty-year-old Afro-descendant lesbian woman from Guanacaste, on the Pacific coast of Costa Rica. We had been introduced by a mutual friend when she found out that I was traveling to San José for work. Gabriela took me on a one day tour of her city, pointing out murals, sculptures, and buildings of historical significance to Black people. We had brunch at Árbol de Seda, the first restaurant opened by a lesbian woman in the city. By the end of the day I knew I wanted to interview Gabriela. I felt connected to her because we shared Pan-African and feminist ideals, and I wanted to understand how her heritage and politics influenced her experiences of sex and sexuality.

A few months later, at the peak of the COVID-19 pandemic, I got some useful tips from Gabriela on how to keep the spark alive when you are forcefully separated from your partner, and learned about her journey of spiritual cleansing, the practice that had enabled her to be in a relationship uncontaminated by stereotypical notions of "romantic love."

GABRIELA

·

SEX IS OVERRATED. Just look at it from a social point of view. Sex is only one way of connecting with a person, yet everybody seems so fixated on it. What I think is important is to be on a journey of understanding one's self as capable of pleasure and connections in many different ways. This includes allowing yourself to experience pleasure in a variety of forms, which can of course include sex. This also allows you to form close connections with a sexual partner when you choose to have one. So for me, sex is an important part of a loving, romantic, sexual relationship but it's not everything. It's as important as other types of connections, which can be emotional, intellectual and political. This includes friendship, which I consider key to a strong sexual connection.

Giving pleasure to myself looks different every day. At its most basic it's eating well, drinking enough water, keeping my environment clean, and doing things that I like to do. Sometimes that's watching TV, other times it's using essential oils or buying flowers. When it comes to sex there are always new things to discover by experimenting with yourself. Touching yourself—and not just your genitalia, your whole body—can be an experience of pleasure. Massaging your head, rubbing oils into your skin, experiencing a nice scent. Practicing self-pleasure in a more holistic way also connects us more deeply to major sources of pleasure like the genitalia and clitoris. Every time you experiment with yourself you discover new ways of experiencing pleasure.

It took me a while to get comfortable with sex toys. I bought my first sex toy years ago and told my boyfriend, "Hey, I want to experiment with this new sex toy that I have." In response, he lost his erection. He thought that meant I wasn't satisfied with our sex life, and subsequently couldn't maintain a hard-on during our encounters. Unconsciously that experience put me off sex toys and it was only recently that I bought some new toys. I bought them in anticipation of a trip to Brazil to visit my girlfriend. When I told her I was thinking of buying sex toys, she got very excited because she'd never used toys before and said she wanted to experience them with me. I sent her the pictures of the ones that I was considering buying and together we chose a vibrator and strap-on. And then the global health pandemic happened and now neither of us can travel.

It also took ages for my sex toys to arrive. When I received the package, we got on a video call so I could show her the toys as I unboxed them. I get to experience the sex toys now while we're apart, and we will also get to experience them together when we next see each other. We're working hard to stay connected in spite of the long distance, and being unable to travel to see each other every two months like we had initially planned to do. We talk every day, and we watch movies together using Netflix Party. Sometimes, if there is a film in one region but not the other, we'll get on Zoom and watch using the screen-share function. What can be hard is when you need to have a difficult conversation—not an argument, just a conversation that's hard to navigate. Distance makes those kinds of conversations hard to have because afterwards you may feel a need for physical connectedness and you can't cuddle or hold the other person. That can lead to an emotional distance, and it can be hard to build up the closeness again. We try to focus on remaining present and enjoying what we have right now because we don't even know when we may be able to travel again, which can feel frustrating on some days.

In 2015, I made the decision to become celibate. I had started a spiritual journey that included being conscious and deliberate about every aspect of my life, including what I ate. I started to meditate regularly and a physical connection through sex was just not fulfilling to me at the time. Celibacy felt easy, natural, and organic. In 2017, I achieved one of my goals, which was to travel to India and live in a temple for six weeks. This allowed me to dive even deeper into my spiritual, celibate practice. By doing that, I learned what a healthy relationship should look like. I feel like I now have the tools to have a more conscious relationship. I am better able to connect with my girlfriend because of the cleansing experience I went through a few years ago. I'm able to be a better listener, to communicate my needs a lot better, and to be more loving. I'm also able to listen, to understand, and not to react. I'm able to accompany my partner better so we can both create a relationship that is much more free, and not as contaminated by the idea of romantic love and limited notions of what a relationship should look like. I'm able to hold space for myself, to hold space for the other person, and also to hold space for the two of us to be together. So whenever conflict arrives, I'm able to look at it more objectively rather than just reacting. This has also allowed me to connect even more with myself, while also interacting with another person. I can ask myself, Why am I reacting like this? Why am I feeling like this? How am I going to communicate this? This means we end up having these awesome conversations that leave us feeling stronger, happier, and more connected as a couple.

I first became aware of sex when I was twelve years old. My cousins and I attended a fiesta patronales, a weekend full of cultural activities. The event was full of young people like us and I remember someone telling me, Go behind that wall, someone wants to see you. When I got there I found this boy. He told me, "You're cute. I like you. I've been wanting to meet you," and then he kissed me. I remember it being a very gentle kiss, and feeling a tingling sensation all through my body. Then some other kids saw us and started calling out, "Look at them. They are kissing." For days afterwards I kept dreaming about that boy. I was always distracted at home and my mum kept asking me, "What's going on? Why do you always seem so far away?" I never got the chance to see the boy again because my uncle told my mum that somebody had seen me kissing a boy at the fiesta and I lived with my mum and my grandmother who were both super protective, and so that was the end of that. One day I overheard my uncle tell my mum, "She's going to get pregnant." I had no idea what that even meant, and when later I understood how people got pregnant, I said to myself, "No way is that going to happen."

At the age of eighteen I moved to the capital, San José, to attend university. That's when I first became aware that people regarded women who originated from the coast as "caliente": hot and perpetually horny. I would meet people and they would say something along these lines, "Oh you're from Guanacaste. You're *caliente*." There was nothing subliminal about this messaging. People told me this to my face. In a similar manner they call me Negrita, or Negra, to this day. They make comments like, "I want hair like yours," or they assume I'm not from Costa Rica and ask me, "Where in the Caribbean are you from?" Costa Ricans have a very limited understanding of the presence of the Black population here. The prevailing narrative is that people from the Caribbean were brought here to work. People from Jamaica, for example, came here to build the railways and work in the banana fields. No one talks about the Black people who migrated here to settle, and mixed with the indigenous population. Yet when you look at Costa Rican culture one can see the similarities to other African Diaspora cultures. It's there in the music, food, and way of life, but because of internalized racism people do not see themselves as Black. Lots of people identify as moreno or mestizo, definitely non-white, but never Black. I always knew I was different; my mum's family is from the Pacific Coast and my dad is an Afro Honduran. So I already understood that I was different, and when I came to university I started reading more about feminism and began to connect with more Black feminists and other Black people from the Caribbean. I started to understand how important it was for me to learn about my own identity and my ancestors, and fully embraced my identity as a Latin American woman of Afro descent.

Ten years ago I also made a conscious decision to explore my attraction to women. Before that I knew that I desired women as well as men but I didn't put any energy towards meeting women romantically. Each time I met a man, I would prioritize my attraction to him over my attraction to a woman. Maybe there were other women who liked me but I didn't know because I wasn't picking up on that vibe. One day I met a woman I was really attracted to. I didn't express how I felt and soon she left Costa Rica as she was only visiting. That's when I made up my mind that I would take action the next time I met a woman I was attracted to. I then had a relationship with a woman that didn't work out, but subsequently I met my current girlfriend, who is a very important part of my life. Nowadays I don't feel like I'm bisexual anymore. I don't desire men anymore, and I do not identify as bi. My love for women is not only sexual, but also political, and in that process I've stopped feeling attracted to men altogether. My relationships with women have been intellectually, emotionally, and sexually more fulfilling than the relationships I had with men. I found heterosexual relationships to be constructed in very limited ways, and my relationships with women have allowed me to understand myself in different ways when it comes to pleasure.

Amina is a twenty-eight-year-old lesbian woman of Sudanese heritage who lives in Egypt. We met in Salvador, Bahia, one of the largest cities in Brazil, a place with the largest number of African people outside of the African continent.

There is a way in which I feel at home in Salvador. It's in how people speak to me in Portuguese, making the assumption that I am a Black Brazilian. It's the easy familiarity of seeing women dressed in print cloths, with head wraps piled up high. It's in the food that reminds me of the food I eat at home, and have eaten in neighboring Nigeria. Gari, waakye, and akara. Salvador was a site of African resistance to slavery with enslaved people creating quilombos, autonomous free spaces. It was a fitting place to interview Amina, a young activist whose life and political choices illustrate the feminist saying, "the personal is political." I learned from speaking to her that the political revolution in the streets and the personal revolution in the sheets are two sides of the same coin.

AMINA

.

"WHAT IS GOING to happen to us after you get married to him?" I asked. "I cannot be showing up after he leaves for work to join you in the same bed that you shared with him the night before." She looked at me; her eyes said one thing and her lips another. "We are not like that. We just got used to each other's bodies. It is unnatural . . ." I barely let her finish. "I know I am a lesbian. We are not sick, we are normal."

After four years, this was the first time we had spoken openly and frankly about our relationship. About being two women in Egypt who loved each other. I fell in love with Fatima in middle school. I was about twelve years old at the time, she loved another girl, it was completely normal in school for girls to have crushes on each other. Everybody knew which girl loved another girl, but I knew I loved Fatima in a special way, in a deeper way, and it took three years before I knew that she felt the same way. We didn't dare discuss our feelings. We only showed it. We lived on the same street and from school we would walk home hand in hand; when we said goodbye we would kiss each other on the cheeks and say "I love you" with all the innocence of youth, until "I love you" started to mean more than just words.

I knew early on that I liked girls. I felt it within my body. I tried to read books on health and reproduction to understand these feelings that I had when I saw Fatima and other girls but none of the books gave me any answers. In my mother's room I found a copy of *Women and Sex*, by Nawal El Saadawi. I was shocked to read that female genital cutting was done to women so that they would not enjoy sex. So people have sex, I thought as I tried to unravel in my mind what that meant. Even more mind-boggling was how Saadawi described female genital cutting. I had always thought tahara was done to purify the sex area. My Sudanese mum would frequently tease me, saying, "You're not as clean as I am. Go change your underwear. Go and wash." Later I realized that I was the first woman in my family not to have been cut. From Saadawi's book I learned what the vagina looks like. Do I have three openings? And where are they? I wondered but did not dare ask my mother these questions. I wasn't supposed to have read this book, or any of the other books about love and romance hidden in her room. Beyond the jokes about female genital cutting, my mother never discussed anything that happens below the waist except to warn me to be careful in using public toilets. "Make sure you clean the toilet seat well before you use it. You don't want any sperm to go into your body," she often cautioned.

The books I read didn't explain my feelings for Fatima or for the other girls and women I had crushes on. I knew my feelings were wrong. I was sick. Nobody mentioned liking girls in books. Sex was between men and women. How could I have children with another woman? But the books taught me other things. I learned about sex, pleasure, and patriarchy. And then, over time, Fatima started to return my feelings. It was her twentieth birthday, and as we sat on her bed, I reached over to give her a birthday kiss. For the first time there was the shock of tongue touching tongue, and then we sprang apart when her mother walked in. "What are you doing? Leave the room now!" she commanded. I was forbidden from entering Fatima's room again, but she managed to convince her mother that we had only been sitting close together. Her mother had no words to describe what she thought she had seen, but she never felt comfortable having me in Fatima's room again. And so we got together in other spaces whenever we could.

My mother had a rule, "You cannot lock the door in any house where I pay the rent," and so we would wait for those moments when my mother, grandmother, and brother were out of the house. Or we would go and watch a film at the cinema and in the dark room sit close and touch each other. After my kung fu class, we would go to the locker room and, if it was empty, go into a bathroom stall and touch each other. We did everything fully clothed. We had to be ready to jump apart in nanoseconds. We touched anywhere we could reach fully clothed: breast, thigh, clit. Just so long as there was no penetration. We needed to stay virgins. We envisaged our hymens as thin coverings just inside us, and we knew that had to be kept sacrosanct.

In the first year of college Fatima fell in love with a man and got engaged. She said, "I don't think I have these lesbian feelings. We just got used to each other's bodies, and in middle school there were no boys around. We need to stop, it's unnatural." But we stopped only during our final term in college, a few months before her wedding date. I knew I couldn't be this secret love for the rest of my life. By this time, I knew for sure I was a lesbian. My command of English was good now and I spent ages on the internet searching for words like "lesbian," "homosexual," and "gay" on Google and Wikipedia. The first couple of pages that came back to me assured me that I was normal, that there were people like me everywhere. For the longest time Fatima and I thought we were the only two girls in Egypt who did what we did. In middle school I had believed that I was sick, but because of Fatima I knew there was at least one other person who was as sick as I was and that was a relief. You're not alone, I would say to myself, you're not alone. And now the internet showed me that I was truly not alone, and that I didn't have to seek asylum in the US and marry a white woman so that I could have a house full of rainbows.

Something happened during the 2011 revolution in Egypt. It was as if someone whispered, "Let's break all our mental chains too." I had just broken up with my girlfriend, Fatima, and walked into a queer space for the first time in my life. I was the new girl and everybody was hitting on me, it felt amazing. We were out, we were free, and we were in the revolution, both politically and sexually. I met this woman, and we fell for each other but neither of us was ready to be in a relationship. The thought of being with a woman freaked her out, and I did not feel ready to jump into another relationship so soon. We decided that we did want to be together, but we did not want to be restricted in any way, shape or form. We wanted to keep our relationship open to possibilities. We were going to be polyamorous, we were going to see each other but allow ourselves the freedom to see other people too. Our only rule was that we would not sleep with the same people or our friends. You have to be really careful as a lesbian woman in Egypt. My lovers come mainly from the leftist and feminist communities. You need to be one hundred percent sure about a woman's sexuality before you approach her because if you make a mistake, and she ends up being a homophobe or tells the wrong person, you could be in deep shit. You could even end up in jail.

Nowadays more and more of my friends are coming up to me and saying, "I'm queer, I'm going to sleep with a woman," and then they come back and say, "It was great!" I'm like, What? I spent my whole life loving women, I did not just get up one day and say, "Guess what, I'm queer." Sex with women is not something that just happened naturally, it took time, and I can't believe these women feel it's that easy. I ask them, "So you didn't freak out the first time you looked at another woman's vagina? You didn't think, 'Shit, I'm sleeping with a woman?' What was it like the first time you were inside a woman? When you were feeling all the things you could not see, when you were touching flesh? You mean it was never weird for even one minute?"

I remember when I first started having sex with my current partner, it was so bad because she insisted on giving me oral sex all the time because in her imagination that was what lesbian sex was. She never asked, "What do you like? How do you like it?" Not that I knew what I liked at the time. Four years ago I still did not have the confidence to speak up about what I liked. That is what living in a conservative society will do to you. Sometimes it is even hard to ask yourself these questions: If I don't have an orgasm, should I fake it or not? Do all women get wet or not? Nowadays you can find a lot of these answers online but that wasn't the case a few years ago. It took a lot of thinking, and practicing, and being part of feminist communities, and being with women who cared for me to learn that if I don't want oral sex right now I should say so. Or if someone is doing something I do not like I need to tell them. And that I need to ask for what I want.

I am really lucky to have found my current partner. We have a completely open relationship with each other. We can discuss anything, we tell each other when we meet someone we are attracted to before we sleep with the person, and we've had a lot of conversations about how it can be really hard to talk dirty in bed or ask for BDSM. The first time I had penetrative sex was with my current partner. This is something that we had both never done before because of the cult of virginity in Egypt. We decided we wanted to take that step together. We had to ask other lesbians about fisting—what do you do? How does it work? So it wasn't that I started having sex with women and it was great straightaway. I always knew I loved women but sometimes my body did not respond the way I thought it should. For me, great sex with women didn't just happen overnight; it took time, growth, and maturity.

Recently, I've had what my partner describes as "a confused boner." I met a man that I felt attracted to. I felt aroused around him. Does this mean I am suddenly hetero, what the hell? I told my partner, "I like this man. I want to sleep with him even though I do not know what this means for my lesbian self." She was supportive even though she also did not understand my sudden attraction to this man, and also felt insecure. There is this fear of the "ultimate man," the one who shows up and cures your gayness. It was a confusing period for me, and a confusion I am still holding on to because after sleeping with him, I went out with a few more men, and some of my experiences were enjoyable and others weren't. I told some of my friends and they started calling me bisexual or queer. That pissed me off. I define myself as a lesbian. For years I have slept with, desired, and been confused as fuck about women, and now that I have slept with a few men people are calling me bisexual as if all my experiences with women before mean nothing. No, I am a lesbian.

There is nothing wrong with being bisexual, but I do not define myself as such. I don't even know why it is so important to me to name myself as a lesbian but it just is. I have not come out to my lesbian circle about having slept with men because I am scared that they will shun me. This is a community that I have contributed to building and feel very much a part of. They will definitely not understand my confused boner, and other communities that may understand that sexuality can be fluid will start categorizing me differently as bisexual. One of my friends said to me, "You used to be a lesbian." I haven't stopped being a lesbian; I have been primarily in a relationship with a woman for the past four years. Doesn't that stand for something? It's fucked up having to deal with this. I did not see this coming at all.

And you get it from both sides. One of my male lovers said to me, "How do you feel after having heterosexual sex?" I said, "How do you feel after having gay sex? You just had sex with a gay woman." Sex with men is different. Their bodies are different, their organs are different, and the way they respond is different. Usually after sex with a woman you will ask: "How do you feel?" "Are you okay?" but after sex with men no one asks anything. None of my friends who know about my relations with men have asked me how it feels to have sex with men. I don't say to my male lovers that I am in a relationship with a woman because some of them set out trying to prove a point, such as, "This is the best sex you're going to have in your life." Only a small pool of trusted people knows that I am in a relationship with a woman. In this country sleeping with a man makes you a whore but sleeping with both men and women can trigger a whole lot of shit if someone reports you to the authorities.

I have a feeling my mother would rather die than know that I am a lesbian. She still perceives me as this asexual being who is going to get married one day. What she knows for now is that I am focused on my career, which she is happy about, but she doesn't see any future in feminism, she thinks I'm wasting my time. She wants me to get married but she wants me to marry a particular type of man. She doesn't want me to marry an Egyptian. If I marry a Sudanese man he has to be educated and rich. Her preference would be for me to marry an American or European who will take me away to live somewhere nice. I think my mother is sensing something, though. I keep my current partner away from her because she was very aggressive towards my ex, and when my girlfriend used to visit she would say, "She looks like a boy. Don't take her to the room with you. What are you doing in the room the whole time? Why does she keep holding you? Why is she touching you like that?" My girlfriend is very feminine and has curly hair. I suspect this is my mother's way of expressing that my partner looks queer, but she cannot express it quite like that. My mother would say, "The way she walks, it's suspicious," rather than make a direct accusation. She cannot entertain the idea that I am having sex, let alone amorous relationships with women.

I met Laura, a twenty-six-year-old mixed-race Black Brazilian/ Italian woman, at a friend's party in Accra. It was December, a month when members of Ghana's Diaspora flock home for the holidays, and Accra, the capital city, becomes congested with increased numbers of people and partygoers. That December was extra special: it also marked the Year of Return, an event organized by the government of Ghana to encourage people from the African Diaspora to return home to the continent. Laura was one of those people who responded to the call to return "home." Ever since I visited Brazil I had wanted to interview a Black Brazilian, and so meeting Laura felt like fate.

Laura and I instantly had an easy connection. At my home she told me about being sexually fluid, and spoke about how her Brazilian heritage helped her gain sexual confidence even though she was brought up in Italy, a country she describes as conservative due to the strong influences of the Vatican. All my life I had bought into the narrative of Italians as romantic, sexually liberated people. My conversation with Laura brought an end to that illusion.

LAURA

·

I GREW UP in Rome with my mum, a single white woman who was determined to give her child as much access to her heritage as possible. In the streets she would stop people who were Brazilian and introduce herself, saying, "My child is also Brazilian." When I was six years old she found out about this summer camp that was only for Brazilian children and enrolled me there. Camp became a permanent fixture in my life, and every year for two weeks I would spend every day with other Brazilian children. As my friends and I grew up, we started partying together, which is how I met even more Brazilians and grew my community.

Italy is a sexually conservative country. The Vatican City is here in our capital, and although most Italians are not practicing Catholics, the majority of people are strongly influenced by Catholicism. People don't speak openly about sex, for example. When I started having sex at fifteen, I couldn't talk about it with my Italian friends. I could only discuss sex with my Brazilian friends, and even then, only with those who had migrated to Italy as teenagers; the Brazilians who had been born in Italy were just like everybody else.

I met Adiel at a party in my neighborhood. We went to these daytime parties that happened every Saturday. Only people of color came to the parties. There were lots of Afro-descendants, as well as Cape Verdeans, Filipinos, Albanians, Chinese, and Romanians. Adiel was part of this crew of Cape Verdean men who were considered to be the hottest guys in the area. He was the stereotypical Cape Verdean guy, curly hair, brown eyes, full lips, and skin color just like mine. He came over and spoke to me at one of the parties. I was completely blown away by him. He had spent four years living in the Netherlands before moving to Italy and so spoke fluent Dutch. Although he had lived

in the country for only three years, his Italian was no different from mine, and
of course he spoke Portuguese. I thought he was so smart. After school each
day I would run home just so I could get on MSN Messenger and chat with
him. I could barely believe that he wanted to be with me. I thought one day he
would just disappear and I'd never hear from him again. Instead, he asked me
out, and we started dating. He was eighteen years old at the time and very
committed to the relationship, but there was a part of me that always held
back. He would tell me that he was falling in love with me, and I would just
come out with this high-pitched nervous laugh that showed that I didn't really
believe him. I had never witnessed real love. My mum and dad had separated
when I was a baby. They met in Brazil and moved to Germany, and after they
broke up my Mum moved back to Italy with me. Although she was from the
countryside, she chose to be in Rome and raised me on her own without any
support from anyone else.

Adiel and I first had sex about three months after we started dating,
although he had been pretty insistent from the very beginning. I had told him
I was a virgin and he'd said, "We can wait, but you should trust me." I wasn't
ready to do that. All the movies I had watched showed me that he would disappear the minute after we had sex. One day we were on the sofa kissing and
he kept trying to have sex with me. I kept asking, "What are you doing?" and
then it just happened. I don't know exactly how it happened but I remember
that it was scary at first and it hurt a bit because he had a large penis. Later that
night I started to enjoy it. I don't think you can ever be ready for your first
time. How can you be ready for something you have never experienced before?
It's impossible. I think you just need to be comfortable with the person you're
with and afterwards everything will be fine.

Recently I was reading that virginity is a social construct and I agree with
that. We hear so much about the significance of the first time but it's only the
beginning of great things. Adiel was a good lover. He was way more experienced than I was. I think his first time had been with an older woman while he
was still in Cape Verde. He was really good when he went down on me. He would
try to get me to give him a blow job but I was terrible at doing that initially.

I used to hate giving blow jobs until much later on when my Brazilian friends shared their tips with me. They told me, "Rub the dick but not too hard. Go up and down. Put your mouth around the whole thing. Keep changing positions." We used to trade stories and ask each other questions. "Do you swallow?" I hate swallowing. I realized it didn't matter because by the time a guy cums he doesn't care what's going on around him. I had a friend who loved swallowing, she said she would take a cup and place it by the bedside so she could catch every drop.

Adiel and I were together for about two years. Even now, twelve years later, I still think that was the best relationship that I ever had. I broke up with him because I felt he would hold me back in life. He dropped out of school and meant to start working but never did. His whole life revolved around me. All he wanted to do was spend time with me. I wanted more with my life.

Adiel and my mum had a great relationship. After we broke up I came home with a guy one day and he was in the kitchen hanging out with her. That was an awkward moment. Later on she told me, "Next time, don't introduce me to a guy until you are sure that you really like him." My mum and I have always been close. We have always had a relationship based on trust. She is a dance teacher and would often have to travel to teach, and so from the age of ten there were times that I was home on my own. When Adiel and I were dating she asked me once if I was having sex and I said yes. She wanted to know if we were using condoms and I said yes. We used to buy condoms from the sex shops. At the time I had no knowledge about sex toys or of any of the other items that you could get from sex shops. All I knew was that for five euros you could get forty-five condoms. It was so cheap because that's where all the sex workers got their condoms.

When my mum traveled I allowed my friends to come over and have sex at my house. One of my closest friends at the time was called Maria. She was very generous and sometimes would come over with an extra guy for me. There was this time that she came over with two boys, and straightaway disappeared into the room with one of them. I was in the living room at the time, and the other guy came over and started kissing me. There was no time to think. I could only feel. I preferred it that way. It gave me no chance to start obsessing about what my body would look like when I took off my clothes. Then there was another time that Maria and I went out clubbing. We met some guys and went back with them to a barbershop that one of them owned. We all went off into the separate rooms in the shop. The guy I was with had a piercing on his dick. It felt amazing.

Then I met Moussa. We started chatting online, and then eventually met up in person. I was disappointed when I first met him because he had permed hair that was dyed blond and cut into this asymmetrical style. All I could see was his split ends. That was during the time that I was growing into my activism, and so I wasn't attracted to his blond permed look, but we continued to chat and eventually that changed. Maria and I teased him a lot about his hair and eventually he cut it. Moussa was from Senegal, and he initially told me that he had traveled to Italy to play soccer. He also told me that the other people he shared a home with in the posh part of Rome where he lived were soccer players. I later found out that wasn't true. Yes, his house was in a fancy part of town, but it was shared accommodation for asylum seekers. I felt hurt that he hadn't trusted me enough to tell me the truth and I don't think our relationship ever healed from that initial betrayal. He used to also go to a lot of tryouts with different soccer clubs but his efforts were not successful. On the plus side he was physically fit and had a great body. Our sex life was amazing.

One Christmas he took me to Paris. We stayed with his sister, a chef whose flat was above the restaurant she owned in the center of town. While she was away, he would grab me in the middle of the day and we'd have sex in the kitchen. After a week in Paris I realized my period was late. We went out and bought two pregnancy kits. Each kit showed the same result. I was pregnant. I called my mum. Her initial reaction was shock: "I thought you were being careful," she said. "I was, I'm not sure what happened." At the time I had forgotten that there was one time we had unprotected sex while I was on day four of my period. I thought that was a safe window but clearly it wasn't. My mum told me, "Don't worry about it for now. Try and enjoy the rest of your holidays. When you get back home the two of you can decide what you want to do." Moussa also told his sister, who was very supportive and said she would stand by us in whatever decision we made.

At the time I was planning a trip to Brazil. It was going to be my first solo trip there as an adult, and I was really looking forward to spending a couple of months there and meeting my Brazilian family. I knew I couldn't travel there pregnant. By this time Moussa had started to do things like put his head on my belly and talk to the baby. I told him not to do that. There was no way that we could have a child. I was in my first year of university and Moussa didn't have a job. I made the decision to have an abortion. The only person who accompanied me to the hospital was my mum. Moussa said I had decided to do this on my own and so I could go to the hospital on my own. None of my friends came with me, and that was hard because I really felt like I needed them. What helped was my mum telling me about her own experiences of abortions. That was such a shock to me. I found out that she'd had two abortions before having me. While pregnant with me in Brazil, she met a Candomblé priest who told her that I was special and that she should keep me and so she did.

Afterwards I traveled to Brazil and spent about three months there. I had always been proud of my Brazilian heritage but I didn't have the kind of experiences that I had dreamed about. I lived with my grandmother, who had a colonized mind. She thought it was a good thing that white people ruled the country. She preferred my white mother to my dad's girlfriend, who was Black, but would completely deny it when I pointed out to her that she only felt differently about my mum because of her race. My cousins didn't pay much attention to me and thought of me as a tourist. I was also shocked by the extreme disparity between the rich and poor in the country. By then I had become an activist in Italy, and so it was especially jarring to see such inequality in Brazil. My dad hadn't been in the country for thirty years but had been an artist and activist when he lived there, so an old activist friend of his took me into her home. She was the kind of auntie I had been dreaming of, and my experience in Brazil improved after I met her. Yet by the time I got back home I was an emotional wreck. Moussa and I resumed our relationship but something had changed. I started seeing a therapist and that gave me the strength to break up with Moussa, although we continued to sleep together for about six months afterwards.

After that experience I made up my mind to stay single and only have casual sex. My friends and I used to travel up north to party in Modena, a city where a lot of Africans, particularly Nigerians, live. I had met this Ghanaian guy there, and so hollered at him during one of our visits. Sex with him was a completely different experience. He was really sweet, really attentive, and also very inexperienced. What I enjoyed most was teaching him about sex. He'd never been with a girl like me before. I wanted to have sex all the time and everywhere.

One evening we were in the car on our way to some random destination. We parked and started making out, and then as it got heated up he said, "I don't have condoms." I told him, "So let's go get some." He said, "How?" I told him, "Start the car and drive to the pharmacy." The pharmacies had these vending machines outside that sold condoms. When we got there, he left the engine running and dashed to the pharmacy topless while holding on to his half-unbuttoned jeans. After a few months of hooking up he told me he was falling in love with me and asked if we could have a proper relationship. I didn't feel the same way about him, and besides, I didn't want to commit to a long-distance relationship. I asked him if he still wanted to hook up from time to time and he said, "No, I'm becoming too involved with you." That was a bare-faced lie, so we continued to hook up until I decided to let things go.

After him I met this Nigerian guy who also lived in Rome. He was one of the smartest guys I had ever met, but he had such low self-esteem. He had these hardworking yet strict parents who I think had beaten all the confidence out of him. He was over six feet tall, had a broad chest and a great butt but would always walk with his shoulders hunched over. I would look at him and think, Why are you walking like that? Like me, he was also recovering from a broken relationship, and so we decided that we were going to only have casual sex. Every Tuesday or Wednesday I would go over to his house after his mum had left for work. We would have sex, take a break and talk about politics, have sex again, stop to eat lunch, and then have more sex. I was having both mental and physical orgasms all the time. I also lost a lot of weight because we were having sex for about six hours each time.

This lasted for about six months, and then one day he told me, "I know we said we were going to keep things casual but my feelings have changed and I can't bear the thought of you sleeping with other men. I already know that you don't want to have a relationship and so I'm not going to ask for that. I'll prefer not to see you anymore. I also started dating someone else and I want to be fair to her so it's over." That was it. He didn't give me any other options, and didn't even give me the chance to think about whether I wanted a relationship with him or not. Things had changed for me too. I was seeing this Brazilian guy I knew from camp years ago but it was really casual. We saw each other once a month and I would have dumped him in a minute for this Nigerian guy. My body couldn't cope with the change, I was horny all the time, and I felt like I was going crazy. I had gotten used to my weekly dick appointment. I lost all my dignity. I called him and said, "You can do whatever you want. You can see the other girl, I don't care. I just need your D. Please give it to me. Please, please, please." I had never begged for anyone's D before. He would just laugh and say, "I've told you already. It's going well with this girl. She's not like you. I can still keep my head around her. With you I get too involved and it's not healthy, it's dangerous for me." I tried talking to him over and over again but he had made up his mind. He told me, "I've already made up my mind. I won't believe you if you say you want to have a relationship with me. You only want the D." It took months for my body to recover. I was just like a drug addict going through withdrawal.

Then I met Felix. He approached me in a club one night, we chitchatted and exchanged numbers, and a few days later we had a date in a restaurant just below the apartment where he was staying. The apartment belonged to his friend's mum. He was a basketball player and played professionally in Siena, a town that is three hours away from Rome. He was Italian but originally from Equatorial Guinea. He was tall and good-looking with a great butt and had the most amazing smile. I felt like I was going to faint every time he smiled. There was this energy between us on our first date. The air practically crackled with sexual tension. He told me from the very beginning that he wanted a serious relationship. After dinner he asked if I wanted to come upstairs; I didn't think it was a good idea, so I said no, but we went upstairs anyway. While showing me around he kissed me and it felt so good but I told him, "If you really want a serious relationship, we cannot have sex on the first date. It's against all the rules." He said, "Yes, you're right." At the time I believed that you needed to wait to have sex with someone you wanted to be in a serious relationship with. Now I know that's bullshit. We continued to kiss and then made love. The minute we were done we heard the click of the door. His friend's mum was home. She was Brazilian, and when she said, "So you're the friend, huh?" I knew that she knew what we had been up to.

Felix and I dated for about three months. After the summer he went back to Siena, and so during periods when I didn't have classes at university, I would travel to visit him and spend up to five days living with him. He trained every day, in the morning and evening, so our routine was that he would come home, we'd have lunch that I had made, have sex, he'd go back to work, and in the evenings we'd either go out for dinner, or have dinner with some of the other basketball players. I was one hundred percent committed to the relationship with Felix. I really cared for him, and our sex life was great, which for me has always been fifty percent of what makes a successful relationship. We had only one issue. He was still traumatized from his last relationship. His last girlfriend had pretended to be pregnant so she could get money from him. He had real money because he played professionally—not NBA type of money, but a solid source of income. Whenever I was in Rome and went out with my friends, he would call me the day afterwards and tell me, "My friends saw you in the club last night and there were all these men around you." I told him, "What do you expect? I am a pretty girl. When I go to the club men come up to me. I'm not going to be rude and tell them, 'Talk to the hand.' Nothing happens with these men, you need to trust me." Then he would say, "I can't trust you. That's what she also used to say."

Then there was the time that my friend and I had planned a five-day trip to Amsterdam. He completely lost it. "Amsterdam is the land of sex and drugs.

What are you going to do there?" I said, "Amsterdam also has a lot of museums and history. There's a lot of culture there that I'm interested in." For over a week he kept complaining about my upcoming trip. I suggested he join us but then he said, "You know I have to play, I cannot travel just like that." I love traveling and I knew that I couldn't continue to deal with such an insecure boyfriend and so I ended the relationship. I was really broken and it took me more than a year to get over him.

During that year I spent six months in Germany as part of ERASMUS, a study-abroad program. Usually students spend a lot of time partying and having sex during these programs but I didn't for several reasons. I was still trying to get over Felix, and I rarely came across people that I fancied. There were one or two occasions when I had sex with people I had randomly met but that was it. There was only one guy I met during the trip who I was really attracted to. His name was Abdul and he was originally from Egypt. He lived in another town that was over five hours away but would come over to the town where I was to visit his friend. Sometimes we all hung out together and I could tell that he also liked me. He was super religious and did not do anything that was not halal, and so I did not dare to ask him if he was sexually active. Plus we never had the chance to spend more than two days together. We became friends and started to chat occasionally over Skype. He later moved to another town in the south of Germany and started to share a house with a Brazilian and a Turkish guy. He started partying, began drinking, and created a Tinder account. By then I was back in Rome.

A few months later he came to Rome with his brother for a visit and we met up for drinks. We ended up having sex that night. That began a pattern which has continued till today. We see each other once a year or so. He'll sometimes come over for my birthday, or I'll travel to Germany for his birthday. He's dating someone now but he's already told me that he knows it's not going to work. He felt under a lot of family pressure to be in a relationship and started dating this white woman. He told me, "When I come home and complain about microaggressions at work she doesn't get it. She tells me the same things that the other white people tell me." Although I really like Abdul and we have a great sex life, I'm not in love with him. We have a good connection, and can talk about my favorite subject, politics, but there's no click that makes me think, I want to spend my life with this man. It's nice when we're together but I don't miss him when we're apart. I suspect that's because I still have my walls up because of the experience I had with Felix the basketball player.

It was important to me that a book about the sex lives of African women would both speak to the infinite identities that African women hold, and show how we can create and re-create our identities, even those that appear fixed and immutable. For this reason, Solange's story is extra special to me because it illustrates that on the inside people already know who they are, while showing the journey that one has to travel in order to come into their full identity.

I first met Solange,* a forty-six-year-old queer trans woman, when she participated in Odyssey of Desire, a festival about sex and sexualities that I co-organized in 2019. Solange's participation at the event was one of my personal highlights. She made the audience laugh and gasp in turn with anecdotes about her life, and the time she spent as a sex worker.

In my subsequent interview, Solange shared with me that she describes herself as queer because it signifies an openness that is expansive and inclusive of her identity as a heterosexual woman who loves men. She originates from Rwanda, lives in Abidjan in La Côte d'Ivoire, and considers Canada one of her homes.

SOLANGE

■

I WAS PRAYING one day and heard a voice within me say: God created you
this way. God does not make mistakes. God had a mission while creating
you just the way that you are.

I realized then that I needed to live my life for myself, and that not being in
accordance with my true self was the real sin. It took me twenty-five years and
being far away from Rwanda, and my family, to have this realization. In Sherbrooke, Canada, people don't tell you what to do or how to dress. You could
choose to walk naked down the street and all the police would tell you to do is
ensure that your nipples and genitals are covered. I was all on my own for the
first time in my life, and had to figure things out for myself. I realized that I
could no longer be that baby who always wanted to please my parents, and
that I had to live my life for myself.

One day I called a helpline and they told me about this bar where I could
meet other people like me. I had been waiting a long time to connect with others
and so, cloaked in courage, I went out one evening to the first queer space I
had ever been in. The bar was filled with white men, but I was reassured to also
see two Black men. Sherbrooke was an extremely white city, and the presence
of people who looked like me took me back to my childhood and hearing a
popular French song over and over again on the radio. It was a song about two
schoolboys who were in love with each other. The words said something to
this effect: ". . . is it an ordinary sickness? Men who love other men."

I remember asking my mum, "They are singing about men who love other
men. What's that?" In response she said, "Oh, we don't have that in Africa. It
doesn't exist in Black society. These things only happen in white society because
white people are rich and when you are rich you want to experience a lot of

things because you have means. You don't have these primary needs where you are looking for food and the basics of life. So that's why they want to try other sexualities and other kinds of love."

I wanted to say to my mum, "The person you call your boy has the same feelings," but instead I nodded, because now at least I knew there were people out there in the world who felt how I did.

Although I was in a bar to meet people like me, I didn't dare approach either of the two Black guys I had spotted the minute I walked in. Instead Tim approached me, and for me it was love at first sight. Tim was a man who loved men. He perceived me as another man, and told me that he wanted to have sex with me. I was twenty-five years old at the time, and had never had sex with anyone before. My body wanted to be joined to Tim but I was scared. I kept giving him the runaround. "We'll go all the way tomorrow. I'm not ready yet." Meanwhile I was dreaming about sex with him. I could imagine myself being naked with him. I could see my body in him, or his body in mine. I could see us becoming one, expressing our love for each other, and coming together.

One day I decided that I was ready, and invited Tim to come over to my studio. It was one of those studios where you could see the bed from every angle, but it was also spacious. My favorite colors are green and red, and so I lit green and red candles everywhere, which filled the room with a lingering vanilla scent. I also bought flowers, which I dotted all over the space. I cooked us dinner: fish with a side of asparagus and potatoes. I opened a good bottle of wine. Tim arrived at about 6:30 p.m. and didn't leave till 2 a.m. We spent the first four hours eating, chatting, and drinking. Finally after 10 p.m. we went to bed. He said to me:

"I want you to take this at your own pace. You can go as far as you want to go, but respect your limits. If anything hurts, tell me to stop. I don't want you to force yourself to give me pleasure. Think of your own pleasure. I'm ready to follow your lead. I know what I want, but I want you to discover what you want. I want you to discover your body, to discover what gives you pleasure. I already know what sexual pleasure is and so I want you to use me to give you pleasure. We're going to take things step by step, and we can stop at any time."

I still feel grateful to Tim for those words, which have stayed with me forever. He helped me understand my feelings, my sexuality, and my limits. When I meet a new lover I am able to say, "No, I can't go there. Stop. I don't feel comfortable."

Tim also taught me how to kiss the body a thousand times. He taught me that every part of the body is sexual. He called our first time a night of a thousand kisses. He kissed all the way from my head to my toes. No part of my body was left untouched. I feel lucky that my first time was with him. It helped me release some of the shame I had long felt about my body and who I was attracted to. Tim wasn't the first guy I fell in love with but he was the first guy I was able to express my love with.

The first person I had fallen for was my best friend in primary school. We must have been around fourteen at the time. We were in the same class at school. In tests he would either come first or I would take first place. We both also loved God. His home was halfway between my home and the Catholic church we both attended, and so part of my ritual would be to stop over at his house so we could go to church together. He was a huge part of my motivation for going to church regularly. My plan at the time was to become a priest. I wanted to go to paradise. I knew that the only way I could have sex was to grow up and get married to a woman, and I couldn't imagine doing that. Being a priest would make me a good person, I could fight my desires and never have sex. I knew that as a good Christian I needed to resist the temptations of the flesh and I was determined to succeed in this effort. I didn't want to be like those other people. I didn't want to be a devil worshipper.

One day my older brother told me about masturbation. He told me that I could think of a girl, touch myself, and cum. It all sounded so stupid to me, and then one day I found myself thinking about my best friend. I dreamed about seeing him naked, touching his hair, his arms. I thought about going down further, and seeing what his sex looked like. My dreams stayed within me, there was no way that I was going to express these desires that I thought were unnatural. Over a decade later, when I started my transition, he was one of the first people I told. He told me that he's jealous that he can't be the first man who touches me as a woman. He's now a priest and credits me for nurturing his love for God.

In those days it was rare to meet Black people in Sherbrooke, let alone other Africans. I had eventually mustered up enough courage to chat with the two Black men I kept seeing at the gay bar, but they were both adopted by white families and not connected to Black culture. One day I was on a bus in Sherbrooke and saw this beautiful African man. He was a god of a man. He looked young, like he was also in his midtwenties. Everything about him was breathtaking. His skin, his eyes, his nose. I felt like I was just going to pass out from looking at him. I have no idea how I found the nerve to approach him but I did. He was also really happy to meet another African. Thierry was originally from Benin, and had been studying in Sherbrooke for three months, but until we connected, he had yet to meet another African. We quickly became close friends, and I fell completely in love with him. We would meet up often to cook African food together, and talk about our experiences of Blackness. I enjoyed every moment that we spent together. I was just happy to be in his company.

A few months later I moved to Montreal to continue my studies, and one day Thierry came over for a visit. It was going to be the very first time we spent the night together. My bed was a tiny one designed for a single student, and it was extremely hard to have an almost naked Thierry in the same tiny cramped space that I was in. I couldn't resist, and made my feelings known to him. We ended up having a night of intense passion. The following day Thierry left, and subsequently I never heard from him again. He didn't respond to any of my calls or text messages. I got so desperate that I even sent him a text apologizing for that night although everything we had done had been completely consensual. That was my first experience of heartbreak. It was hard to believe that everything we had together was gone because of one night of passion. I had loved everything about Thierry. I loved to listen to him talk passionately about soccer or about winning a programming competition at school. I even loved his silences. When I look back on that night I recognize that Thierry had just not been prepared. We went through experiences without naming them, and afterwards we each knew who the other was. When I think back on that moment I know he connected with the woman in me because he is a man who loves women, but he had no idea that someone shaped like a man could be a woman. So he was troubled by his feelings towards me because he did not see me as a woman.

My mum says she knew I was a girl from the moment I was in her womb. She had given birth previously to two boys and two girls, and so she knew how children of different genders acted in the womb. So she was surprised when she gave birth to me and I had male genitals. From the age of two or three I knew I was a girl. I wanted to be with people who had the same energy that I did, who felt like I did, and those people were girls. It wasn't until I was around nine years old that I started to feel attracted to boys. That was a moment of shock for me. Why would I be attracted to this same group of people who were rejecting me?

Part of what I find really interesting about being trans is how it allows you to connect with different people while you are on the different phases of your journey. I think of transitioning as taking a step towards the different people you love. Before the transition the gap can seem too wide, but afterwards it's a shorter path to travel for the people we love. There was one time I met a man on a dating app. By then I was living fully as a trans woman. I was taking hormones and my breasts had developed. He knew I was trans, and he had previously told me that he loved trans women. When he came over to my apartment I thought he looked familiar but couldn't quite place him. We had a good time, and ended up having sex about three or four times.

One day when he came over he said to me, "I knew a guy at university who was also from Rwanda. He used to be in love with me. The two of you really look alike. It seems like you all look alike in your country." That's when the memories came rushing back. I was the same person he was referring to. At university I had been in love with him, and I had opened up to him. At the time I had said to him, "I love men. I describe myself as a woman," and he had said, "No, you're not a woman. When I see you, I see a boy." Now ten years later we had come full circle and he was now in love with me as a woman.

Not everybody is able to stay on the journey with us during transition. I spent five years in a relationship with a Haitian man. We bought a house and a car together. He even met my parents. I loved him and wanted to get married but he was not ready to do that because he was not fully out. When I started to transition, that was too much for him. He felt that if his parents saw me they would perceive him differently and know that he was not as heterosexual as he had been portraying himself to be. He had been telling them that he was living with a male friend, but now this man was becoming a woman. He was especially worried about what people back home in Haiti were going to say. That brought our relationship to an end.

In my relationships with women, there's been a peacefulness that doesn't exist in my relationships with men. I was seventeen years old when I first fell in love with a woman. At the time my family and I had moved to Congo because of the war in Rwanda. She was the daughter of our landlord and we lived together in the same compound. My brother had a crush on her and I told him, "You can have any girl you want but not this one." He was surprised. "You've never been interested in girls. Why do you want to marry her?" I didn't want to marry her but I knew I loved her. We had a close friendship and would spend ages teasing each other. We kept in touch throughout the years even when my family left Congo and moved to Zambia. Years later she expressed an interest in also moving to Canada to study and I was able to share tips with her on how to find a good university.

I opened up to her when she moved to Canada. When I told her, "I like men," she said, "I already know." I asked her how, and she said the other guys who liked her behaved differently. Being open with her allowed an intimacy to develop between us. My feelings for her were more than physical. I felt at peace whenever we were together. Sometimes we would kiss, other times we would kiss and touch each other, sometimes we would not kiss but do something else. I loved holding her in my arms, feeling her hair on my shoulder, touching her skin. Each experience with her was different. Nothing felt forced. There were no expectations. When she came over, she came over because she wanted to be with me, and not because she wanted to have sex with me. This was different from my relationship with men. With men they have this attitude, "I have to cum. If I didn't cum we didn't have sex." When I started my transition she was supportive. She's also a queer woman and told me that our intimacy and lovemaking had always felt like being with another woman even though at the time I was in a man's body.

When I started transitioning I also started to embrace the experience of exploring my changing body through sex. Every stage of the transition was an opportunity to get closer to different types of people. There are people who like feminine men, there are people who like cross-dressers, there are people who like folks that have started hormone treatments and have breasts. At every stage of the transition there will be people who love us as we are. The only challenge is that some people want us to stay at the stage where they met us. They don't understand that we are evolving, and so you have to be strong and say, "I haven't reached the end of my journey yet." Experiencing sex at every stage of my journey allowed me the opportunity to really get to know people.

I was now in my body as a woman and I decided to start traveling the world; I wanted to experience different cultures and meet different people. Doing sex work allowed me to travel, and also allowed me to connect with people all over the world. Sex work allowed me to come back home to Africa, and to experience love with my brothers and sisters. Sex work allowed me to get in touch with the real me. I still have some clients from my time as a sex worker who are now my friends and lovers. Most of them are people who describe themselves as heterosexual. Some of them are married and I am their second or third lover. Some of them are single men. At the beginning there was some questioning because of the presence of my male sex. Some were initially not comfortable but in time they learned to love me, love my body, and love my personality. They learned to enjoy sex with me, and I learned to understand them, to understand their way of life, and to not push them because most of them had never been with a trans woman before.

My experience of sex with women is also very different now that I am a trans woman. I realize now that women did not sufficiently recognize me as a woman when I was in a man's body. There was this charge of being privileged, of benefiting from the patriarchal system. Now I feel more accepted by women. My experience of sisterhood with other women is much easier. We meet as women who have common experiences around the male gaze and that creates an intimacy where no one woman is superior to another.

My lovers know that I have multiple partners and they are comfortable because we are not in an exclusive relationship. They know that my experience of sexuality is in a state of freedom. I feel very rich when it comes to my sex life. I feel sexually fulfilled. I can experience different aspects of my sexuality with different people. In French we describe that as épanouie. *J'ai une vie sexuelle épanouie.*

I met Yami,* a thirty-year-old Canadian femme of Malawian heritage, in the Caribbean. We had both traveled to Grenada for Carnival, an important period to celebrate Black resistance and culture. It's also a time for fun, decadence, and hedonism, and the group we had traveled with was there for all of it. Yami and I were there for some of it. We were those people in the group who were always the first to leave the party, and so while our friends were still having fun past midnight, we would catch a taxi back to our hotel.

During our trip, I had overheard Yami chatting with her partner, and sometimes sharing an anecdote about their relationship. I knew Yami was in a relationship with a trans person, and that their heritage was Indian. I don't know many Black people who are in relationships with people from East and Southeast Asia, and so I was especially curious about the dynamics of their relationship, especially where extended families are concerned.

What I especially appreciated from speaking to Yami were the insights into how second-generation immigrants in the diaspora negotiate their identity and sexuality with parents whose own views on this issue have been firmly shaped by their countries of origin, traditional culture, and religious beliefs. It made me think of the more limited conversations I have had with my parents about sex, and I found myself often thinking, Wow, Yami's parents are very open-minded, which is not how she read her folks at all.

YAMI

.

I REMEMBER YEARS ago going to see my gynecologist *and* my naturopath because I was concerned that I could not orgasm through sex. "Is my pussy broken?" I asked. They said, "No, you're just having bad sex." It took me a while to realize that part of the issue was bad sex, the other aspect was trauma.

In most of my former sexual relationships, I had rarely orgasmed. Sex at the time was more about the performance. It's the opposite in this relationship. We talk about desire, what is going on with our bodies, what we like, what we don't like. Nothing is weird in our relationship, absolutely nothing. I'm very femme-presenting and people often assume that means I'm passive. I feel comfortable in this relationship and so I'm able to be dominant. I've gotten to know my body in a very different way. I now know what my body likes because there's been space created for me to figure that out. Grinding on my partner, for example, feels amazing. The other day I was pinching my nipples and got really aroused although usually I don't like nipple play. This is the first time in a relationship that I have felt that everything is on the table, and nothing is off-limits sexually. When we first started dating, we would fuck like rabbits, I would have multiple orgasms and then weep uncontrollably. I thought, WTF is wrong with me? Why am I crying? Then I realized that too was okay. My body was healing. I was connecting both with myself and with another person. The only challenges we've experienced sexually have been around my own body dysphoria, feeling disconnected from my body and dissociating. But when I'm present with them, I'm really present with them.

I fancied my partner from the moment I saw them at a conference in Ottawa, where I lived at the time. They had traveled from Toronto, also to speak about sexual violence. I thought they were hella cute from the moment I saw them.

They are very masculine presenting, and just had this swag. When they look at you, their eyes pierce right through to your soul. Plus, they were this super-confident executive director, and in Ottawa there just weren't that many racialized queer folks I found attractive. Then I looked at their fingers and thought, I see your ring, so I guess not.

Fast forward to a year and a half later; I moved to Toronto, and invited them out for a coffee. I made sure to look good for that date. It turned out that the ring was meaningless, they just recklessly wear rings on any finger. Then we went on a second date, and because we worked in the same neighborhood, they started to ask, "Do you want me to drive you home?" and soon it was the December holiday season, so we started to spend all of our time together.

This is the first "out" relationship I have ever been in, although I initially came out to my mum when I turned twenty-five. On that day I was going to get a tattoo of the map of Africa, and she offered to drop me off. On the way I said to her, "Mummy, I have something to tell you but I am really scared that you're not going to accept me." She asked, "What is it?" and then I think I told her that I was bisexual because I was still coming into my queerness and so that seemed like the simplest thing to say at the time. She said, "Okay, so you like the P and the V," and then proceeded to give this long speech about how she'll never disown me for being queer or gay. I got very emotional and started to cry. It was also very anticlimactic.

My parents are Malawians, we moved to Canada as refugees when I was about three years old, and we grew up in this strict Catholic household that was extremely sex negative. Sexuality was always something that had to be conserved. I was always told, "Cover your body, you don't want people to think you're a ho," so I started to react. I said, "Hos are great. #Ho." It feels like the process of coming out has been a continuous one. I've always felt that I had to conceal parts of myself. I remember being four or five years old and being really attracted to my friend Alice. I just didn't have the words to name what I was feeling. I just knew that I liked hanging around her a lot.

My current partner and I have been together for close to two years, and that's been a challenge for my family because my previous partners were cisgender men. So bringing home this transmasculine human really shifted what my family thought of me. They always knew I was the radical child, yet it continues to be a painful process when it comes to my sexuality. No matter who I bring home, they react as stereotypical African parents and say, "Oh, that's your friend, that's your friend . . ." That's been a constant refrain whether I'm with a cis man or woman or a nonbinary person.

At the same time, my mum always tells me, "I knew for the longest time that you were a lesbian." My parents have the language. They may not always have the conceptual clarity, but they have the language for sure. Part of what has been really difficult with my mum is that in her quest to seek understanding she's always asking me questions about sex and my queerness specifically. That's another difficulty. People perceive queer relationships as purely physical—as about the physical act of how we have sex. It's taken therapy for me to understand that our parents have their own processes too. Just like we do. When we go through different experiences in life, we have to ask questions to get clarity. I know for some of my queer friends that feels really scary: Are you asking questions to try to invalidate who I am? Over time, I have come to understand that part of the questioning is because my mum is trying to wrap her head around sexuality because she's from a generation where these issues were not discussed openly, especially with children. Recently, she told me that she had been talking to her friends about her daughter being gay, and they said, "That's okay." That was a big deal for me because even though I know she feels some shame about my sexuality, she was still having this conversation with her friends.

With my dad I've never openly discussed my sexuality. There was a time he sent me a poster of my queer uncle who was delivering a talk in London about gay men and sexuality in Malawi. He didn't say anything else, just sent me the poster. He also sends me these long WhatsApp messages about how he loves me and says he's okay with my choices. I told him, "Daddy, it's not a choice!" He sends me other random stuff like #LoveIsLove during Pride. I guess that's his way of affirming who I am as a whole person.

My family is very big and friendly so they've always been welcoming to my partner when they visit. Recently they joined us to celebrate Christmas, which was a first for them because they are Hindu. I've also celebrated Diwali with their family. I was so nervous to meet them. I thought first-generation Indian immigrants who are also practicing Hindus would be ultra conservative. I also had a fear that they would be anti-Black. When my partner and I first met, we talked about anti-Black racism and how it shows up in Brown families, and what that experience could be like. The reality has been very different.

Their family has embraced me, and shown me a lot of love. We all go out together to predominantly Indian restaurants in Toronto for dinner. If I miss a dinner they always ask, "Where is Yami?" Their mum taught me to make parathas. We're planning a family trip together to India, and they have openly discussed which places we can travel to and the places we'll avoid. The only time that I've felt like a bit of an outsider is when they speak Hindi. I always sleep over when I go to their house, and my partner and I sleep in the same bed, which is also a novelty. At my family's home that doesn't happen. My mum said, "Just because you're gay doesn't mean you can sleep in the same bed. I'm still an African, and so that can't happen until you're married." I'm sure that even when we get married, we'll still sleep in separate beds when we visit my parents.

A year into our relationship I proposed. We were lying in bed one day and I said, "Babes, we should get married." Their response was, "Huh," and then *they* proposed a couple of months later. I had a feeling it was going to happen because they had told me that we were going away and that I should "wear a cute dress and look really nice." I told them to just leave me alone to live my best life. When they picked me up they brought roses and chocolate-covered strawberries. We drove about an hour away to a five-star hotel near Niagara Falls. There were roses strewn all over the bed and there were candles everywhere. It was like a Keith Sweat music video. They drew me a bath, and then afterwards we had lobster and shrimp. Then they gave me this pink blinged-out ring that I had tried on in a jewelry shop a few weeks prior. I felt like the princess that I know I am. I rang all my friends up afterwards and said, "I'm engaged!"

A few months down the line we were in Ottawa for a long weekend. We went to this fair trade jewelry store and my partner chose their ring. It was a simple, eco-friendly one. One morning we were lying in bed, they were still sleeping and snoring away, and I was thinking about the perfect moment to propose to them. Then I thought, Keep it simple. When they finally woke up, I pulled out the ring and said, "Babe, will you marry me?" They were still groggy at the time but the moment felt beautiful, and each proposal was fitting of our personalities.

My mum was going to drop me off at the airport and then I told her, "I have something to tell you." I pulled out my ring, showed it to her, and then ran out of the car. I didn't wait for a reaction. She texted me and said, "We'll talk about it later." It took two months for us to have that conversation. I said, "I'm gay, it's not a phase." She explained what her struggle was. She just couldn't understand why I wasn't with a man if I was so attracted to masculinity. I had to explain gender and transness to her, and then she decided to do her own research.

I want to have children, and so does my partner. Our plan is to undergo in vitro fertilization (IVF) with me carrying all the pregnancies. My partner is very clear that they never want to carry. For the first pregnancy, we intend to use their eggs, and then use mine subsequently. For me it's really important to have Black children. It's political. We live in a world that continues to erase Black people, and so the process of birth is a radical act against state sanction, the prison industrial complex, and violence against Black bodies. I have cystic fibroids so I am hoping those don't impact the pregnancies. The expense is also a huge concern. Where I live, the first IVF trial is free, and then subsequently it costs CAD$10,000. We're going to have to prep even to get pregnant just because of how challenging that process is. I know that my prep will be mostly emotional especially in terms of how I will relate to my body during that time. We're also going to take parenting classes.

When my partner and I first met, they asked, "Are you polyamorous?" I don't think I fully understood then what being poly was all about. I think open, honest communication is key in relationships (which is also what being poly is all about) and so I've always been very explicit with them. When we are out in the community, people come on to me a lot. I've had folks tell me, "I am in love with you," and then I go to my partner and say, "Hey, babe, someone told me this." We have lots of late-night conversations about our relationship, what our limits are, what we feel comfortable with. We've decided that our relationship is monogamous with an exception. If either of us are on vacation we can have fun. If we meet someone abroad and want to hook up we can do so. The only caveat is that person cannot be from Toronto because that's where we live. Personally I'm not interested in vacation romances. That's just not my thing.

As my partner's gender expression changes, and they've decided to fully medically transition, other factors have come up. People's sex drives tend to increase when they are on testosterone. We've had conversations where I've asked, "What if you start to find other people attractive? What would that look like?" For me that level of honesty is really important because I have been cheated on in a lot of my previous relationships. I think if you want to have sex with someone else, by all means do so, but let's navigate that in a way that feels good for both of us. It's okay to be sexually attracted to other people or to have sex with other people. That's just a reality of relationships. We've talked about going to play parties together, for example. We've discussed what would feel good or not feel good at these events even before we've experienced them together. They have been to play parties before; I haven't, but I know I'd much rather watch than participate. I'm a bit of a voyeur. They said, "Guaranteed, Yami, people will want to have sex with you." That's one of the things that is so interesting about my relationship. It is the first time that nothing has felt off-limits. Everything is consensual and desire is all that.

PART 3: HEALING

Atiadonka, katrikwa donka,

Womp3 mia gyia me
M3nya na)p3 me

A sixteen-year-old family friend taught me this song. It was an ode to the girl I was, whose frequent bouts of asthma and an inability to keep food down had led me to become a skinny child. I would sing the words he taught me:

Leave me if you do not want me
I will find the one who wants me

I must have been about seven or eight at the time that I learned this ditty from a friend of the family. I remember following this family friend to the boys' quarters where he lived, and putting his wee wee thing in my mouth. I remember lying down on a mat, him heavy above me, trying to put his thing inside me. It wouldn't fit and he stopped.

At eleven I went to an all-girls Catholic boarding school. I was a year younger than most of my classmates and smaller than most of my contemporaries, but in about two years I was bigger than most of the girls in my class. The bulk of the weight appeared on my chest. I walked with my chest tilted forward like I was oppressed by the load I carried. My classmates nicknamed me Madam Stiff. I remember walking into the hostels one day and suddenly coming across a group of girls at the base of the steps. We had just returned to school from the long vacation and before seeing them I overheard part of their chatter:

"Have you seen Nana's breasts? I think she did *it* while we were on holiday."

I walked by awkwardly as if I had heard nothing at all.

I wasn't the only one girls spoke about in school. There was Ama, who everyone knew had gotten pregnant, left school to have a baby, and returned. I guess all the talking got to her because she left school again and this time did not return. But there were plenty of people who stayed, like Beth, whom everybody called "Kaneshie mattress" because it was said that all the boys in Kaneshie had slept with her. She was one of the cool girls, and the cool girls strutted around confidently, not hearing or caring what people said about them.

We all need healing of some sort, and when it comes to sex there is a whole lot of healing that Black and African women need. Healing from child sexual abuse, healing from abusive relationships, healing from the violence perpetuated on our bodies, through so-called traditional practices and culture, including those fostered by religious institutions. We also need healing from state-sanctioned violence, as well as from the harm and trauma we ourselves perpetuate. One of the ways in which women heal is by speaking up about the sexual harm they have experienced.

Salma El-Wardany,* a well-known poet, writer, and media personality with roots from Egypt and Ireland, chose to allow me to publish her story using her real name because she recognizes how being in a bad relationship robbed her of her voice for far too long. Speaking out is a deliberate part of her activism. This is something I identify with. I spent two years working on this book before it dawned on me that I needed to interview myself. I struggled initially with what aspects of my life to share in this book, and then I decided to follow the same process that I had followed for all the women whose stories I have shared here. I asked my friend, the writer Valérie Bah, to interview me about my experiences of sex. I was struck then, as I am now, of how the experience of being molested as a child always comes out as a central theme in my personal story.

Many of the women I spoke to are already doing the work of healing. Some have sought therapy, others journal, some practice self-love challenges, as was the case with Shanita, who started out by embarking on a hundred-day self-love challenge that included being celibate, and then extended her practice to a thousand days. These women are actively doing the work to feel whole, and many are inspiring others to go on their own healing journeys too.

Good sex is also healing, as is having partners who desire you, love you, and reflect your best selves back to you. This is the kind of healing that I wish for myself, and for all Black women.

I met Salma* in 2019 when we were both invited to Lagos, Nigeria, as guests of the Lagos International Poetry Festival. The title of our conversation was Wild Geographies, which brings to my mind the volatility within nature and humankind. There is something extremely freeing about tapping into our wild side. The parts of us that we tend to keep hidden, even from the people who are closest to us. The desires we cannot speak of. The fantasies we dream of. The love we keep hidden.

Although Nigeria is a homophobic country (as is my own country, Ghana, and the vast majority of countries throughout the world), it is also the place on the continent where I see a diversity of visibly queer people taking up space in the arts and creative sector. Queer people living their best lives is the most dynamic resistance to state-sanctioned homophobia. It is this resistance that also created space for Salma and me to share a public stage in Lagos and to speak about our experiences of sex, including sharing anecdotes of sexual experiences with other women.

After being in conversation with Salma publicly, I knew I wanted a more in-depth conversation with her. At the time I had imagined that the story that would emerge would be one of high jinks and sexual romps. What I hadn't expected is the story you are about to read. One that comes from a place of deep vulnerability, and yet another reminder of how the world tries to clip the wings of girls and women.

Salma is a thirty-one-year-old cis heterosexual woman. She was born in Cairo, Egypt, to an Irish mother and an Egyptian dad. At the age of four, she and her mum moved to the UK and she currently lives in London.

The following story includes experiences of rape and sexual assault.

SALMA

·

I WAS ADAMANT that I wasn't going to have sex until I was married. I was really clear about a couple of things. No alcohol. No bacon. No sex. In my first year of university I met Paul. We had mutual friends, and so would all hang out together. One day we kissed and it felt like the most beautiful act. That kiss marked the start of our relationship. I told him, "I'm not having sex until I'm married," and he said okay. For the first year of our relationship we did everything but penetrative sex. It was like a year-long foreplay, and then one night we went all the way. It was so beautiful that I cried. By then we were in love, and I fully trusted him. Our relationship lasted throughout all three years of university. Afterwards we both decided that we wanted to spend a year abroad. He traveled to Japan, and I traveled to Egypt, where my dad's family is from. Before we left I gave Paul a box of letters. I had written him 365 letters so he could open one every day that we were going to be apart.

I went to Egypt in 2010 and quickly became immersed in the culture and religion of my identity. It was everything that I had been yearning for. As a Muslim, I had been raised to understand that I needed to marry a Muslim man. That tension had always hung over my relationship with Paul. I was a practicing Muslim and he didn't even know if God existed. I could no longer see how I could make this relationship with a white man from Yorkshire work. There were no models that I could look to. No one else in my community at the time had married a non-Muslim. I broke up with Paul, broke his heart, and in the process broke mine too.

I started teaching at a school in Cairo and every summer break would go back to the UK to see my family. On one trip back home I noticed this man while queuing for my flight to Heathrow. When I got to carousel six at baggage

claim, he was there too. Our bags were the last to arrive and in the interim we
began chatting and exchanged contact details. We kept in touch throughout
the holidays, speaking often on the phone as I lived in Newcastle at the time,
while he lived in London. He was exactly the kind of man that I had been told
that I needed to be with. Both his parents were Egyptian, he spoke Arabic
and, like me, was a British-bred Muslim. We had also both fought in the 2011
revolution and were filled with a passion for Egypt. At the end of the summer
we both went back to Egypt within a day of each other. In Cairo we reunited,
began a relationship, and moved in together. To this day no one in my family
knows I ever lived with him as both sets of our parents lived in the UK.

One time, we went on vacation to Dubai and I spent hours in the mall
looking for a bikini that he would find acceptable. Even though I was a size 8 at
the time, I ended up buying a bikini in a size 16 because I thought it would
provide more coverage. On a previous vacation we had been on the beach
together, and I had pushed my straps down so that I could tan more evenly. He
had screamed at me, "You're lucky that I am even allowing you to wear a bikini."
If I wore clothing that he considered revealing he would make me change. In
time, I started sewing up the cleavage of my clothing. He hated that I had male
friends. It drove him mad that I would end text messages to them with xxx at
the end to signify kisses.

One time he called me a whore for being with another man before him. He
said he didn't know if I could ever be the mother of his child. At night I would
feel panicky about going to sleep. I talk in my sleep sometimes, about anything
from ketchup to Harry Potter, and he started to say to me in the morning,
"You were talking about your ex again." I started to google "how to stop sleep
talking." There is no cure for sleep talking. No tablet you can take to stop talking in your sleep. I didn't even know if it was true that I had been talking about
Paul in my sleep. I wasn't thinking about Paul, and I don't even remember
dreaming about him. I lived in fear of going to sleep and not knowing whether
he was going to wake up angry or not.

After two and a half years in Egypt we moved back to the UK. There's
only so long that one can deal with political unrest and the constant state of

curfew in Egypt. I found a job in London and moved to the city where he already lived. I got my own apartment and met his dad, and he also met my parents. Our relationship continued on a downward spiral. One day he said to me, "I'm going to Egypt for a month because I am super stressed. For that month we can't speak to each other. There can be absolutely no communication between us." I was trying to be a supportive girlfriend and so I said, "Yes, take all the time you need."

After a month he came back, looked me in the eye, and said, "Salma, I don't love you anymore, and I don't want to be with you." I said, "That's fine, but let me just tell you, I've loved you so much and you've been an absolute bastard to me." He continued to look me dead in the eye and replied, "I know, and don't let anyone ever treat you like that again because you don't deserve it." A month later he was married. That trip he had taken earlier to Egypt had been to arrange his wedding.

I've never been the same since that relationship. There is a lightness that I had before that has never returned. I learned that you can take your ribs out for a man, bend over backwards, twist yourself inside out, and change everything about you, but he will still leave if he wants to. I learned that you can change your friends, change the people in your life, and change everything about yourself, but it's never enough. The biggest lesson I learned is that you should never change for anybody because they will still leave you anyway and you can only ever be true to yourself. I faded in that relationship. I became someone else. I stopped going out to bars and clubs even though I don't drink because he didn't like it. I stopped talking to some of my friends. I stopped talking to one of my best friends because he's a man. I became a shadow of myself.

When that relationship ended I was silent for years. For a long time I didn't speak about the abuse. Even now there is a lot around that relationship that I cannot go into. Sometimes it feels like if I do, I might never come back out again. I might never come up for air. That's the same silence I experienced when I was raped.

For the longest time I said, "I was almost raped." During my second year of university my friend and I went to Greece for the summer. We wanted some sunshine and to have some fun. We were on a small island, and I worked on one side as a waitress and she worked on the opposite end, also waitressing. At night, the restaurant I worked at turned into a bar and a club. One evening I finished work late. It was around 3 a.m. and I and a big group of other English friends started walking home, as we all lived in the same direction. When we got to the junction, everybody in the group had to go one way, and I had to go the other way. The guys in the group offered to walk me home but I said no. I lived less than five minutes down the road, and they were all drunk and tired. I jokingly said, "If I get raped it will be your fault." We all laughed about it and went our separate ways. I carried on down my road and soon realized there was a car behind me. I started walking faster. There was a Greek man in the car and he pulled up alongside me and rolled down his window and tried to talk to me. I said to him, "Leave me alone, please," and walked even faster. He then sped off round the corner. I thought he had gone. When I walked around the bend I saw him walking towards me with his dick in his hands. He was motioning to me to suck it. I turned and started running down the road. He caught up with me and pinned my arms to my side. I remember thinking, You should scream, you should scream now, but I couldn't speak. It felt like I was outside of my body just watching. I remember thinking, This can't be happening. Then suddenly I felt his hands relax and I jumped up and ran, and ran, and ran. He had his trousers around his legs and couldn't chase me. I ran until I saw two British women out on their balcony smoking. I ran to them and they took one look at me and said, "Cut through here. You can climb up from over there." I told them, "I need to call my friend." I called my friend and the lads I had been with earlier. Bless them, they came running out of their apartment armed with bottles, and walked me back to my place.

The really scary thing was that the man continued to drive past my apartment several times that night and each time the guys would throw a bottle at his car. In the morning I went to the police station and made a report. I also told my employers what had happened and described the man to them. They said, "We know exactly who he is," and told the police who the suspect was. Apparently he had a reputation. The following day the police went to look for him but he had already left the island. I remember thinking to myself, "I can't tell Paul what has happened while I'm still away because he will be so worried."

When I got back to London, Paul came to see me and I told him, "I have something to tell you." He looked sick when I said that. I knew he was probably imagining what in his mind would have been the worst-case scenario. That I was going to say that I had been out partying on a Greek island for a month, and I'd had sex with somebody else. When I told him what actually happened he cried and held me. I told my mum that I was "almost raped." That's how I spoke about it for years. I said to myself, "He never got to finish and so maybe it wasn't rape. He didn't ejaculate, he didn't cum, and so it wasn't a full rape." I wrote down this line in my journal, "I called it almost rape. So I could almost talk about it." I didn't know how to speak about what I had been through. I told two of my friends what happened and then I was silent. Years later I finally told my mum what happened. She looked at me and said, "I knew he raped you. I knew it wasn't just almost rape."

Subsequently I've done a lot of work on myself. I started therapy, and worked on my sense of self-worth. I want to be in a healthy relationship one day. I want a relationship like the one Paul and I had. A beautiful, kind love. I know I need to work on myself to make that a possibility and so that's what I have been doing. In the past year I've felt ready to be in a partnership, whereas prior to that I felt scared and fled from anything that wasn't just sexual or fun. Now when I'm dating someone I'm really communicative. If I just want sex from someone I tell them. If I want to date someone I let them know straightaway. I'll also tell people if I am not that into them. I don't keep them around to see what happens. I know what it's like for someone to hold that kind of power over you, and so I never want to be that person.

I now have a compulsive need to speak up about everything because I was silent for so long. Silence leads to damage and I am a product of that. For me, having a healthy relationship with a person of the opposite sex is about unlearning those patterns of silence and coming to each experience with honesty. When you have two consenting adults, and you're open about your wants and desires, that's the goal, right? Your needs and wants may not always match up but if you can vocalize them you can decide an appropriate action. If you say, "I don't want you the way you want me," then the other person can make a fucking choice to go or realign how they feel about you. Or they can say, "It's too hard for me to realign and so I'm going to save myself." I was never given the chance to save myself.

I feel extremely passionate about the rights of children to learn about their bodies, and to be given access to comprehensive sex education (CSE). I was told very little about sex growing up, a sentiment also expressed by the majority of women I have spoken to about sex (both for this book and for other projects, including the blog I cofounded, "Adventures from the Bedrooms of African Women"). Part of the reason why I feel CSE is so important is that I hope it will help children recognize when they are being abused, and will equip them with language to express any instances of violence to a responsible adult.

I know that in my own case that may have helped my younger self speak to my mum about the abuse that I experienced while I was only eight years old. So in a visceral way I felt connected to the experiences that Mariam Gebre* had been through as a child. Mariam is a twenty-six-year-old Ethiopian American woman who identifies as heterosexual. When she told me about being five years old and the gardener next door holding her hand and walking her down the path, I remembered following a friend of the family to the boys' quarters where he lived. Women often do not get the chance to speak about the abuse they have suffered, whether as children or adults. When we spoke, Mariam told me that was the first time she had ever felt able to open up about her experiences of being sexually abused as a child, even though she had previously worked in a shelter for survivors of gender-based violence.

The following story includes experiences of child rape and sexual assault.

MARIAM GEBRE

■

IN COMPANY PEOPLE would say, "Do you see your daughter? She is playing with herself." My mum would look over and see me: legs open, my fingers in my vagina. Sometimes I would put flowers inside me, other times plants, or rocks. "Stop it," she would say. "Don't do that."

Our house in Harar was encircled by a veranda with smaller living quarters in the sprawling compound. As Tigri people who had moved from the north to the western region of Ethiopia, we frequently had family members dropping in to visit and stay. They would usually sleep in the smaller quarters. I remember one of my male relatives saying to me, "Let's go and take a nap," and then touching my body. When my teacher would visit my parents at night he would sit on the dimly lit veranda and put me on his lap while chatting with them. He would put his fingers in me, or touch my nipples. He had told me previously, "I am touching your boobs so they will grow." I thought that was a good thing. One time in school, my second-grade classmate chased a boy all over the schoolyard yelling, "Touch my boobs." He eventually stopped, turned around, and said: "You are so weird, why would you want me to touch your boobs?" She said, "Teacher said it would make my boobs grow."

One of our science projects in school had been to bring seeds to school, which we had been taught to cultivate in little bags. By the end of the term everyone had a little plant, which we were asked to take home to nurture. Being a small community, our teachers would frequently drop by to see how our plants were doing. I discovered a love for planting and grew tomatoes, onions, and potatoes in a little bed at the front of the house. One day I was pottering in my garden as my mum was heading out. She asked the gateman next door to keep an eye on me. He came over and said, "Let's go to the backyard and see what's there." My mum had a huge vegetable garden at the back of the house, and off we went down the pebbled path, and down the stairs. I sat on the bottom step and suddenly he pushed me to the ground, lay on top of me and tried to put his thing inside me. It was so painful. I screamed, "Aiiiiiii, aiiiiii, aiiiii." He got up and went back to the neighbor's house. All this happened between the ages of five and six. I remember clearly because my dad got a new job, and we moved when I was seven.

In my orthodox Christian household we never spoke about sex. The word never came up. If anybody tried to bring up anything related to sex they were told to hush. When my mother saw me touching myself she never asked me why I was doing that, she only told me to stop.

Things didn't change much when I moved to America at the age of twelve after my dad died. My uncle who adopted my brother and me treated us like his own children. We went to a Christian school where sex was never discussed. When my period started in the eighth grade I thought I was bleeding to death. I had previously seen big boxes of pads in the bathroom at home and wondered, Who is the baby in this house? In tenth grade we were taught about the human body. "This is your shoulder. This is your arm. This is your vagina." The end.

I started traveling in the summer of my freshman year. I told my aunt and uncle that I would stay on campus and left for London for six weeks. Since then I travel whenever I can. I work three or four jobs just to travel. I don't care where I stay at my destination, and I never make any reservations. I just want to get there. Sometimes I've ended up in a posh hotel, other times I end up at the cheapest backpackers' hostel. What matters to me is what I see, eat, and drink, the people I meet, and the experiences I have.

When I was twenty-one I met the only official boyfriend I have had to date. We met in South Africa. He was from Guyana, in South America, and he was my research advisor. The first pleasurable sexual experience I had was when he went down on me. Then another time we had penetrative sex. It lasted about a minute. I said, "That's it?" and he said, "When it's your first time you don't really cum." He never said, "It's your first time, let me teach you." Our sex life didn't get better. He seemed content with how things were. We would do missionary or doggy style, he would orgasm and that would be the end of sex. I never came from penetrative sex. When I returned to the US we continued to have a long-distance relationship and saw each other about four times a year. I think the distance was the reason why we managed to stay together for four years.

The first time I began to acknowledge that I was molested as a child was at my first job working in a women's center in the US. A lot of the women who came there were refugees, or students from other countries. They shared stories of molestation and rape. I used to sit there, listen, and weep. I was crying for myself. My family still doesn't know I was molested. I don't know what they will do if they find out. My friend told her mum that she had been raped and her mum told her, "Never say that aloud again, I don't want to hear this, you're a liar." I have only told one other person that I was molested as a child. Sometimes I think I have come to terms with it, and then certain things happen and it all comes flooding back. I don't want to be a victim to my past. Maybe talking to more people will take it out of my head and it will become normal.

Some of my friends see good-looking men with six-packs and go, "Damn, I would love to fuck him." I have never felt like that. I never see anyone and think, I would love to fuck him. When guys I'm dating try to get physical with me I think, Is this all you want from me? It takes me a while to want anyone to touch me. It still blows my mind when my friends tell me about one-night stands they have had. I used to say to myself, What kind of directionless ho must you be to have a one-night stand? But now I think it must be the ultimate sign of liberation to have sex without any emotions.

I told the guy I'm currently dating that I am celibate. I don't want to force myself to have sex with men anymore. I want someone who is stable to be intimate with: physically and emotionally. The next time I have sex it will be on my own terms. I want to be more open and assertive. I feel like I shouldn't have to ask for certain things but maybe I should. If I don't cum the next time I have sex, I'm going to charge the guy $100. You cum and then you pass out? What about me? I might as well get paid for it.

One of my rituals is to go on vacation at the start of every year. I'll usually go to the beach either by myself or with a group of girlfriends, and at least one of those days will be dedicated to setting goals and intentions for the rest of the year. At the end of the year, whenever I look back at my goals, I'm always surprised by how much I have achieved, even in years when I didn't regularly review and check in on my captured thoughts, wishes, and desires.

The one area of my life where I have consistently struggled to create a firm goal has been in the area of personal romantic relationships. There are some years that I think, I would like a boyfriend, and then in other moments I say to myself, I would like a partner, but they have to be just like me, with similar values and beliefs, but what I consistently fail to do is to visualize my ideal partner(s), and also, frankly, I spectacularly fail at what I need to do to attract said partners into my life.

My conversation with Shanita* made me want to grab a journal and write down in glorious technicolor all the characteristics I would want in my romantic partners. Shanita is a thirty-six-year-old heterosexual woman who was born in the US. Her parents originate from Barbados in the Caribbean. As an act of self-love, she initially decided to practice a hundred days of celibacy and eventually extended the practice to a thousand days.

SHANITA

·

I'VE BEEN CELIBATE for almost a thousand days now. In that period I have focused on loving myself, raising my son, and opening a salon of my own in Boston. If I hadn't chosen to stay away from men, I wouldn't have been able to achieve all that in the last three years. Previously, I was so distracted by men, relationships, and desires of the flesh. Now I can see the rewards of patience and sacrifice. I've learned so much about myself. I never realized how much self-control I had, for a start. I now know that I'm able to stick to my goals. I also love the new me that emerged. I used to find the old me annoying. *She* was a shopaholic, constantly spending money and partying. Being celibate was not just about sex; it was also about breaking free of all forms of distractions, and delving deep into myself so I could understand why I used these as a crutch.

I wasn't ever extreme when it came to sex. I wasn't a sexaholic, for instance. I was a serial monogamist and I often found myself staying in relationships way after I should have moved on because of my desire for the other person. A few years ago I was in a relationship with a man. We had fun, we had a lot in common, we also had a friendship. When that relationship ended, I had to ask myself some tough questions. Why do I constantly end up in this kind of situation? What is it about me that I need to change so that I don't end up with someone who doesn't want me as much as I want them?

I decided to spend some time retreating into myself. I read a lot. I prayed a lot. I sat through many dark nights until I had a realization: I am the light. I am what I need in this world. Everything starts and ends with God but through me, and so the only things that I can experience are those things that I allow to happen. I realized that I needed to take back control of my life. This meant that I had to focus on myself. I had to take some time away from people. This resulted in me pushing a lot of people away. Some of those were good folks but that was just where I was in life at the time. I got really quiet and out of that stillness emerged my hundred days of self-love practice. All I wanted to do in that period was nourish my body and soul.

During those hundred days I ate healthily, I barely drank alcohol, and I took myself on dates. At the end of the period I decided to take a solo trip to Saint Martin and Anguilla in the Caribbean. I had never traveled alone before. The mere idea had always been scary and so I decided that I needed to conquer that fear. That also meant dealing with mom guilt as I left my son home with friends and family. During that entire hundred-day period I also stayed away from men. The only men that were ever around me were purely platonic friends. That was how my celibacy journey began, as part of my practice of self-love. At the end of my trip I decided that I wasn't going to have sex with anybody who wasn't worthy of me and the celibacy vow that I had made to God.

There are different schools of thought on whether one can masturbate or not while practicing celibacy. I believe in keeping my chakras open and aligned. Sometimes your sacred chakra just needs to be taken care of because otherwise you can get blocked creatively. Practicing masturbation while celibate allowed me to focus more on pleasing myself. In my previous sexual relationships I never focused on myself. It was all about the other person. I felt happy as long as my partner was satisfied. I never thought about my own pleasure. That's no longer the case. Through self-pleasure, I have learned how to satisfy myself, and I can go to a place in my mind that allows me to orgasm. I have also learned that sex is more than physical. My practices of meditation and getting more in touch with myself and my spirituality have helped me experience more orgasmic pleasure. I've also learned that it is possible to tap into your sexual energy to manifest your wants and desires. Those heightened sexually charged moments can also be really powerful times to think of the things you want to create or want to make real in the physical world.

Then there are periods when I practice complete abstinence, when I don't masturbate. That's the phase I am in now. I am communing with my spirit instead of being driven by the desires of my body. In any given situation I can pause and ask myself, Who is really feeling this way? Is it you, or is it your higher self? That's also what I am looking for in a future partner. Someone who is in touch with their higher self. I am seeking a divine connection. I'm at a stage in my life where I no longer want lessons. There are people who come into your life to teach you, to mold you. There are people who may cause you hurt and pain. They lead you to ask yourself some tough questions: What is it about me that keeps choosing this kind of person? In many ways those relationships are also divine because they take you to the next level. I'm at the next level. I am done with the lessons and ready for my blessings.

Dating while celibate has been interesting. Initially I would tell people on the first date, "I am celibate." I wanted them to know what the deal was, and in a sense, I wanted to know why they were on the date. Were they there because they were hoping to have sex with me? And then I realized it was unfair of me to make those kinds of assumptions. People don't always know what they want on a first date, and I may also have been scaring off people who might have been prepared to wait for me to be ready to have sex again.

You have all sorts of experiences when you're dating but sex is firmly off the table. You meet men who assume that all they need to do is to be patient and that eventually you'll change your mind about sex. With some of these men, it's taken a while for them to realize that my self-control is real. My male friends, for example, never believed I could be celibate this long. I think this says more about them than about me. They don't have that level of self-control and determination, and so they find it hard to imagine that I can practice this and stay the course. I told them, "Trust me. There is nothing that anyone can say or do that will make me change my mind until I'm ready to. Determining when I next have sex is totally my decision." It doesn't matter how handsome or successful the man is. You have to bring a lot to the table to get me to be interested in you. Being celibate has also allowed me to pay close attention to the men I date. When we're together, I find that I am paying a lot more attention. I really look at the person, I pay close attention to what they are saying. I am interested in who they are as a person, and what kind of character they have. All this has made the dating experience very different from what it was before.

Two months ago I started seeing someone who I think may be the right person for me. He is the chef and owner of a popular restaurant in my city. I'd heard a lot about his restaurant and so started going there. I loved their food and so would go there often. I started running into him, so we would chitchat. He would ask, "Hey, how are you doing?" One day he said to me, "I was talking to a friend and wondering if you are single." At the time I was feeling ready to meet someone. I had just opened up my salon and so was in a good place. I said, "Yes, I'm single." He invited me out on a date.

When he came to my house to pick me up, he got out of his car, and stood by the bottom of the stairs and waited for me. I was wearing heels and so he held my hand while I walked down. He was so physically present in a way that initially made me feel uncomfortable. I and my celibacy had a lot of walls up. In spite of that, we had a good date. I'd admired him and his work for a long time and so we spoke about business. We also had a friend in common and she encouraged me to get to know him. She told me, "He's a really good guy." That endorsement made a difference, and I'm glad that I allowed myself to get to know him. In time I realized that he also has a deeply spiritual side to him. He's not scared by the side of me that sages or practices full-moon rituals. He understands the healing and spiritual journey that I am on. He also practices self-care.

At the time we met I was close to hitting the thousand-day celibacy mark. I felt like the universe was tempting me. Here was this man who I was really attracted to. He would turn up at my door with food. He would call me and say, "I'm outside. Please come out for just a few minutes." Everybody knows that I do not like to be disturbed when I'm working but he ignores that. He says, "I want to do this for you, so let me." I'm looking right now at an orchid he gave me. When he brought it over I was in the shower. I heard the doorbell ring and so I told my son not to go to the door. When I came out he had sent me a text message saying, "I only rang the bell so you would know that there were flowers at the door for you."

I've realized that he feels he has to tiptoe around me, that I might ask him why he was at my door. I'm recognizing that I need to let down my walls a bit.

I have gotten so used to being by myself. It's hard to have someone close to me. The temptation is to say, "No, stay out there." I've really grown to like him and so this is something I'm working on. At the same time I want to make sure we're not rushing it. We started dating two months ago and time has gone by so quickly. I want to slow it down. I want to make sure that this right here is where I'm supposed to be. I want to be in a relationship where the man can meet my son. Where I don't need to say, "You have to leave before he wakes up in the morning." As a single mum, you have to protect yourself and your child. I once had a friend who told me, "Men don't ever take baby mamas seriously. They want to have sex with you, but they don't want to be with you." That's something I never want to internalize. I want the man I allow to share my life to be there for my son too, and to be the kind of person he can look up to. Someone who can play the role of a mentor.

One of my self-care practices is to journal. I'll ask myself questions like, What do I bring into a relationship? What do I want somebody to bring into a relationship? What kind of relationship do I want? Recently I found this list that I wrote describing the characteristics of my future partner. I wrote: "He is emotionally intelligent, he loves kids and wants to raise a king. He is handsome, successful, and stylish; he has a big dick and knows what to do with it." The last sentence made me know that list was real. The guy I am seeing now seems to check off most of the things on this list but of course I don't know what his dick game is like. There's something else that was on my list that he doesn't have. He's not as tall as I would have liked, although he's taller than me so that's okay. I want to be able to wear heels when I go out with my guy.

It's very important to trust the timing of your life. I know that because I have now had the chance to work on myself and to improve myself, I can attract my equivalent into my life. You can have all manner of items on your list, but the real question is, do you have those characteristics yourself? I used to be terrible at communicating. I would bottle up stuff and just feel so angry and upset all the time. It took me a while to realize, Being unable to communicate is your real problem. So I got a life coach and worked on that. My coach also taught me how to allow myself to be more vulnerable, and to tap into my femininity. That was a part of me that had become dominated by my experiences as a single mum who was also a business owner. At the time I was at a point in life where I felt, I don't need a man, I don't need anyone to do anything for me. I also couldn't ask for help because I literally did not know how to speak about my wants and desires. I also felt that I couldn't trust people. That folks would let me down. Those were all issues that I needed to work on, and so I did until I no longer felt blocked by these.

I don't know when my celibacy journey will end. For me it's not necessarily about waiting for marriage. It may be when I and a man agree that we're in a partnership. All I know is that I need to be patient and to trust my intuition. Patience is a lesson that I am constantly having to learn. Last year, for several months of the year all my lessons were around patience and discipline. This year I was hoping for a different lesson. Why can't my lesson be self-care, for example? But no, it's still patience. I know it's a virtue. I understand why I have to control myself and wait for what God and the universe have in store for me. I know that all I have to do is to practice patience and things will come to me in ways that I could never have anticipated. I know that I have to wait to create this long-lasting relationship that I want.

At some point in time, I was feeling down about the many stories of sexual abuse that I was hearing, and so sent out a tweet asking people to get in touch with me if they were living their best sex lives. Maureen* sent a tweet back saying, "I am not living my best sex life but I would love to be interviewed for your book."

Maureen is a twenty-nine-year-old heterosexual woman who was born in Côte d'Ivoire and raised in France. I interviewed her at my home in Accra, while she was a participating artist in a festival that had become controversial due to allegations of sexual abuse and violence on the part of its cofounder. Maureen and other feminist artists participating in the festival had made efforts to take a public stance to denounce sexual violence, and subsequently had been harassed by the police.

On the night that Maureen called me she was feeling particularly vulnerable, and so I drove to her guest house and brought her to my home to spend the night. On my way to pick her up there was a voice in my head saying, *This is madness, you can't bring a total stranger into your home,* but the other voice, saying, *You can't leave someone who is a stranger in your town distraught and alone,* won out. Later that evening, Maureen and I sat down to chat.

What I found particularly heartbreaking was that although Maureen has had several lovers, she has never had an "official" boyfriend apart from a brief two-month-long relationship. On a grand scale this may seem like nothing, but feeling like she's never chosen has had a huge impact on Maureen's sense of self-worth and *confidence. This conversation made me wonder how my sense of self would have been affected if I too had grown up in a majority white country where I was reminded time and time again that I am not the standard of beauty.*

MAUREEN

.

I WAS IN Abidjan when I heard about the Chale Wote festival happening in August 2018. I thought to myself, You need to be there, and so I jumped on a bus and traveled ten hours to Accra. I remember when I first saw Akwete. He had dark skin and thick black hair. There was also this other woman from South Africa who clearly liked him, and so I made up my mind to just admire him from afar. I knew I didn't have a chance with him. We were often in discussion groups together but we never spoke. After the festival, we followed each other on Instagram. One day, he posted a picture of a joint in his stories and commented, "Who wants to come and smoke with me?" Although I was back home by then, I replied, "Me, me, me," and that's how we started chatting.

By September, our conversations had gotten intense and we were Face-Timing each other a lot. When he started flirting with me, I said, "Where's this going? You cannot handle me. Most men cannot handle me." I couldn't keep up my defenses and very quickly our chats became intimate. Part of my attraction to him was because he came across as a conscious and feminist African man, which is really like meeting a unicorn. Plus he was good-looking and creative. By then we were planning some joint work together. The idea was that I would travel to Ghana the following year and shoot a film. He was also supporting my application as a participating artist for the next edition of the festival where we had originally met. Then in December he told me he wanted to end our relationship.

I was devastated. I thought it was my fault because I had told him off when he slut-shamed me. I had traveled to New York and sent him a picture I took there. In the image I was wearing a top that showed off my boobs. His comment was, "You look like a woman who has nothing else to offer." That cut me deeply, and I told him how disappointed I was in him. He quickly backtracked, saying, "I'm so sorry, I still have a lot to learn. I was a Christian kid, let's keep talking, no one is perfect." I thought to myself, "At least he knows the issue."

We had several incidents like this. This was all happening at a really difficult period in my life. I have a difficult relationship with my family, and at the time I was living with my mum. There were moments when I recognized that I was transferring the anger I felt at my family towards him. A part of me also felt that I sabotaged the relationship. I thought, If it ends now then you won't need to put all of this work into it. When he stopped talking to me I cried for three weeks straight. I couldn't stop thinking about him.

After three months I sent him a message. "I miss talking to you." He said, "I miss talking to you too. I'm in a much better place now. I had my heart broken before and you were going too fast." I told him I was done with all that and we were going to stay in touch as friends but soon we started flirting again. He told me, "I want to start a family so if you start to show me even a small amount of love and attention I might fall in love with you." He even said he wanted to FaceTime with my mum at some point in time.

Around this period my sister had a baby with her husband so was spending all her time at home so my mum could support her. In a fit of anger, I tweeted one day, "Men are so useless." He sent me a DM saying, "You can't say that." I replied, "Fuck you. I can say anything I want to say." He went on to say, "You think men are useless yet you want me to talk to your mother?" "Yes," I said, "she's married to my father, she's used to it." Eventually, I apologized. I recognized that I had been treating him like a troll and I shouldn't have because I knew him. We resumed being friendly with heavy doses of flirting. One day I suggested we FaceTime. That's when he said:

"I can't. I have a girlfriend now."

"What? You couldn't tell me this to my face?"

"I can. I'm not scared of you."

I wanted to know who she was but he refused to tell me. I concluded that he had found somebody else in Accra.

Later on I posted on Instagram that I was going to participate in the Chale Wote festival. This girl who I was friendly with online commented: "Go girl." I responded: "Thank you! Will you be in Ghana for the festival?" "No, but I knew you were going to be there because my boyfriend is on the organizing team."

I could feel my heart beat faster.

"Who is your boyfriend?"

"Akwete."

I felt so sad. In many ways we were so similar. She was also an African living in the Diaspora. I had assumed that he had broken up with me so he could be with someone in the same city.

In August I returned to Ghana for the festival. On the first night he said to me, "I know you've been talking to my girlfriend." On the second night he tried to chat with me as if we were friends. I sent him a text saying, "In case my attitude is not clear, we are not friends. We can talk when you are ready to drop this imagined fuckboy attitude of yours. I hate you."

The following day there was a party for all the artists. He came over to me and said, "Let's talk." I was drunk. I told him, "What really bothers me is that you wasted my time for a whole year until you found someone you really like. I spent all of this time thinking about someone who didn't care for me. Did you ever have any feelings for me?" I spent the rest of the time at the party crying. He could see me. I didn't care. I'm not capable of hiding my emotions.

I feel trapped in this pattern with men. They meet me. They like me. They don't want to date me. I've had lots of lovers but only one boyfriend. He was a Kenyan guy who suffered from bipolar disorder and eventually committed suicide. Sometimes I wonder if that relationship counts. Did he only date me because his own emotions swung from one extreme to another? We dated for a really short time—two months. We met about five years ago. At the time, I was working in the Democratic Republic of Congo and had a trip to Kenya, so a few weeks prior to that, I went on Tinder and started browsing. We met up when I arrived in Nairobi and started dating. I didn't realize that he had a mental health condition when we first met. In retrospect it all makes sense now. It explains the hard drugs and why he was always drunk. I can now see that was his effort to self-medicate and control his moods. Our relationship was a difficult one. He would either be very sweet or extremely violent. He was also unpredictable.

One day we went to a party together, and he got so drunk that I had to physically prop him up. Later that evening he vanished, leaving me to pay for all the drinks. He also never had any money. At the time I was working for the United Nations and so I was earning a good salary. I decided to rent us a love nest in Malindi on the Kenyan coast so we could go on vacation together. He couldn't even find any money to make the trip. I felt that I couldn't pay for our accommodation as well as the cost of his travel there, and so I went on the trip alone. Eventually we broke up because I told him about a time I went out for drinks with someone else during a period when we had not been talking. I was back in Congo then and feeling very lonely. I wanted to get back at him, so I told him that I was pregnant, which wasn't true. That wasn't my smartest move. He was the only guy that claimed me as a girlfriend and told me that he loved me.

As a dark-skinned Black girl growing up in France, you're never chosen. Nobody sends you a letter saying you're not desirable. You can just see that the girls who have boyfriends are not like you. They don't even look like you when they're Black. They are the girls with good hair, or they are white or Arabs. That didn't bother me in my teens. I had no interest in boys and none of my friends were dating anyone either. It was only when I went to university that I started to become interested in boys. I had no idea how I could meet someone who would like me back. And then I traveled to Spain for an internship. There was a stereotypically good-looking German man who lived on the floor above mine— tall, blond, with blue eyes. I was twenty-one to his thirty-five and ready to no longer be a virgin. There were also three white girls who stayed in the same apartment block. One of them also liked this man. I had an argument with her and told her, "This one is mine." He ended up choosing me.

It was only when I traveled to Liverpool in the UK to study that I realized that men were attracted to me. I was in an environment where there were lots of international students. I particularly remember one Indigenous student from Mexico who had a huge crush on me. I wasn't interested in him at all and it was only years later that I realized that I too had been brainwashed and guilty of the same thing that I was accusing Black men of. I had only been interested in dating white guys. Like this other guy who I also met in Spain but was originally from a village in Bavaria, Germany. We kept seeing each other intermittently even after I moved back to France and he was back in Germany. This went on for about three years. I was always the one pursuing him. I told him, "Let's date." He said, "No, you're too young." I was too young to date but I wasn't too young to fuck. We stayed in touch until I realized he was fetishizing me. He only dated Black girls. In bed he would say things to me like, "I love your features. I love your arse." One day he told me that as a child he had watched a lot of MTV videos and seen Black girls shaking their arses. That's where his desire for Black women sprang from.

The last white guy I dated was Italian, although we met in France. He used to call me chocolate. I felt really uncomfortable with that but just didn't have the language to express my feelings. When he went back home to Italy I visited him. People there were racist. They would try and touch my hair and make fun of me. All he said was, "Ignore them, they're from the village." There was one particular occasion that I have tried really hard to wipe from my memory. We were with a large group of his friends. We must have been about twenty-five in number. Most of the people in the group were men. One guy asked, "Where are you from?"

"I'm from France."

"You're Black, is your pussy black too?"

All of this time the guy I was with said nothing. It was a random guy in the group who eventually told this other man off. The final nail in the coffin of our somewhat relationship was this Italian guy claiming to know more about racism than I did because he had a PhD on the subject.

I once had a chat with a Black Portuguese friend of mine. I told him, "I don't really like Black boys."

"That's racist thinking."

"It's not racist, it's my preference."

In the years that followed I began to realize that my preference had been built in a society that demeans Black people. I've always loved reading romantic books. As a child I read Coeur Grenadine, a collection of romantic books targeted at teen girls between the ages of twelve to sixteen. There were no Black people in these stories. In France you barely see Black people on TV, and in the few instances they appear they are never shown as part of a community. For example, Black people are never coupled on French TV. You might see on screen a mixed-race woman who is dating a white person and vice versa. So when I came to that realization, I said to myself, "No more white guys. I'm going to focus on Black guys."

That's when I learned about Black love and how it's more than just romantic love—it's love for you, love for your people, love for your history, and for your children. This was really powerful to me as someone who grew up in France, where the imperialist strategy has been assimilation. We're told to be as white as possible, which means we end up hating ourselves. This is something I have observed in my own family. Like the time that my sister wanted to move out and live in a new neighborhood. My mum's reaction was, "This place is nice, but if one or two Black families move there, the neighborhood will start to become a ghetto." I had to point out to them, "You are the Black family moving there."

When I decided to proactively try to date Black guys, I went on a couple of Tinder dates that were actually really horrible because the men were simply trying to get me to go to hotel rooms with them. At the time I still lived with my mum, whose house was an hour outside Paris, so logistically even trying to socialize was difficult, as I always needed to leave town by a certain time.

One of my dates was with a man from Martinique. He seemed sweet, and told me that he was in a polyamorous relationship and thought I would get along with his girlfriend. I told him that wasn't my scene. A few months later after months of no sex, and with no prospective lovers on the horizon, I called him and said, "Invite me over, I just want to have sex." He told me to come over to his place after work. When I got there he made us dinner. He seemed really quiet and shy. As it got late I asked him, "Am I spending the night here?" He said yes. The whole evening he had been constantly texting on his phone. We got into bed and he was still on his phone. Eventually he said, "Sorry, I'm just texting with my girl. She doesn't want me to sleep with you." I was so angry. "Why did you invite me over then? Now it's too late for me to go back home and I have to spend the night here." I could barely sleep that night. At 5 a.m. in the dead of a freezing winter I woke up and let myself out of his place and caught the first train home. He didn't even bother to wake up and see me out. He didn't even text me later to check if I had gotten home safely.

I decided then that I needed to change my strategy. I would stop chasing men and allow them to chase me. A couple of months later I got a message from Pierre; he told me that he was coming to visit his parents in Paris and wanted to know if I fancied meeting up. Initially I couldn't remember him and then he reminded me that we had originally met in Ghana at the 2017 Chale Wote festival. At the time, I was in a good space in my life. I had just moved from my mum's house and was feeling really good about myself in general.

I put on a cute outfit and met him for dinner. He was hot, I looked hot, you could practically feel the chemistry sizzle. We went back to my place and started to kiss and fondle each other. Usually I rush through foreplay because I want to get to the physical intercourse, but since developing endometriosis, penetration can be painful, especially when I'm having a flare-up. So we're kissing, making out, and then he goes down on me, which feels really good. Then he starts to finger me, which I don't enjoy. I try to communicate this to him but it's a struggle. He's the first French guy I'd had sex with and for the first time I'm fucking in French. The words don't come easily to me. I'm used to fucking in English. I watch porn in English. I don't have the language for sex in French. I tell him: "I don't like being fingered. It kind of hurts."

"Why? What's wrong with fingering?"

"Nothing. It just kind of hurts."

He stops for a few minutes and then later starts fingering me again. I try to tell myself, "Relax, maybe you'll like it." It was still painful, and I didn't enjoy it. Later I beat myself up. "How can you call yourself a feminist and not even speak up when you're not enjoying sex?" Recently he got back in touch with me and told me that he was coming back to Paris on a short visit. I told him, "If we're going to sleep together there is something I have to tell you. I suffer from endometriosis. Sometimes penetrative sex is painful. I told you the last time to stop fingering me but you didn't listen." He was really apologetic and said, "I didn't know you had that condition. Let's talk about this the next time I'm there."

I was really surprised and I know that's setting the bar really low. I've had bad experiences when I've previously told other guys about endo. There was this mixed-race guy—he was German and Black Brazilian, we originally met back in 2012 and had stayed in touch. It felt really rough the first time we had sex, and more like an act of solo masturbation for him. I might as well not have been there. One time he called me up and asked me if I wanted to accompany him on a trip to Portugal. This is something I experience quite a bit, men wanting me to travel with them to a different country but not offering to buy my ticket or cover any of my expenses. It's like they think I am a traveling sex toy. I said no. Sometime last year he got in touch. He was in Paris and wanted to know if I wanted to meet up in his hotel. I went over. I had a bad case of endometriosis at the time, and sometimes that would cause me to have my period randomly. I told him I couldn't have penetrative sex. He suggested we have anal sex. I said no. He became very insistent. I told him, "That's not okay. I have told you that I don't want to have penetrative sex and you're being insistent." He demanded that I suck his dick. I said no. He lost his temper. "Why are you exaggerating? It's always like this with you." That was the last time we saw each other.

Sometimes all I want is for someone to hug and caress me. I miss intimacy. As an adult no one touches you unless you're having sex. I feel this lack especially in winter. At least in the summertime you can be outside, you can dance and let go that way.

Sometimes I think I would have been able to be in more long-term relationships if I wasn't a feminist because I would cut men more slack. I don't really like men but unfortunately I am sexually attracted to them. This just proves that sexuality is not a choice. All my friends are LGBTQ people of color. They are the people I feel comfortable with. I go to queer parties where I am unlikely to meet straight Black men but those are the spaces where I feel safe.

I've missed out on romantic love, and I've missed out on experiencing young love. My friend coined this term, "hetero decadence." It describes how Black girls experience love in the European context. Of knowing that you are regarded as the bottom of the pyramid, and yet trying to navigate equality in your relationships with men. Recognizing that you still desire men even though they are not good for you. I really identify with this. Hetero decadence captures my life.

I wonder if I will ever have an equal relationship with a man. None of my strategies work. I'm back in Ghana for the Chale Wote festival and I'm still sad about Akwete. I ask myself why I've allowed him to get under my skin. I've spent a year obsessed with him and he wasn't even my boyfriend. I feel so tired of it all. I'll be turning thirty soon and I'm asking myself all sorts of questions. Will I have children one day? How will this happen when I'm perennially single? I feel like I'm never going to end up in a loving, committed relationship. My therapist says that the fact that something has never happened, doesn't mean it will never happen. That's not how I feel. When you have never been desired or wanted, it is difficult for you to imagine that you will be desired. When you've had several boyfriends, you can think, This is just a dry spell. I can't think like that. I don't have a lot of self-confidence even though it looks like I do. My friends tell me, "You're flirty with everyone," but I'm not flirty with the people that I am really interested in because I feel like I have no chance with them. So now I'm giving up on Black men. I'm not going to date anyone anymore.

When I initially met Esther over Zoom, she had on a bonnet and explained that she was going to need to multitask while we were chatting. She was prepping signs for a Black Lives Matter protest that she was going to attend right after our interview. Esther was one of the folks who DM'd me after seeing one of my callouts via Twitter. I tended to ask the women who responded to my invitation, "Why are you interested in being interviewed for a book about the sex lives of African women?" Invariably they would say something along these lines: "I am a feminist and I think it's important that these stories should be told."

Esther is a twenty-eight-year-old cisgender, heterosexual woman who is originally from Cameroon, was raised in Kenya, and is currently studying in the US. In speaking to her I remembered all the stories that I had heard as a young person about the children of pastors. In Ghana at least it was well known that the most rebellious children were the offspring of pastors and extremely religious people. I had always read that as a logical act of resistance to growing up within a very strict or fundamentalist environment.

I hadn't thought of what I now think all parents should be aware of. A well-behaved child who suddenly starts to "act out" may not just be rebelling for no good reason, but could have experienced an extremely traumatic event.

The following story includes experiences of child rape and sexual assault.

ESTHER

.

I STARTED LOOKING up websites on sexuality and found Lust Cinema, a feminist site run by a woman who specializes in creating erotic videos for women. All you need to do is send in your fantasy, and voilà, an erotic video is created specifically for you. The people she works with are well paid, not people who have been drugged or are being forced to engage in sexual acts. I paid $13 a month and for that entire semester kept up my subscription. I also kept a journal during that period and would write down how I felt as I watched the films. At the beginning I used to feel a lot of guilt. My inner dialogue would say things like, Why would someone fantasize about doing something like this? or, What on earth is going on here? but as I continued watching I started to become less judgmental of other people's desires.

I decided the next step was to buy a sex toy and to practice on myself. I bought the toy and hid it at the bottom of my closet. It remained there for two months. I would ask myself, Why did you even bother to buy that toy? You spent so much money on it. I made up my mind that I would take out the toy at the last possible minute, when it was almost time for me to hand in my project for my human sexuality course. At the beginning of the semester we had been given this assignment: Go out of your comfort zone and do something you have never done before sexually. Or interview a person from an older generation, like a grandparent, about what sexuality means for them, and how it has evolved over the course of their life. My only living grandparent lives in France, so that assignment option was not a viable one for me.

In our human sexuality course we had been exposed to so many alternatives. Our professor brought in guest lecturers from different sex clubs, including people from the BDSM world. I didn't feel like I wanted to explore

BDSM and so thought I could start with sex toys. It was while searching for sex toys online that I initially came across Lust Cinema.

I kept an eye on my essay deadline with a mixed sense of dread and appreciation, and as the date drew closer I decided to experiment. I went to my room, closed my curtains, and lit some candles. I took off my clothes and laid a fresh towel on my bed. All the reading I had done about masturbation had advised that you do that. I clicked play on one of the erotic videos, got out my toy, and turned it on. I just kept saying, "Ohmygosh, ohmygosh, ohmygosh." I not only came three times, but also squirted. Afterwards I continued to lie on my bed in a dreamlike haze. I said to myself, Just enjoy this, but I kept hearing the sounds from the video, which I had left running. I started to feel dirty so I turned it off.

That was the first time I squirted and no man did that for me. I had done that for myself. I remember thinking, I know what my body can do, and I know how to get there.

Throughout my teenage years, sex with men had been them saying to me, "Nitaguzisha tu." I'll just touch it, let me just tap it. I would usually start by saying "No, no, no," but would eventually give up because this scenario would often happen at a guy's house after I'd gone over so we could watch a film together, or after visiting during the day. I also gave in to persistent requests for sex frequently because jumping through all the hoops to maintain my virginity had made no difference in the long run.

At thirteen I went to a party with my best friend. We had told our parents that we were going to the mall. I even asked my parents for money even though I knew that I was not going to use it. We were on vacation because we were waiting to enter high school, and so a lot of children in the community where I lived would regularly go to the mall to hang out. At the time we lived in a gated community and we had heard about this party that was happening outside our estate. My best friend had been invited by her boyfriend, who had just finished high school. I had a crush on her boyfriend's friend but had never spoken to him before, even though we regularly saw each other because our friends were dating, and we lived in the same neighborhood.

At the party, everybody was on the dance floor while I stood in a corner. I was a pastor's child and so I didn't drink or smoke weed at parties like all the other kids. I was also a bad dancer and so I just stood on the sidelines of the dance floor and watched everyone else. People would walk out for a smoke or to chat with friends, and then come back on the dance floor. My best friend was dancing with her boyfriend. And then *he* came over to speak to me. It was the first time we had ever spoken. He told me, "I've been watching you. You look really nice." I thought, Yes, he's finally noticed me. After chitchatting for a while he said, "I need to go home and get a jacket. Are you also cold?" It was about 9 p.m. at the time and a chilly Nairobi evening. I agreed to accompany him home. When we got there I initially stood outside the gate until he insisted I come in. In the living room I perched on the arm of the sofa as he went into his bedroom. He turned me around, helped me into the jacket, and turned me around again so I was now facing him. Then he leaned down and kissed me. That was the first time anyone had ever kissed me. I kissed him back until he started pulling me down towards the sofa.

"Sit on me."

"No. Can we go back to the party now?"

"Why are you scared? Is this your first time?"

"Please, let's go back to the party."

By now we were tussling on the sofa. I kept saying no, and he kept saying, "You don't need to be scared." We were in this unholy dance for what felt like hours. I realized nothing I said was going to make a difference. No one was coming to rescue me. All his housemates were at the party and he was stronger and bigger than I was. I stopped struggling and it happened. I felt so ashamed when it was all over. I turned and buried myself deeper into the sofa. I heard him walk out and after a while he came back in.

"The party is over and your friend has left."

"What am I going to do? How am I going to get home? What am I going to tell my parents?"

I felt sore, it was a struggle to move. I remember noticing that there was no blood. I had always thought there would be blood. I ended up spending the night at his house because I couldn't face my parents. I thought the Holy Spirit would tell them what I had done. After all, I had willingly gone to the party, accompanied him to his house, and kissed him back. How was I going to tell my parents that I had done all of that?

In the morning I still couldn't face the thought of seeing my parents, so went to see one of my aunties instead. She took one look at me and asked, "What's wrong?" I told her that I had gone out the day before, and hadn't yet returned home. She responded with a barrage of questions: "Where did you sleep? You can't just say you blacked out. Were you drunk? Have you been smoking drugs?"

I kept saying no, no, no. She kept asking, "What happened?" I told her I had gone to a party and met a group of guys. They had told me about another party and so I had gone with them only to find out when we got there that I was the only girl at the party. And then the guys left me in the room with a guy I didn't know. I made up this story because I didn't want anybody to know who the guy actually was. He lived in my neighborhood and was considered one of the good guys.

My aunt took me home, and my parents took me to a newly opened women's hospital. My mum kept crying and I remember thinking, Why is she crying? At the hospital they examined me and gave me antiretroviral drugs. I told them I didn't know who the guys were and so they didn't file a case but told me they had opened a file in my name and that whenever I remembered we could open a case.

Months later my parents decided to hire a home tutor for me. The guy they selected was the same one who had raped me. That is when I finally told my mum the truth. My parents were really angry but they did what they always do whenever anything bad happens. They decided to fast and pray and forgave him.

I have never forgiven him nor have I ever forgotten his name. I know everything about him. I knew when he got married. I know about his family. I know about his children. For years I stalked every detail of his life. I was determined that I was the one who was going to turn him in to the police. He caused me years of damage. I grew distant from my family. After that experience I thought there was no point in abstinence and so I started sleeping around. After school I would go out, and sleep over in the homes of friends. My younger brother started to act up too. He would say, "You're always going out so I can go out too." He even started doing drugs. It took years for him to straighten out. I held on to so much guilt for so many years because he would say, "I'm following my big sister. I can do whatever she's doing." It made no difference when I said, "But I'm not doing drugs."

By the time I turned fifteen my parents were at the end of their tether. I went from being someone who taught Sunday school, served in church, and sang in the praise and worship team to being a girl who openly defied her parents. I would say to them, "I don't like you. Are you even my parents?" By then my parents had gotten to the stage where they would ask the house help to lock me in the house whenever they were going out. Then they decided to send me home to Cameroon. I think they made that choice because that is where our church is headquartered.

When I got there I found out that they had told everyone about me because people kept saying to me, "We're praying for you. This is just a trying moment." I felt so angry. Why were they telling everyone my business? I decided to move away from the church family they had placed me with and moved in with some of our relatives. I became friends with the other pastors' children, who were also seen as the rebellious ones. All we were interested in doing was partying. It was in Cameroon that I first tasted alcohol, but even then I was always careful to keep myself safe. I had made up my mind that I wanted to go back to abstinence. I felt like trash. I had already slept with so many people and I was no longer interested in dating boys. All I wanted to do was party and then come home. I spent two years in Cameroon before returning home to Kenya. That's when I met the guy who would become the father of my child.

I'd missed my period two months in a row and so bought a test kit. One evening, while helping my mum in the kitchen, I slipped upstairs to use my bathroom so I could pee on the stick. I left the cup there and went back downstairs to continue helping my mum. Our relationship had improved and we were starting to spend more time together. We finished making the meal, and the whole family sat down to dinner. When I went back upstairs I checked on the stick. I was definitely pregnant. I didn't say anything to anyone until I started showing. I didn't even tell the boy I had gotten pregnant with because by the time I realized I was pregnant, I had broken up with him—I had found out that he was seeing other girls. I must have been five months pregnant when I finally opened up to my mum. She said, "I already knew, I was waiting for you to tell me."

I had a defiant attitude towards my pregnancy. I knew people would say, "What did you expect? She was such a rebellious child." I was determined not to care what people would say about me. My father, who was the lead pastor of our church, delivered a letter of excommunication to me. I was told that this was a unanimous decision taken by the church, whose members were now forbidden to speak to me. Members of my own family could only speak to me about particular issues of concern to the family at large. As my father handed me the letter he told me what the conditions were for being accepted back into the folds of the church. I had to repent of my sins and to pray for forgiveness from God, the members of the church, and my family. He also had a personal condition. I needed to name the person who had made me pregnant. At the time I had refused to tell them who the man was.

I ended up apologizing to my family. I still loved God and the church, and I had just found my way back to enjoying all the activities in the church again. I also knew that sex before marriage is a sin. I felt that it was wrong of me to have gotten pregnant and to have shamed my parents, who were highly regarded as religious icons. I had let them down in the worst possible way.

When I was six months pregnant my ex found out about the pregnancy and called me. He asked what I was going to do about it. I told him, "I'm not going to answer that," and hung up. When I was eight months pregnant, I was out with my friends at a restaurant and saw him. He was with another woman. When he noticed me he sent the other woman away and came to my table. He knelt down, cried, and said, "Can I feel your belly?" I said no, and my friends told him to get away from me. I still hadn't told my family who had impregnated me, but my dad involved the police, who found out who the guy was, and one day we went over to his family's house. His family and my family made some agreements, which his family never honored. To date, my family have been the only ones who have supported me in raising my son, whom I had at eighteen.

I am now twenty-eight and I have found that being a single mother shapes the types of relationships I am able to have. There are some people who do not want to date mothers, or they want to be with me but not my son. Sometimes people don't understand if I turn down a date because I need to take care of my son, or be with him. My last boyfriend told me when he broke up with me, "You're a good person. It's not you. I just don't see myself being happy with you, or being able to make you happy." I hadn't ever said to him that I was unhappy. On the contrary, I had wanted the relationship to deepen, but when I tried to quiz him about why he really wanted to end the relationship he said, "Let's drop it." I've been in that situation a few times now and it always makes me wonder, Is it because I have a child? Sometimes I break up with someone, and then a few months later I find out that they have married someone else. It's like I was a stepping stone on their path to bliss.

In my relationships I've sometimes found it hard to express my sexual needs. I'm concerned people will judge me and think, No wonder you're a single mother. It's easy to feel guilty for wanting sexual pleasure. I've had guys break up with me because I told them they did not prioritize my sexual needs. There are moments where I wonder, Am I going to be alone for the rest of my life? I'm tired of having flings. I want a relationship. I would like to get married one day. I'll keep on praying.

Baaba, a twenty-nine-year-old Ghanaian woman, was the very first person I interviewed for this book, in 2015. I had been mulling the idea of writing a nonfiction book about African women's experiences of sex and sexuality for a year when she sent me a long DM that included the following query:

"I'm getting serious urges to be with a girl although I'm in a relationship. It bothers me, and at the same time intrigues me. I hardly get turned on by heterosexual porn. Lesbian porn does it for me. So Nana, am I bi, a suppressed lesbian, or just confused? Help."

My wannabe agony aunt kicked in and I responded:

"In my opinion we don't rigidly fit into boxes so we are never really completely straight, bi, or lesbian. I think of sexuality as a spectrum. It is just that society makes us feel guilty about anything outside societal norms and that is the issue. As long as a sexual act involves consenting adults then it's all good. Enjoying lesbian porn doesn't make you lesbian. On the other hand, so what if you are lesbian? And so what if you're bi? What's important is that you love yourself and experience love."

For the next three months we chatted back and forth. Baaba asked if we could meet in person, and I in turn asked if I could interview her, which she agreed to. In our first meeting she was super nervous, and I was probably a bit unsure of how to go about the interview, and so we just chatted and drank some wine. In our next meeting I turned my recorder on and we started our conversation in earnest. In total we ended up having three interview sessions.

The following story includes experiences of rape and sexual assault.

BAABA

.

HE TOLD ME that if something like this ever happened he wouldn't turn his back on me, but that was exactly what he did. He said, "I can't do this." I was confused. I didn't know what to do, where to go for help. Maybe if he had stood by me I could have been stronger. I was old enough and I was studying for my master's at the time.

My mum, a strict Christian, had always warned me and my sisters, "No sex before marriage. Don't let anyone touch your breasts. No kissing." She was very polite to male friends who came over, but after they left, she would come to our room and ask, "Who is he to you? Remember, you come from a good Christian home." My response was always, "I know, I know . . ."

He took me to a clinic. The nursing sister asked if I'd had a pregnancy test done. I had; I was just over four weeks in. She wanted to know how old I was. Twenty-five.

"Are you sure you want to do this?" she asked.

"Yes," I lied.

I knew I would have it on my conscience forever. She gave me two pills. I took one. I was supposed to take the other in a couple of hours.

"Make sure you are home resting when you take the second pill. There will be some pain."

I took the pill later on that night. At that moment, I didn't feel much. It was just a litany in my head: You are committing an abortion, is this really going to work, do you even want this to work?

In the morning I still felt fine, so I started prepping for class, as I had to participate in a group presentation. Initially, it felt like menstrual cramps—my lower abdomen felt heavy, then my legs started to wobble. I decided to warn one of my group members that I was going to be late. Suddenly, the pain ripped through my stomach, it felt as if someone was wrenching out its contents. It surpassed the worst of menstrual cramps. I cursed those pills.

My boyfriend had to call one of my friends and tell her that I wasn't going to make it to class that day because I was sick. He called his employees and told them he couldn't come into the office. He just sat there holding my hand and looking at me. This was in 2012; by then we had been in a relationship for three years.

Soon after my boyfriend and I started dating in 2009, I noticed an abnormal smell in my panties, and I would feel a burning pain whenever I peed. I went to the clinic, they gave me some pills, and I felt better. Two years later I had the same experience. I told my boyfriend about it. He said maybe I needed to take better care of my hygiene, iron my panties perhaps, or that I had gotten something from shared bathrooms. I went back to the campus clinic again, was given some medication, and got better. The third time it happened was in 2013. I was out of university then so went to see my family doctor. He asked me how many times I had experienced this. He wanted to know if I was sexually active. He told me to be more careful, to use protection, and that my partner would also have to be tested and treated. I ended up in hospital for five days. I was given three different types of drugs intravenously. *He* only needed to go to hospital for one shot. My mum assumed that I had picked up an infection of some sort from school or some other public toilet. I couldn't tell her the truth.

He kept asking me for a threesome. I thought this particular friend of mine wouldn't mind. There was that one time when she had been bored and asked me to come over. We started off watching straight porn, and then lesbian porn. I felt turned on. I asked her if she wanted to play. She was up for some fun. I sucked her nipples and played with her boobs. That turned her on so much that she came. I licked her clit a bit. She didn't return the favor. That put me off. It was my second experience with a girl.

The first time was at my university. I was twenty-one at the time. I was in a room with this other girl, my then boyfriend, and his friends. They dared the other girl and me to kiss. It ended up being more like a peck on the lips.

And afterwards she started being overly friendly to me. She would call to ask how I was, and come over to my hostel to see me. She told me about her previous experiences with girls in secondary school. She told me about how she and her previous girlfriends used to touch each other. I was very curious and always asked her lots of questions about what sex with another woman was like. One time she came over to my room and my roommate was not around. We kissed a bit; she touched my boobs, sucked on my nipples. She wanted to touch me down there but I had my period. She said, "What a shame. I would have loved to lick you." I couldn't help but think, Oh no, first I was having sex, now I'm having sex with a woman. Later on we progressed to tribbing, but I wasn't that into her, so things trailed off. She was quite round, and big. I am not into big people. After that I started watching more lesbian porn to try and understand what really goes on between women. I found out that lesbian porn turned me on more than heterosexual porn. Even when my boyfriend and I were watching porn together I would ask for us to watch lesbian porn. At first he was surprised, and then he asked if I have a thing for girls and whether I had ever been with a girl. He said to me, "Tell me if you ever want to have sex with a girl."

One evening we went out drinking with my friend. The same one I had hooked up with previously. She got tipsy, I got tipsy. It was too late to drop her off at her house so we decided to crash at my boyfriend's. He gave us his room and went to sleep in the living room. My friend fell asleep. I went back out and asked him to come to the room. He asked if I was sure. I said yes. We started having sex on the bed. My friend was lying next to us. I think she was more drunk than I was. I asked him to touch her—so he was touching her and fucking me. After we were done he asked me to touch her. I think that was only when she realized what was happening. Then my boyfriend asked me if he could fuck her. At some point in time I found myself looking at them thinking, My boyfriend is fucking my friend. It wasn't a good feeling.

In the morning it was so awkward. He was still asleep when she woke up. She went into the bathroom. I followed her. The only thing she said to me was, "This never happened." After she left I told him it didn't feel good to see him fuck my friend. He said he understood. A few months afterwards he asked for another threesome. Then he started asking to have anal sex. I said no. Regular sex with him was already uncomfortable. There were times I would feel pain so would push him away during sex and he would get upset. He would say, "You should relax, you should relax . . ." He would say it in a way that would make me feel that I was being boring. He was very aggressive in bed. He liked rough sex. There were a few times he would ask if I was okay because he could see the pain on my face. He would get some lube. It helped somewhat but he always stayed hard for a long time. I would end up getting uncomfortable so he would have to pull out and touch himself. I never came through vaginal penetration. I would have to touch myself or he would rub my clit till I came.

I feel like I gave up so much for him. And yet the one time I made a mistake he never let me forget it. We were lying in bed one day, he got a phone call, and afterwards went to the bathroom. When he came back he said, "How long have you been having an affair?" I denied everything. That made him even more angry. He said he had evidence, messages between me and the other guy. It was then that I confessed. Do you know how he found out? There was this girl who was a friend of his. He would go out of town to meet her. He said he was mentoring her, helping her with her writing. I felt very insecure about their relationship. He told me there was nothing going on between them. I had also started to write but he wasn't interested in my writing. And then I became friends with this other guy. He was also creative, and in the same industry as my boyfriend; in fact they had worked together on a big project. This guy started sharing his poetry with me. He said, "I hear you're a shark, just have a look through this and let me know if there is anything missing." I told him that I had also started writing and shared my work with him. He told me, "You're pretty good for someone who has just started writing. You should definitely continue." We started chatting over Black-Berry Messenger about random things. My boyfriend was often away working so when I was bored I would send him little jokes and things I found amusing. Usually when I messaged my boyfriend he wouldn't reply because he was busy, or would respond much later. This guy was the opposite.

One day he asked me to meet him at the mall so we could hang out, but when I got there he said something had come up and he needed to rush home, so I should come with him for a short while and then I could go back to campus. That was the first time we had sex. It was rough. He fucked me like he had a point to prove. I still remember his smokers' breath. That put me off. At the same time there was the excitement of sleeping with someone new I was attracted to. He was quite athletic, but not overly so, and taller than my boyfriend. I felt guilty about cheating and when I got back to campus sent him a message. "This can't happen again." He said, "It won't happen again. I'm not going to worry you with such things. Can we stay friends?" We went back to our normal friendship and regular chats. One day he wrote, "I miss you and what happened. Is there no chance of this happening again?"

And so I was in shock when my boyfriend found out about the affair. The whole thing had been a setup. The guy I had slept with had wanted to get back at my boyfriend for something that had previously happened between the two of them. He selected those messages that made it look like *I* had been pursuing him and sent them to the girl that my boyfriend said he was mentoring. She was the one who called him that day before he went to the bathroom. When he went to work later that day he had been acting strangely, so one of his colleagues took him aside to find out what was wrong. Later on I got a call from the girlfriend of that colleague. He had told them what had happened. They had tried to calm him down; they said to him, "These things happen, just try and fix it. You guys have come too far to let this end. You should be able to fix it."

When the girl called she told me to leave the house that day, to find somewhere else to go to so that things wouldn't turn violent. I packed my things and went to his sister's place. After he finished work he came by and would just sit and stare at me, mainly in silence. When he spoke he would say something along the lines of, "Why would you do that? I can't believe it. With that guy of all people?" I kept begging for him to forgive me. I told him it had only happened once, and I had ended things that very month. His sister's room had two twin beds, that night I slept on one, and he on the other, except he didn't sleep much, and neither did I. He would lie down, get up, stare at me, and ask me the same questions over and over again. In the morning he left for work, when he came back he said, "I don't think we can go on. This is a mess. I don't know how I can deal with it. It's best to end things now." I begged him to forgive me, to not leave. We stayed together for a while in a hell-like existence. He became very abusive. He would have sudden outbursts, insult me, and later on become apologetic. I felt like the worst person on earth.

In that period it felt like all that we had gone through together was worthless, even the abortion. Three months went by like this. On Christmas Eve I was at home with my family when I got a call from him. He said, "What else have you not told me? How many times did you sleep with that guy?" Do you remember that girl he was mentoring? She had sent him some more messages which proved that I had slept with the guy at least twice and not once like I had told my boyfriend. I had been too scared to tell him the truth initially.

My boyfriend had been out of town the second time it happened. The guy had messaged me saying, "I want to see you, nothing would happen this time." I was gullible. I went over to his house one evening and he said to me, "Your boyfriend doesn't deserve you. Why are you even with him? He doesn't have time for you. At least I have been a great friend to you. Why don't you give us a chance?" I said, "I can't. I've already messed up once." He responded, "If you've messed up once why can't you do it again? It's not like anyone will know. If it comes out it will hurt me as well." He told me he needed to take a shower and went to his room. After a while he called out, "Can you come and check out something?" When I went to his room he only had a towel wrapped around him. He locked the door and said, "I know this shouldn't be happening but I just can't let you go." I felt some fear—what had I gotten myself into? He started to kiss me, and dropped his towel. I could feel his erection. When you are in that situation with a guy who's stronger than you, it gets to a point where you just let it happen . . . This time he wasn't as forceful as before. When I got back to campus I sent him another message. "This can never happen again and this time we can't even stay friends."

Of course my boyfriend didn't believe me when I told him it happened only twice, and that I had ended things the very same month. When he called me that Christmas Eve he accused me of lying to him and said he was coming over. It was almost midnight. My parents were asleep; the gates to the house were locked up. I had no idea how I would even get to see him. I called him back to try and persuade him not to come over. He didn't pick up. Within ten minutes of his call I could smell the burn from his tires. It would normally have taken at least thirty minutes for him to arrive at my house. He reeked of alcohol and weed. He started shouting, "You're lying to me again. What haven't you told me? How long did the affair go on? Tell me the truth."

I tried to reason with him. "It's late. The neighbors will hear . . ." He was still swigging from a bottle of Guinness in his car. He smashed the bottle on the pavement. I don't know how I managed to persuade him to go home but eventually he left. The next day he turned up at my house for Christmas lunch like nothing had happened. He sat down, and said hello to everybody. I was scared to sit by him. He asked me why I was behaving strangely. I didn't know how to act. I was confused. Was he pretending for the sake of my family? He sat there quietly for most of the day. He told me not to worry about it. He said he had forgiven me.

I had a talk with his mum. He had told her what happened. He said he needed to talk to someone. She told me that these things happen even in marriages, and that she believed that he and I had come too far and "beating one side of the drum" will just keep the wounds open. She said, "Stay away from the past and focus on forging ahead." I couldn't tell anyone in my family about what had happened so hearing those words from his mum gave me hope. In spite of how understanding she had been I was very worried about the future. I thought one day she would remind me of my past, and how filthy I was.

Even though he said he had forgiven me, his behavior did not depict that. He kept bringing up the affair. He would say, "I can't forget the past. I want to get back at that guy. I want to hurt him." He would wake up in the morning full of anger and rage. One time I walked into a restaurant and he was there having lunch with this girl. He didn't say a word to me. That was when I realized that he had started cheating on me again. Later on I found out that all along he had two girlfriends on the side that I didn't know about. I don't think I can ever forgive him. He doesn't care about anything I went through for him, especially the baby.

Once I started this book I was always seeking out African women to interview wherever I went. In 2015 I went on holiday for the very first time to São Tomé and Príncipe, an island in Central Africa. While sitting in a tour bus, I struck up a conversation with the friendly male guide and asked him if he knew any São Toméan women who would be open to being interviewed for a book about sex. He later introduced me to his friend Vera Cruz, a thirty-two-year-old heterosexual woman.

This was the most challenging interview I did for the book because Vera Cruz and I had no languages in common. She's most fluent in Portuguese, and my first language is English, and so with my eyes and body I did my best to convey warmth, sharing my motivations for this book project before launching into a mediated conversation with the help of the guide I had hired as a translator. In our conversation I was struck by one key difference between São Toméans and other African cultures that I know. São Toméans are not obsessed with marriage. At least according to Vera Cruz. When a São Toméan woman gets pregnant, for instance, she just moves in with the family of the man who has impregnated her. I pressed Vera Cruz on this point several times, although of course it is extremely possible that something was lost in translation. "So before you move in with a man do you go through any traditional marriage ceremonies?" "Do you have to get married in a church before you move in with a man?" The answer that came back to me time and time again was "No, no, no."

VERA CRUZ

·

IT MUST HAVE been around 10 p.m., I was on my way home from night school, and from the corner of my eye I saw his car start to slow down behind me. I have never been good with cars so I can't tell you what make and model it was, but it was a decent car; after all, he was a lawyer. I recognized him when he pulled up next to me. São Tomé is a small city, everyone knows everyone. He gave me a lift home, and took my number. The next day he took me out for dinner. Our relationship started soon afterwards. He was twice my age and treated me far better than my previous boyfriend had. He provided financially for my daughter and me. In my relationship with him I discovered that women too could experience sexual pleasure, and not just provide pleasure to others. The very first time I had an orgasm was with him. But he had two wives, and I wasn't prepared to be his third, so after three years I ended that relationship.

With my first boyfriend, sex had only been for his pleasure. We would lie on the bed, and we would each cover ourselves with our individual sleeping cloths. There might as well have been an ocean between us. I never felt I could reach over and touch him, or embrace him. The only time we touched in bed was when he wanted sex, and then he would mount me, cum, and then fall sleep. He was machismo, he never cared about my feelings, whether I wanted more sexually or was satisfied. We never spoke about sex or anything else for that matter.

In São Tomé, parents do not talk about sex with their children, at least my parents didn't. Sex is a taboo topic. What I was taught in biology class in school was very clinical. This is what a man's body looks like. This is what a woman's body looks like. This is how the body changes during puberty.

I met the father of my daughter when I was sixteen years old; he was twenty-four and taught at my school. He told my cousin that he wanted to get to know me, and so both of us went to visit him. Lots of girls in my school were involved with teachers, sometimes it was real love, other times it was because the girls wanted good grades. The first time we kissed it felt strange, my body was hot and tingly. One day I went to visit him, and as we were kissing and hugging he decided that was the day he was going to take my virginity. There was no discussion or conversation. Afterwards I bled for eight straight days. It's hard for me to say now why I stayed with him, or why I decided to have a child with him. Maybe it's because my grandmother told me that women cannot just change their men like they change their underwear, and that no man would want a woman who had been with other men.

At eighteen I decided to try to have a child with him; he wanted to have a child, he was of an age where people expected him to have a child, and when I soon got pregnant he told his parents who came to see my parents. Both families decided that it was best that I move in with my boyfriend and his family, which is the normal thing to do in São Toméan society. There was no formal wedding or church ceremony—that is not in our tradition. I joined my boyfriend in his parents' home; his older brother also lived there with his wife, as well as his younger brother. For a large family they were not very close. Each person just did his or her own thing. I found it very strange. They never ate together as a family; when people were home they stayed in their own room. I was always working like a "masace," an enslaved person.

A year after my daughter was born I decided to leave. My dad was very upset, and is still unhappy about that decision to this day. He told me, "I don't want a daughter who keeps changing her man." My mum, on the other hand, said, "If your relationship is not good, and you have decided to leave, you can count on me." I think she understood because she left my dad when I was eleven years old. I had saved some money from my job working as a secretary in my dad's factory, and built a small room as an annex to my mum's house, where I live now.

A few years ago I met another man and we had a son who is now five years old, but he went to Angola to work, and I don't know what is happening to us. I am still waiting for him to decide whether we are going to stay together and where we will stay. I am now thirty-two. I feel like I am getting old. It is tough to have two children and no husband.

I met Tafadzwa, a thirty-two-year-old bisexual Zimbabwean woman, while visiting Harare. She mentioned to me that she had a Ghanaian boyfriend, and I responded, "Ah, you're my sister-in-law," referencing an insider connection between Zimbabweans and Ghanaians. Robert Mugabe, the former president of Zimbabwe, was initially married to Sally Hayfron, a Ghanaian woman. Allegedly, she had been able to control his excesses, and until she passed, he had been a more benevolent leader.

Like Tafadzwa, and I assume many other children around the world, I also grew up playing mummy and daddy. Like Tafadzwa, and many other girls around the world, I was sexually abused as a child. Like Tafadzwa, my sex education as a child was a variation of "Don't play with boys, otherwise. . . ." The implication being that "playing with boys" would lead to pregnancy, which would of course naturally be followed by societal condemnation of the young girl (it's rare for the boy to be blamed), who then becomes condemned to a life as a struggling single parent. Luckily, that wasn't Tafadzwa's story. Like many women I spoke to for this book, she needs healing from sexual trauma and abuse, and is navigating a journey towards sexual freedom.

The following story includes experiences of rape and sexual assault.

TAFADZWA

·

Don't play with boys.
If you play with boys you will get pregnant.

I didn't really know or understand why I shouldn't play with boys. Nobody explained these things to me. I was just always being told off. When I was about four or five we used to play house. I was always the mother, different boys would play father. We would take off our underwear, the father would lie on top and push inside me, I would lie on the bottom, and then we would make the sounds. I knew that is what mothers and fathers did.

You're a problem child.
You'll get pregnant.

Condoms had fallen out of my skirt.

What do you want to use the condoms for?

It didn't matter that we had discussed condoms in school that day. No one asked me anything. I didn't even know if I had wanted to use the condoms or not. As usual, I got another beating, this time from my older siblings.

Do this.
Don't do that.
Here's a packet of pads.

That was the nature of my relationship with my mum. A series of do this, don't do that. We didn't even talk about periods. I didn't even know how I was supposed to use the pads she gave me.

By the time I was twelve or thirteen I was having sex with boys two or three years older than I was. At fifteen I was having sex with men who were ten years older than I was. Married men, men who were bosses, ministers, heads of military units . . . I realized that when they came they were reduced to nothing. By the time I was seventeen I had a voracious appetite for sex; I started masturbating, which is how I grew into being sexually confident.

Namazzi is an amazing lover. With her, I have come to realize that I have the most incredible orgasms when sex is not penetrative, when someone is playing with my clit. She has helped me understand and explore my body more. She plays with my breasts in a particular way. She is amazing with her tongue. One time she started to gently kiss my tits, played with my navel, and then went down. Just before my pelvic area is one of the most sensitive parts of my body, she lingered there, and then she touched me, put her mouth on me, and oh my god, her tongue work down there was amazing. In Uganda they practice a type of lovemaking known as *kachabali*. She has mastered the art of kachabali with her tongue. I started to tremble. She climbed on top of me and we started to rub our clits against each other. It was one of the most amazing sensations I have ever felt. We came together.

Namazzi claims to be in a polyamorous relationship, but I get the sense that her other woman doesn't know about me. Why else did she keep calling her at 3 a.m., when Namazzi was visiting me in Zimbabwe? What really made this obvious to me was when I visited her in Uganda. She had invited me to come over, she even bought my ticket, but after two days I had to move out of her bedroom into the spare room because her girlfriend had come to visit. One night we went clubbing. All three of us, like one big happy family. I was wining on her, shaking my booty, twerking on her. She was holding me close and feeling on my body. When we went home we were all over each other in the kitchen. And then we heard the sound of her bedroom door open, so we just stopped and pretended to be doing something else. I started washing the dishes, and she started warming up some food. I'm sure her girlfriend could sense something had happened when she got to the kitchen. It was obvious; there was a lot of tension in the air.

Our relationship has been strained ever since that visit. I came home feeling hurt. Even though I was also seeing someone else, I gave her my full attention when she was in my country, but that's not how she treated me when I visited her.

I met my Ghanaian boyfriend while I was attending university in South Africa. He realized I was from Zimbabwe and came over to chat with me. He called me "my in-law," referencing the relationship between Sally and Robert Mugabe, the first Zimbabwean president and his Ghanaian wife; we exchanged numbers, and he asked if we could go out for a drink sometime. The next day we bumped into each other on the Gautrain. He said, "I want to see you after your day is over." I agreed to visit him in his hostel. We spent hours lost in conversation. I didn't want to leave, and then he said: "It's too late for you to leave."

He had a tiny bed because he resided in student quarters. He then made what sounded like a complicated proposition to me.

"You can sleep on the bed and I can sleep on the floor, but can you allow me to sleep on the bed for a few minutes and then I'll sleep on the floor?"

"What is the point of you sleeping on the floor?"

"If you allow me to sleep me on the bed, can I touch you?" he asked.

"I don't mind if you do."

That's how our relationship started.

When we have sex he always makes sure I cum. The minute I get to his place we undress and make love. Two minutes later, we're at it again. He brings out the tigress in me; I can never tire of sex with him.

Recently I told him I wanted to have anal sex. He was reluctant. He thought having anal sex with a woman would mean he is homosexual. I think that's the most ridiculous thing. I bought lubricant, took it to him, and said, "I want anal sex." The experience with him was different than it had been with a previous lover because of the difference in penis size. It was pleasure pain. He withdrew after a while because he still couldn't get over his associations between anal sex and homosexuality. I said to him, "Are you a dog when you do doggy style?"

Not all my lovers have been amazing. There was this guy I used to date. One day he brought a friend over. We all sat in my lounge chatting, and then his friend fell asleep. My guy started to make moves on me. "Let's go to the room," I said, but he insisted that his friend was asleep and that we should stay in the room. We started to have sex and at some point in time his friend stood up, walked over, and put on a condom. My boyfriend held me down and his friend started to fuck me. They took it in turns, first one, then the other. I wanted to scream. I started crying, I cried the whole night. Eventually they left.

I had never felt so violated. I was raped that night. We had spoken about a threesome previously but I had not given my consent, it was just two men who decided to violate my body. I was just a lifeless body that they decided to do whatever they wanted with. I felt dirty; I felt my body didn't belong to me anymore. They had taken my body and made it their own. They went away with my soul that night. Afterwards I found it difficult to trust people. I had trusted that guy. I couldn't even make a report to the police. A part of me felt that I had invited that situation. I decided to block it out of my mind. It took me a while before I could start having relationships—I didn't want to see anyone, men or women. This was over four years ago. A part of me feels that I have dealt with the situation, I have cried, and had to pick the pieces up. A part of me feels I am a strong woman.

Retrospectively, I can see that the men I slept with in my teens were taking advantage of the fact that I was a child. My whole life I was sexualized. People would always say to me:

You have a big bum.
You have hips.

At the time I thought I was in relationships with these people but I can now see that what they had was a young person they could have sex with. All of them used to use protection religiously. Clearly this was to protect them in case anything happened. I see it for what it was now. I was just there to give them sexual pleasure.

I am a sexual being, and I do not want to be limited by who I have sex with. I am attracted to a person's intellect and not necessarily the body they sit in. I haven't told my Ugandan girlfriend about my married Ghanaian boyfriend, and I haven't told him about her either. With my boyfriend I am scared of what his reaction would be if he knew I was also seeing a woman, although he knows I have previously been in relationships with women. My ideal would be for both of them to know that they exist in my life for different reasons. They are fulfilling different needs that I have, sexually, emotionally, and intellectually. I want them both for what they bring into my life. I'm not sure I want to fully commit to either one of them. There is something that is lost when you fully commit to a relationship. Or maybe I am afraid of what commitment looks like, feels like, and what it could do to my relationships.

I started corresponding with Tsitsi, a heterosexual Zimbabwean woman in her thirties, when she started contributing stories to the blog. I thought her stories were super important because very few African women write about their experiences of navigating sex while living with AIDS.

Speaking with Tsitsi also took me back several years, to a time when I worked in London as a coach running personal empowerment workshops for women living positively. At the time of my interview with Tsitsi she was in a great period in her life. After years of struggling to accept her diagnosis, she had started to take medication, got married, and had a healthy three-month-old baby.

TSITSI

·

I SPENT MY days counseling patients who had just been diagnosed with HIV, but I had received no counseling for my own diagnosis. Every day was like trudging through thick, viscous mud. I would see patient after patient and would ask them the questions that had already been predetermined by the clinic. It was a revolving door of person after person, and like a well-trained robot, I would feed their answers to the machine that would generate statistics about the epidemic of HIV and AIDS in South Africa. I performed my duties without passion. How could I be passionate when I was dead inside? It had been a year since I had tested positive, but even though I was continuously advising people to get on treatment, I myself was not on any medication. Deep down, all I wanted was for it all to come to an end.

And yet I did not die. I went to work day after day and still saw patient after patient. There was very little time spent getting to know the people who needed our services, and to find out how they were really doing. I yearned to spend more time with folks who had come to the clinic because they were having a bad day, but how could I do that when there were many more people sitting in the waiting room waiting their turn to see me? Many of those who came to the clinic were undocumented migrants who had moved to South Africa in search of that utopian dream of "a better life," but now many of them could barely afford the good-quality food that they needed to eat in order to get the nutritional value that was now key to sustaining their life.

Despite this I started to see a difference. Patients who had been forlorn during their initial appointment would be cheerier on their second or third visit. They would look at me, smile, and say, "Madam, I've started taking my medicine. I'm feeling better." I started to think, Come on, you need to pull yourself up. Your life hasn't ended. There's still so much out there for you to do and experience. Around that time, a group of friends and I decided to create a booklet of poems and stories that we dedicated to people living with HIV. I churned out poem after poem. That writing healed me. It enabled me to go deep within myself, and to tap into all the pent-up anger I had felt since my diagnosis. It helped me process the incompetence I felt to truly counsel my patients in the ways that I thought would be most meaningful for them. All the words, hurts, and feelings came out in black and white, in a little booklet that very few people bought, and which we mostly gave away for free.

And then I came back home to Zimbabwe, and moved to a small town where I could walk home from work in ten minutes. He came to the clinic with his sister one day and asked me about particular drugs that he needed for his animals. He was a vet and so that made all the sense in the world. Humans and animals are more alike than many of us realize, and for certain conditions we can all get healing from the same medicine. He started dropping by the clinic more and more, asking to spend time together. I had spent four years withdrawn from people. Yet I would occasionally flirt with people online. Sometimes I would even go so far as to meet up with someone in person but my most intimate experience in that period was a hug or a kiss and then I would disappear. I didn't know how to speak about my diagnosis to any potential lover.

I couldn't disappear from him. He knew where I worked and could drop by any time. Then he started following me home from work. I was frustrated by his insistence and so told him my truth: "I'm HIV positive." He acted like everything was okay and we started dating. I began to mellow and started to feel like my old carefree self. Our sex life was amazing. And just as I was starting to think that this could be my new forever, he told me that we needed to end things. His dream was to find work in the US and he couldn't afford to get infected. His dreams clearly came true. For years now there has only been silence between us but for the past few weeks he's been blowing up my WhatsApp from a US number. He says he regrets ending our relationship. He says I should give him another chance. He says it doesn't matter that I am married and have a child. He says he can give me a better life.

I had almost been married before. That time I was still wide-eyed and excited about wearing a white dress and being the center of attention for a day. I hadn't yet gotten to the stage where I looked around at all the married couples thinking, Why do people do this to themselves? We listened to all the ads urging young couples to get tested before marriage and so we did, although at the time we had already been physically intimate. The results showed that I was positive and he was negative. I didn't know how to take the news. We went to a bar and I had shot after shot. He stayed drinking with me but I knew and understood that he wasn't going to be there in the long run. I had only been with one man previously and so I knew exactly who to call. The last time I had seen him was at his sister's house. He had showed up with another woman who kept touching him as if he would otherwise vaporize into thin air. We weren't "official official" but he had met my family, and I had met his too. Later on his sister called me to apologize: "I am really sorry. You were the one I wanted him to date."

I texted him and told him that I needed to speak to him NOW. When he arrived at the car park of the bar I told my almost fiancé that I needed to do this alone. He insisted on staying at the bar within sight of me.

"I just found out that I'm HIV positive. Did you know that you had this illness?"

The news was clearly not the shocker to him that it had been to me. His response was:

"I didn't know at the time when we were together."

I could feel my legs start to melt into nothingness. I could hear the loud *thud thud* in my chest. I wanted to shout. I wanted to scream aloud, "You fucking gave me HIV!"

He continued, "I thought you hadn't caught it because we had only had sex raw a few times."

I turned and walked back to the bar.

We avoided each other for years but we live in the same small town and so couldn't do that forever. Now we've both moved on with our lives. He's also married, and when we run into each other we stop, say hi, and chat about our children. The man I married is reliable. He's given me a better life. He's the kind of person who answers the phone when you call in the middle of the night. Recently my dad was diagnosed with cancer and my husband spent a lot of time running around various black markets to acquire the precious dollars that we needed to pay the specialists. He doesn't have a lot of book knowledge but he's all heart. He's a man who works with his hands, a contractor, and similar to my dad in that regard. When we have sex he's not in a rush to enter me. He takes his time to touch me all over. When I told him I had HIV he said, "It's something that happens." He realized I was pregnant way before I did. He bought a pregnancy kit and said, "I think you need to use this." I was adamant that I was fine. My periods have always been irregular. The little stick showed he was right, and later, a scan showed that I was almost three months pregnant. I wasn't sure I wanted to get married but it's difficult being a single unmarried working mother in her thirties. He wanted to stay in the picture and have access to the baby. Family members on both sides also kept saying, "You need to get married," and so we did.

Waris is a thirty-nine year old woman who lives in London. She describes herself as a sexually free woman who is also a work in progress. She was born in Somalia, and her family moved to Saudi Arabia when she was only ten days old. Her dad worked for an Italian company, and so as a child she spent her holidays in between Somalia and Italy, and her life has been shaped by these three patriarchal cultures.

Speaking to Waris helped me grapple with the many complicated feelings I have around Female Genital Mutilation (FGM) or cutting, a practice that she experienced and describes as child sexual abuse. I found this description helpful because it allows one to think about all the ways in which children are abused around the world, and to recognize FGM/C as a systemic issue rather than a practice done by "those savages over there," which is the framing that I still see in many mainstream media platforms today.

My conversation with Waris also reminded me of how much we all absorb societal messaging around sexual pleasure, even when we work consciously to rid ourselves of those influences. At one point in our chat, Waris was describing a pleasurable sexual experience and I found myself mentally stuck. I kept thinking, How can she enjoy sex if she has been cut? And so I asked a more nuanced version of the thought that has been floating around in my head. Waris generously reminded me of how large and expansive the clitoris is, and how far it travels within our bodies; the clit is only the tip of the entire clitoral system, and so women who have had theirs cut can still experience sexual pleasure.

The following story includes experiences of child sexual assault.

WARIS

·

EACH LOVER I have had has taken me to the next level sexually, and Kamau was the ultimate. We initially met in November 2018. We connected via Tinder while I was on a work trip to Kenya and when we met I told him the stereotypical things women tell men on dates. I was looking for a serious relationship. A commitment, one that could lead to marriage, and more children. He told me he wasn't looking for that. What he wanted was a real human connection. I thought that was a weird thing to say to someone on a first date. We agreed that we wanted different things and so would explore a friendship instead.

In February 2019 I was back in Kenya for work and met up with Kamau again. In the interim I had undergone MDMA therapy and part of what I had learned was that it is important to let people know exactly who you are, and so I decided to tell Kamau about the experience I'd had. When I told him he cheesed so hard. He told me that he had been using psychedelic drugs for the past four years and that is why he had been so honest with me when we had originally met. He uses drugs in ceremonial and group sessions. It's why he knew that he didn't want children. Kamau changed my whole outlook on life and sex. I never thought being with a man would help me heal from the wounds of my previous relationships with other men but that's exactly what he did for me. He taught me about the importance of creating a sensual environment. How to set up the room, the importance of lighting, food, and mood. Every time I had sex with him was the best sex I ever had. He was the first person I had tantric sex with. One time we had sex and it stimulated my vagus nerve—I could feel the orgasm in my spine. Kamau had been on a healing journey of his own. We would often meditate together before having sex. Then we would smoke a joint. With him I learned how to enjoy weed without fear and now

I associate weed with sexual pleasure. We referred to each other as lovers. When we decided to end our physical relationship, we meditated together, and gave each other gifts to mark the end of that relationship. We are still very good friends today.

In December 2018 I had a crisis. On the surface I was this successful woman whose public profile had rapidly risen, and then I took my daughter to visit her dad in Minnesota and had a breakdown. I called one of my friends in the US. He's a rich, well-connected man and he said, "Waris, let me pay for you to go to San Francisco for MDMA therapy," and so I did. The clinician I saw asked me, "What do you want to work on?" and I said, "Sex. I enjoy sex but I feel guilty every time I have sex. I feel like I'm going to go to hell, and it affects my relationships. I can't just have sex and go home. It becomes this destructive behavior which is not good for me, and I know where it stems from."

Up until that point I had never tried any drugs, not even weed, but what MDMA did for me was that it gave me six to seven hours of feeling no guilt or shame, and a part of my brain switched on that I had never felt before, and that was compassion for Waris.

I got married when I was eighteen. I met my husband physically for the first time when he came to London for our wedding. It was an arranged marriage, as is customary for Somalis. A member of his family had asked for my hand in marriage, and my parents did not want to be rude, so they said, "Just talk to him for a little bit, and then we'll say no." They didn't anticipate that I would come back saying, "I am in love! I want to marry him."

That was the first time any man had paid me attention. I was unhappy as a teenager. I wasn't part of the in-crowd at school. I was a nerd and often on my own reading a book. I also felt self-conscious because I developed very early; I had big breasts that to this day I hide by wearing loose-fitting tops. I also felt a lot of desire towards older men. I would masturbate and then feel bad. I questioned myself a lot: What's wrong with you? You're going to go to hell. You shouldn't be feeling like this, you need to get married. From childhood my mum had spoken to me about sex. She said it was a wonderful thing to do but only with your husband.

After we got married, my dad insisted that I needed to stay in London a while longer, although my husband lived in the States. He said I was too young, and that I needed to grow up a bit. When I turned twenty, I moved to live with my husband in Minnesota, the largest Diaspora for Somalis in the West. I arrived there on September 10, 2001, and the next day woke up to 9/11. The eventual breakdown of my marriage caused a similar kind of reverberation in my life. While still in the UK I had dropped out of university, but my husband had reassured my parents that I could continue my studies in the US. Once I got there, he said he wanted me to stay at home. He wanted me to stop wearing trousers and cover up with a burka instead of the small head scarf that I wore.

At the beginning our sex life was good. We would have sex two or three times a day but only when he initiated it. When I tried to initiate sex my husband would get upset and ask if I had been with other men before him. Meanwhile he was sleeping with other women, some of whom he had been in a relationship with before marrying me. I realized that he had married me because he wanted me to be the mother of his children. He didn't want me to be his lover. Other women were his lovers. I found out that I was pregnant the day after I had decided to leave the relationship. I thought, Fuck. I'm stuck with him now.

I began to feel really sick all the time. I couldn't eat and would throw up everything. In the initial months of my pregnancy I was hospitalized twice. I didn't want to have sex anymore but my husband insisted. After he had his way I would run to the toilet and throw up. My dad called and said, "Maybe she's homesick. Send her to us for a while and she'll come back to have the baby in the US." The more time I spent in London, the less I wanted to go back to Minneapolis. One day Dad asked, "So Waris, why don't you want to go back?" I broke down crying and told him everything. Dad was supportive throughout but my mum really struggled at the beginning. Here I was, twenty-one years old, pregnant, with no university degree and no prospects. I never did go back, and it took years for my husband to sign the divorce papers. In the interim he had another baby with one of the women he had been having an affair with during our marriage.

All I had wanted was a marriage like my parents had. At home they held hands, and cuddled on the couch. Their marriage had not been an arranged one; they were from two opposing clans but had defied their families to be together. As a child I loved to tidy up Mum's wardrobe and try on things I found. One day I found a basket of silky delicates. It was her lingerie collection. She in turn gifted me with lingerie when I got married. Mummy always spoke about sex in a direct way. The first conversation I remember was when I was ten years old. War had just broken out in Somalia and my family, like all the other wealthy families, were planning their escape. Mum warned my sister and me that we needed to be really careful so that no one violated us.

Three years earlier she had already taken steps to ensure that we wouldn't have sex with anyone before we got married. I remember waking up that day to a house full of women. The only men around were outside killing a cow. My dad had traveled for work, and so when I saw my mum's regular caterer bringing in piles of food, I wondered why she was throwing a party while Dad was away. It was obvious that there was a big event being planned but it wasn't my birthday or my little sister's birthday either. It was the nine-year-old girl who lived next door who told me what was happening. "This is an important day for you. You're going to have guudnin." As I asked her what that was, and she described what was going to happen to me in the next few minutes, all I could think of was, But Mummy said no one should touch our bodies. Then I heard a scream from the other side of the house. I could hear my sister calling for my mother and then me in rapid succession. At that moment I felt my soul flee my body and I wanted to follow suit. When it was my turn I fought with everything that was within me. I kicked, I bit, I punched and scratched the women holding me down. I fought so hard that the doctor had to summon his male assistant. I have never forgotten the sight of him. He was dressed from head to toe in white. It was him who held me down and took a blade to my genitals.

We were considered Diaspora kids and so no one had informed us of what was being planned. My mum had deliberately planned to do this while my dad was away because she knew he wouldn't approve. On her side of the family her dad had made sure his daughters were cut, whereas my paternal grand-father took his daughter to the village and threw a big party so that everybody assumed his daughter had been cut. Both my grandfathers were doctors but they made very different decisions when it came to controlling the sexuality of their children. As I grew up I began to understand that the act that was carried out on me as a child was serious sexual abuse. I no longer refer to it as FGM, which is othering. It is a serious sexual assault against women and children. I was assaulted publicly and what's most disturbing is that your mother picks the women she trusts the most to be there with you. Mothers are usually not there in case they get distressed and can't cope with the screaming. So they pick women they trust, usually aunties and neighbors. For a long time I struggled with being around Black women. I didn't know if they were going to harm me.

Being back in London as a single woman with a child was tough. People have these ideas of single women, especially Somalis, and so for years I didn't have sex because I didn't want anyone thinking that I'm easy. After about three years I started dating another Somali man. We were together for about seven months. We didn't have sex during that period because I did not want him to judge me, and I was hoping we would get married. I had been warned, "Men are only interested in having sex with single mums. They won't respect you or marry you." When he broke up with me I found out that he had impregnated someone else. The breakup was only two months after I had lost my dad and so at the time it felt like my world was coming apart.

A month later I met a Nigerian man who became my secret lover for ten years. We never dated officially. He was basically a friend with benefits. By then I had decided that I didn't want a man in my daughter's life. I was also very clear then that I wanted to have sex, and in my relationship with my buddy I learned about my body and what brings me pleasure. All our hookups were planned. I would put my daughter to bed by 6:30 p.m. and by 8 p.m. I would be getting my groove on. When we started seeing each other I never thought the relationship would last a decade. None of my friends or family ever met or knew about him. He was the guy who got me out of my vanilla, wife, missionary-sex-type life. He got me to feel comfortable with my body, especially my boobs, which I've always been self-conscious about. The relationship eventually ended because he started to want more than friendship but by then I was in a different phase of life. I had become focused. I wanted to get my career on track. I didn't want to be financially dependent on a man or to be anyone's girlfriend or wife. I felt that going back to that way of being would suffocate me, and that no matter what, the man would end up cheating or having a baby behind my back.

Although I made the decision to have sex while unmarried, I still felt a lot of shame and guilt. I would fall into deep pits of depression and harm myself emotionally. This affected my relationships. My next relationship was with a Gambian man. This time it was official. He, like me, was a single parent who was divorced from his wife, with whom he already had two children. All my friends knew and loved him, my siblings met him, and I told my mum about him. I fell in love, and then he ended the relationship because his wife got pregnant and they decided to try and make their marriage work. I ended up in bed with depression for a month. My friends would come over and drag me out of the house. Somehow, along the way, he and I managed to become friends.

A few months ago, before the world locked down, we met up for dinner and I said to him, "Thank goodness I never became your wife." He was also a Muslim and wanted a wife who would be home. He wanted a religious woman who was going to cover up. I loved him so much that I think I would have done it. I think I would have found some sort of compromise, but from where I am today I can see that breaking up with him was the best thing that could have ever happened to me. All my previous relationships helped me to get to where I am today. I needed those men to be taken out of the equation so that I could go and find myself. After that breakup I made a rule. After the end of every relationship I would give myself a detox. I didn't want to take the issues from one relationship into the next. I wanted time to explore and figure out why a relationship didn't work before jumping into the next one.

One of my closest friends got married and the priest who read out a prayer was a George Clooney–looking type of man. He had a grey goatee and wore a grey suit. I said to one of my friends, "I want to have sex with that priest." The wedding took place really early in the morning, and it was all over by 9 a.m. Afterwards a group of us went up to the bridal suite, which was really huge, it was the size of a flat. We started popping bottles of champagne and drinking whisky. The priest joined us and we started chatting. It turned out that he wasn't a priest. He was an atheist who was a friend of the groom and had been asked to read a prayer. At some point in time everyone fell asleep and he and I had sex right there in the suite.

I learned a lot about sexuality from that relationship. He was bisexual, and honest about his attractions towards men and women. He and I would also role-play a lot. At the time I had a job that involved traveling all across the country, and he would come and meet me wherever I was and take me out for intimate dinners. After a few months it got a bit hard for him because he wanted more and I wasn't ready for another relationship. So I took another detox and didn't have sex for a year. Well, I had lots of sex with myself but not with other people.

MDMA therapy saved my life, and helped me become the person that I am today. I'm at a stage now where I want to get away from a lot of social conditioning, including sexual orientation. The world would probably define me as a heterosexual woman but that's not a label I put on myself. I'm now open to all kinds of possibilities when it comes to relationships, including being with another woman. If I had to define myself I would describe myself as a sexually free woman. Or, more accurately, a work-in-progress sexually free woman.

I was thirty-eight years old when I started having extensive conversations with women about their experiences of sex and sexuality. I am now forty-three years old. During the intervening years I have continued to think deeply about my various intersecting identities. First and foremost I identify as a Pan-African feminist. In a sense that identity trumps the other identities I also hold: Ghanaian, a person of dual nationality who was born in the UK, a bisexual woman who also considers herself at this moment in time to be a solo polyamorist.

As a feminist, I couldn't ask other African women to share their vulnerabilities without revealing myself to you.

My own story includes experiences of child sexual assault.

NANA DARKOA

·

THE FIRST TIME Yaw and I had sex I remember thinking afterwards, Ohhhh shitttt, I have been dickmatized. I knew then that my relationship with Ngugi was over. It made no logical sense that I ended up in bed with Yaw that day. When I first met him I told him, "I have a boyfriend." He had responded, "I am not going to disrespect your boyfriend," yet we had ended up that night with his head between my thighs, my stomach muscles tying into tighter and tighter knots until it felt like my whole body was melting into pools of pleasure. It made no sense that I had ended up in bed with Yaw on the very evening when he had told me, "I have a girlfriend." I had looked at him in shock.

He had first told me, "I'm really attracted to you," two months before, and in the interim there had been no mention of a girlfriend, and no mention that he and his girlfriend lived together. While I was still trying to sort through the various thoughts tumbling through my mind, the waiter at the beachside bar we were sitting at said, "Sorry, we're closing now." I looked at my watch; we had been there for barely an hour. Perhaps it was the magical sounds of waves crashing on the beach, or the chill in the air that had led Yaw to sit closer to me and wrap his arm around me, or perhaps it was because by now we had been chatting and intermittently spending time together over a couple of weeks, but I had found myself saying to myself that night, I'm really beginning to like this guy, in spite of all the ways in which I knew we were different, and remembering stories he had told me of being brought up in the zongos of Takoradi, and the gang violence that plagued his neighborhood; his love for his paternal grandmother who raised him on her own, yet kept him indoors when other family came to visit and called him "frafra," the mixed-up one, in scornful reference to the heritage of his mum, who came from Burkina Faso. Finding herself in an unhappy marriage, she had left, leaving behind a young son who years later was still hurting from growing up motherless.

I had started to fall for this man who in some ways was still a boy, who was ten years younger than me, and who was now telling me that he had a girlfriend whom he was in a common-law marriage with. It was too much to unravel even as he tried to untie the knots. "I have been trying to end the relationship for a while," "It's a violent relationship," "I'm just waiting for her to go back to the States in two months' time and then it'll be really over because she would have left." We went to mine to continue the conversation, and ended up in bed. I waited a few weeks to tell Ngugi over WhatsApp that it was over, that the long-distance relationship was not working for me. I asked if he wanted to talk about it; he didn't. "I just need to be on my own right now," he said.

Yaw's breakup with his girlfriend was more complicated than my breakup with my boyfriend had been. She reached out to me via direct message on Instagram a few days after I had surgery to remove the remnants of the baby that had been growing in my womb. "I'm sorry about your loss, sister," she said, "but I think you should know the kind of man you're with." "So why do you still keep trying to get back with him?" I countered. "My self-esteem is low," she said. I WhatsApp'd my boyfriend when the call was over. I was sleeping on my friend's couch in London, grateful that I had been away from home when the miscarriage occurred. Grateful for the good hospital care I had been able to get, that when I had started to bleed unexpectedly in the middle of what was meant to be routine day surgery, I was in a country where I had been able to get the emergency transfusion of blood I needed. I knew that if I had been in Ghana, I would have had surgery at my private gynecologist's clinic, and that in an emergency I would have been rushed to a public hospital where the blood banks are, and there would have been no free beds, my dad would have needed to make a call to a contact to try and get me admitted, and my relatives would have had to donate blood before I in turn could be given that lifesaving blood, and by then it might have been too late. I got through to Yaw on the first ring.

"Guess what, I just spoke to your ex, and she told me you and her had phone sex a month ago," I said. I was practically laughing when I told him. A month ago I was about six weeks into my pregnancy and we were spending our time debating baby names and imagining what our little girl would look like. I was adamant I was going to have a girl. I have long dreamed of my little feminist baby girl, and how I was going to raise her to be the fiercest, sassiest feminist that ever strode this earth.

"It's true," he said. "What?" I asked. "It's true," he repeated. "I have been trying to figure out how to tell you." I could feel my eyes start to water and I started to cry. I never knew I had so many tears in me. I heard him start to cry too. "I am so sorry, I was feeling sorry for her, she said she hadn't had sex in months," he said. I didn't need that detail. "I need to go," I said, and put down the phone. I snuggled into the duvet and wept. I wept for the dreams I had lost, for the little girl I had imagined nurturing, for the happy family I had envisaged.

Later on, Yaw and I made up and ended up having a three-year relationship. In general I felt loved and desired by him. In what ended up being the last year of our partnership, we moved to London so that I could undergo fertility treatment. The experience of the first miscarriage had scarred me, and I had decided that because we were both sickle cell carriers, I did not want us to try to get pregnant naturally. After a few months and due to visa restrictions, Yaw had to return home while I continued my treatment in the UK. Alone in my cold London flat I would pinch the fat of my belly and self-inject hormones while looking at myself in the mirror. I would travel to the nearby fertility treatment center on my own to check how many eggs I had. My aunt accompanied me to the hospital the day my eggs were harvested. I was grateful to have her support. I was on the train alone a few days later when I got a call from the treatment center. None of the eggs that had been harvested had progressed to the blastocyst stage. The fertility treatment had failed.

I started to reflect on what *I* really wanted to do. I had not been sure whether I wanted biological children or not but I had always known that I wanted to adopt. Yaw, on the other hand, had insisted that he wanted a biological child, and his concession to me was that after we had a child on our own, we could adopt. I had also begun to question the model of relationship that Yaw and I were in—a heterosexual, monogamous relationship that had started with both of us cheating on our respective partners. Over the years I had come to realize that this wasn't a model that I personally bought into anymore. I knew from my own life and family that other legitimate relationship models existed. I ended my relationship with Yaw. I wanted a fresh start. A new beginning. A chance to go on my own journey of discovery, and an opportunity to find out for myself what my personal sexual freedom could be. Today, I'm charting my own path accompanied by my daughter Asantewaa. She brings a lot of laughter, joy, and sleepless nights to my life.

A FINAL NOTE

Over a five-year period I interviewed Black and African women from all over
the world about sex. In London I was welcomed into the home of a stranger
and drank tea while she showed me the rubber costume drying in her bathroom, one of the outfits she wears while pro domming. In São Tomé I told my
tour guide about my book project, and asked if he knew any women who would
be willing to share their personal stories with me. The chapter featuring Vera
Cruz was a result of that trip. In Rwanda a friend introduced me to Bingi, and
in a café she shared the story of the man she loves but cannot be with, pausing
whenever the waiter came to check if we needed anything else. In many countries around the world, women I had never previously met responded to the
intimate questions I asked of them. "What's your earliest sexual memory?"
"How did you guys meet? I want to know all the details," "What was sex like
with them?"

From across the African continent and throughout a vast global Diaspora in Europe, the Americas, and the Caribbean, Black and Afro-descendant
women shared stories that spoke to our similarities and differences, our
desire for freedom, our need for healing, and the journeys that we embark on
to achieve wholeness.

In person and through the interface of various digital platforms, I went
through a gamut of emotions as I spoke with the women featured in this book.
I felt most inspired by the women living life on their own terms, who buck
tradition, and fearlessly create and re-create their lives. Women like Alexis,
Laura, and Helen epitomize a freedom that I wish for all. There were many
stories that were difficult, especially those who spoke to the abuse that too

many women face as children and adults. I remember Maureen saying to me, "I don't have a happy story to share with you," and my conversation with her was an important reminder that many Black women, particularly heterosexual Black women in Europe, feel unloved, undesired, and unseen by straight Black men.

The women I interacted with who seemed to be dealing most positively with sexual trauma were or had been on healing journeys. For some this looked like tapping deeply into a spiritual practice, abstaining from sex and journaling. For others, like the above-mentioned Bingi, sex was the therapy. A reminder that healing is different for everyone.

I feel lucky that I got to tap into the eroticism and sensuality of Black women. An eroticism nurtured by bodily confidence, nurture (including good food), and experimentation. I was often reminded that good sex takes practice and starts with the self.

For many of the women I interviewed, their conversation with me was the first time they had ever shared deeply personal stories with anyone else, and some described our conversations as therapeutic, a healing that I benefited from and hope that you, the reader, gained as well.

HOW WILL THIS BOOK CHANGE YOU?

An invitation to join us on a journey of self-discovery, freedom, and healing

One of the most interesting questions I have been asked since this book initially came out was, "How has this book changed you?" The answer is, in so many ways. Writing this book has been part of my own journey of self-discovery—a way to process my experiences by reflecting on my own growing understanding of the complexities and dynamic nature of sex and sexualities. Writing this book has also been part of my political work as an African feminist—born out of a desire to contribute to the knowledge created, shared, and conceptualized by so many African feminists who came before me, those who are my contemporaries, and those yet to follow. Writing this book has challenged me, blown apart some of my own misconceptions and limiting beliefs, and encouraged me to stay open to the myriad possibilities that blossom when we allow ourselves to work on our own healing and explore what possibilities exist in the here and now for our collective sexual freedom.

Freedom is not an individual pursuit—it's a collective process that embraces the least among us. When the most marginalized people are free, we can all be collectively free. When LGBTQI people are free to love, when queer people can walk down the streets around the world with pride, when sex workers can perform labor with dignity, we will all be the better for it.

The work of self-discovery, freedom, and healing is an active, ongoing process. It requires that we question everything we've been told. It requires that we go back into our histories and bring back those aspects that are positive. What my people, the Akan of Ghana, refer to as Sankofa. We must look back, rediscover, and reimagine those aspects of our culture that were positive. For instance, creating space for young girls to learn about their sexuality—and this time making them active agents of their own pleasure, and not vessels for the pleasure of men.

I invite you and your community to deepen your own journeys around self-discovery, freedom, and healing. Over the next few pages, I am providing some prompts that you could either reflect on by yourself, with your partner(s), or in community. Feel free to take notes in the blank pages provided for this purpose, or if you want to share, take a picture and tag @thesexlivesofafricanwomen on Instagram or @SexLivesAfrica via Twitter.

Enjoy your journeys of self-discovery, freedom, and healing.

Much love,

Nana xoxo

JOURNALING PROMPTS

SELF-DISCOVERY

What were you told about sex as a child, and how has that shaped your
experience of sexuality?

_____

_____

_____

_____

_____

_____

In what ways has your culture (and/or other cultures) shaped who you are
today as a sexual being?

_____

_____

_____

_____

_____

_____

Which myths and misconceptions about sex and sexualities have you bought into, and are now ready to shed?

_____

_____

_____

_____

_____

_____

_____

How has your sexuality evolved over time?

_____

_____

_____

_____

_____

_____

_____

_____

What resources, voices, and experiences would you like to read, listen to, or watch to learn more about sex and sexualities?

_____

_____

_____

_____

_____

_____

_____

_____

_____

_____

_____

_____

_____

_____

FREEDOM

How can you prepare your mind and body for an experience of intense pleasure?

_____

_____

_____

_____

_____

_____

_____

What can you do to learn more about your own body, and what brings it the most joy?

_____

_____

_____

_____

_____

_____

_____

Which pleasurable rituals can you incorporate into your sex life?

_____

_____

_____

_____

_____

_____

_____

_____

Outside of sex, what are the ways in which you can experience deep
pleasure?

_____

_____

_____

_____

_____

_____

_____

_____

_____

In an ideal world, what would your experience of sexual freedom be like?

_____

_____

_____

_____

_____

_____

_____

_____

_____

_____

_____

_____

_____

_____

HEALING

What trauma do you need to heal from in order to live your best sex life, whatever that means for you?

_____

_____

_____

_____

_____

_____

_____

_____

What does healing look like for you, and how will you know you are making progress in this area of your life?

_____

_____

_____

_____

_____

_____

_____

_____

In this book, whose healing journey did you find most inspirational, and what can you take away from her story?

_____

_____

_____

_____

_____

_____

_____

What would a practice of self-love look like for you?

_____

_____

_____

_____

_____

_____

_____

In what ways could you contribute to building a community that practices collective care?

_____

_____

_____

_____

_____

_____

_____

_____

_____

_____

_____

_____

_____

_____

_____

_____

GLOSSARY

El Árbol de Seda—The Silk Tree

Épanouie—blooming

Frafra—a subset of the Gurunsi people living in Northern Ghana. In local usage the term is often used in a derogatory manner in reference to people from the Northern region of Ghana.

Gautrain—a commuter railway system in South Africa

J'Ouvert—a day celebrated during Carnival to mark enslaved people breaking free of their chains

Kachabali—a sexual act indigenous to parts of East Africa that involves a rhythmic stroking of the clitoris

Machismo—aggressively masculine

Mumu—a person who is stunned into silence

Na wash but best wash ever—it's a lie, but the best lie ever

Shark—a super smart person

Sleeping cloth(s)—a printed piece of wax cloth used to cover one's self while sleeping

Tom(s)—a slang term used in London in reference to sex workers

Wine—a sexy dance that involves gyrating on one's partner

Zongos—settlements in West African towns traditionally inhabited by people from the Northern Sahel region

)w)—a Twi word for snake

ACKNOWLEDGMENTS

I would like to thank my parents for their love and constant support—my dad who kept asking, "So when are you finishing your book?" while simultaneously telling me that he wasn't going to read it, my Mum for encouraging my love of reading—and my siblings Abena and Kweku Sekyiamah for always being in my corner.

I have an immense amount of gratitude for all the writing spaces I have benefited from, including the tutors of the 2012 Farafina Trust Creative Workshop: thank you for giving me much needed confidence in my voice. I am also grateful to the tutors of the 2014 FEMRITE/Karavan writing residence and my 2016 residency at Hedgebrook, which gave me much needed space to work on my first ten chapters.

There are so many African writers who have supported me in numerous ways: Sulaiman Addonia, Yewande Omotoso, Minna Salami, thank you for all your advice and support during this publishing journey. My writing community: Famia Nkansa, Rita Nketiah, Kobina Graham, Nana Oforiatta Ayim, and the entire Hairy Hermits crew (shout out to Martina Odonkor and Nii Ayikwei Parkes). Thank you for the fun writing dates and accompanying me throughout this process. Thank you to my BFFFL Malaka Grant and the Adventures from the Bedrooms of African Women blogging community; without our blog I wouldn't have written this book.

I feel so lucky to have been published by Alessandra Bastagli and have felt held by the wonderful team at Astra House. Thank you to my agent, Robert Caskie, for believing so passionately in this book.

To the numerous African women who openly shared so much of themselves with me for this book, my biggest thanks goes to you. Thank you, thank you, thank you.

ABOUT THE AUTHOR

Nana Darkoa Sekyiamah is a feminist activist, writer, and blogger. She is also cofounder of Adventures from the Bedrooms of African Women, a website, podcast, and festival that publishes and creates content that tells stories of African women's experiences around sex, sexualities, and pleasure. She lives in Accra, Ghana, with her daughter, Asantewaa, and her dog, Romeo.

It takes a village to get from a manuscript to the printed book in your hands. The team at Astra House would like to thank everyone who helped to publish *The Sex Lives of African Women*.

PUBLISHER

Ben Schrank

EDITORIAL

Alessandra Bastagli

Rola Harb

CONTRACTS

Stefanie Ratzki

Angelica Chong

PUBLICITY

Rachael Small

MARKETING

Tiffany Gonzalez

Sarah Christensen Fu

Jordan Snowden

SALES

Jack W. Perry

DESIGN

Jacket: Rodrigo Corral Studio

Interior: Richard Oriolo

Jeanette Tran

PRODUCTION

Lisa Taylor

Alisa Trager

Olivia Dontsov

Rebecca Baumann

COPYEDITING

Janine Barlow

COMPOSITION

Westchester Publishing Services

ABOUT ASTRA HOUSE

Astra House is dedicated to publishing authors across genres and from around the world. We value works that are authentic, ask new questions, present counter-narratives and original thinking, challenge our assumptions, and broaden and deepen our understanding of the world. Our mission is to advocate for authors who experience their subject deeply and personally, and who have a strong point of view; writers who represent multifaceted expressions of intellectual thought and personal experience, and who can introduce readers to new perspectives about their everyday lives as well as the lives of others.